A HANDBOOK
on
PAUL'S LETTER TO THE GALATIANS

The Handbooks in the **UBS Handbook Series** are detailed commentaries providing valuable exegetical, historical, cultural, and linguistic information on the books of the Bible. They are prepared primarily to assist practicing Bible translators as they carry out the important task of putting God's Word into the many languages spoken in the world today. The text is discussed verse by verse and is accompanied by running text in at least one modern English translation.

Over the years church leaders and Bible readers have found the UBS Handbooks to be useful for their own study of the Scriptures. Many of the issues Bible translators must address when trying to communicate the Bible's message to modern readers are the ones Bible students must address when approaching the Bible text as part of their own private study and devotions.

The Handbooks will continue to be prepared primarily for translators, but we are confident that they will be useful to a wider audience, helping all who use them to gain a better understanding of the Bible message.

UBS Helps for Translators

Handbooks:

A Handbook on . . .

Leviticus
The Book of Joshua
The Book of Ruth
The Book of Job
The Book of Psalms
Lamentations
The Book of Amos
The Books of Obadiah, Jonah, and Micah
The Books of Nahum, Habakkuk, and Zephaniah
The Gospel of Matthew
The Gospel of Mark
The Gospel of Luke
The Gospel of John
The Acts of the Apostles
Paul's Letter to the Romans

Paul's First Letter to the Corinthians
Paul's Second Letter to the Corinthians
Paul's Letter to the Galatians
Paul's Letter to the Ephesians
Paul's Letter to the Philippians
Paul's Letters to the Colossians and to Philemon
Paul's Letters to the Thessalonians
The Letter to the Hebrews
The First Letter from Peter
The Letter from Jude and the Second Letter from Peter
The Letters of John
The Revelation to John

Guides:

A Translator's Guide to . . .

Selections from the First Five Books of the Old Testament
Selected Psalms
the Gospel of Mark
the Gospel of Luke

Paul's Second Letter to the Corinthians
Paul's Letters to Timothy and to Titus
the Letters to James, Peter, and Jude

Technical Helps:

Old Testament Quotations in the New Testament
Short Bible Reference System
New Testament Index
The Theory and Practice of Translation
Bible Index

Fauna and Flora of the Bible
Marginal Notes for the Old Testament
Marginal Notes for the New Testament
The Practice of Translating

A HANDBOOK ON

Paul's Letter to the Galatians

by Daniel C. Arichea

and Eugene A. Nida

UBS Handbook Series

United Bible Societies
New York

Books in the series of **UBS Helps for Translators** may be ordered from a national Bible Society or from either of the following centers:

United Bible Societies
European Production Fund
W-7000 Stuttgart 80
Postfach 81 03 40
Germany

United Bible Societies
1865 Broadway
New York, NY 10023
U. S. A.

L. C. Cataloging-in-Publication Data

Arichea, Daniel C.
    [Translator's handbook on Paul's letter to the Galatians]
    A handbook on Paul's letter to the Galatians / by Daniel C. Arichea and Eugene A. Nida.
       p. cm — (UBS handbook series) (UBS helps for translators)
    Originally published under title: A translator's handbook on Paul's letter to the Galatians.
    Includes bibliographical references and index.
    ISBN 0-8267-0163-9
    1. Bible. N.T. Galatians—Translating. I. Nida, Eugene Albert, 1914- . II. Title. III. Title: Paul's letter to the Galatians. IV. Series. V. Series: UBS helps for translators.
BS2685.5.A74 1993
227'.4077—dc20
                                   92-20511
                                      CIP

ABS-1993-250-4,050-CM-6-102690

PREFACE

This Translators Handbook on Galatians follows in format and emphasis the pattern established in the preparation of the corresponding Handbook on Romans in that special attention is paid to the structure of the discourse as a means of revealing as clearly as possible the closely related series of themes.

As in the case of other volumes in this series, no attempt is made in this volume to identify the various languages in which particular renderings are employed, except the major European languages. The texts of Scripture cited in translations appearing in these languages are readily available to translators who may want to consult them, and therefore they are mentioned.

Though the sources of scholarly opinions are cited in particularly important instances, no attempt is made to identify all the possible sources, since this volume is not designed to be an analysis of scholarly opinion but a guide to translators who attempt to deal with the many difficulties involved in rendering this important part of the Bible into meaningful language. A bibliography is provided for the benefit of those who may be especially interested in the major scholarly sources. Those who make use of this volume may obtain most of the relevant supplementary data by noting the treatments of the corresponding passages in the various commentaries.

Special thanks must be extended to members of the United Bible Societies Committee on Helps for Translators, who have carefully reviewed the manuscript of this volume, and to Paul C. Clarke, Elizabeth G. Edwards, and Lucy Rowe, who have assisted so materially in the editorial processes and in the preparation of the text for offset reproduction.

Daniel C. Arichea, Jr.
Eugene A. Nida

June 1976

CONTENTS

Abbreviations used in this volume viii

Translating Galatians. 1

Chapter 1 3

Chapter 2 27

Chapter 3 52

Chapter 4 86

Chapter 5 118

Chapter 6 144

Bibliography 161

Glossary 163

Index 175

ABBREVIATIONS USED IN THIS VOLUME

Bible texts and versions cited (for details see Bibliography, page 161):

Brc	Barclay
GeCL	German common language translation
JB	Jerusalem Bible
KJV	King James Version
Mft	Moffatt
NAB	New American Bible
NEB	New English Bible
Phps	Phillips
RSV	Revised Standard Version
TEV	Today's English Version

Books of the Bible:

Col	Colossians
Cor	Corinthians
Deut	Deuteronomy
Eph	Ephesians
Gal	Galatians
Gen	Genesis
Hab	Habakkuk
Heb	Hebrews
Isa	Isaiah
Lev	Leviticus
Matt	Matthew
Phil	Philippians
Rev	Revelation
Rom	Romans
Thes	Thessalonians

Other abbreviations:

A.D.	Anno Domini = "in the year of [our] Lord"
cf.	confer = compare, or see also
e.g.	exempli gratia = for example
ff.	= and the following [verses]
i.e.	id est = that is
LXX	Septuagint (see Glossary)
UBS	United Bible Societies
v., vv.	verse, verses

TRANSLATING GALATIANS

Paul's letter to the Galatians is one of the most significant books of the New Testament and of the whole Bible. Sometimes described as "the Magna Carta of Christian Liberty," it discusses in clear, emotional, and intensely personal language the basic issue of how a man is put right with God. In Paul's own words, the basic question is: "Does God give you the Spirit and work miracles among you because you do what the Law requires or because you hear the gospel and believe it?" (3.5). And the answer comes in similar language: "A person is put right with God only through faith in Jesus Christ, never by doing what the Law requires" (2.16, emphasis added).

The occasion for the letter is a situation that has arisen among the Christians in Galatia. Predominantly non-Jewish, they are therefore confronted with the problem of what to do with the Jewish Law. There would no doubt have been a tendency for many Jewish converts to Christianity to continue to observe at least some of the regulations of the Law. But what about non-Jews? Are they bound by the Jewish Law? Should they first submit to circumcision and other Jewish ritualistic practices before being accepted as full members of the Christian community? In other words, must they become Jews before they can become Christians?

An affirmative answer to the above questions is advocated by some persons who relate in some way to the Galatian churches. These "false teachers" seem to have some connection with the Jerusalem church (2.11-14). They advocate not only circumcision but also observance of Jewish feasts (4.10). Obviously, their position is that to be put right with God, it is not enough to have faith in Jesus Christ; one must also obey the regulations in the Law of Moses.

To this issue Paul addresses himself. He does not write a cold theological treatise, but an intensely personal letter, for he knows the Galatians personally. He founded the churches there, and, according to one possible interpretation, he visited them more than once (4.13). He considers them as his children (4.19). He is therefore deeply affected by their situation and troubled by their receptiveness to this new doctrine, this "other gospel" (1.6) which is encroaching upon them. So despite his closeness to them, he calls them "foolish" (3.1, 3). In many places in this letter, he even seems to get angry with them (1.6-9; 3.1-4; 4.8-11; 5.7, etc.). But he keeps a personal, intimate tone throughout, calling them "brothers" very often, including the final salutation (6.18). His concern is clear: he wants the Galatians to be faithful to the Good News which they have received; he wants them to remain in unison with Christ, and therefore to remain free in the life of the Spirit.

The letter to the Galatians falls easily into six divisions. (1) The first five verses of chapter 1 form the introduction to the letter, and (2) in the next five verses (1.6-10), Paul presents the problem which is the occasion for the letter. (3) From 1.11 to 2.21, Paul defends his position as an apostle of Jesus Christ and justifies the message which he has been preaching among the Gentiles, a message which is centered on trust and commitment to Jesus Christ, and not on doing what the Law requires. (4) In 3.1—4.31, this message is now expounded

[1]

and defended from criticism by means of theological and biblical arguments and through the use of illustrations both from the Bible and from Jewish and Roman practices. (5) In 5.1—6.10 Paul deals with the implications of this message for the life of the Christian and of the church, defining Christian life in terms of freedom in Christ, life in the Spirit, and concern for others. (6) Finally, in 6.11-18, Paul concludes his letter by a reference to his own handwriting, summing up the main points, and, what is more important, reiterating his concern for his readers and his closeness to them.

CHAPTER 1

TEV	RSV
1 From Paul, whose call to be an apostle did not come from man or by means of man, but from Jesus Christ and God the Father, who raised him from death. 2 All the brothers who are here join me in sending greetings to the churches of Galatia:	1 Paul an apostle--not from men nor through man, but through Jesus Christ and God the Father, who raised him from the dead--2 and all the brethren who are with me,
	To the churches of Galatia:
3 May God our Father and the Lord Jesus Christ give you grace and peace.	3 Grace to you and peace from God the Father and our Lord Jesus Christ, 4 who gave himself for our sins to deliver us from the present evil age, according to the will of our God and Father; 5 to whom be the glory for ever and ever. Amen. (1.1-5)
4 In order to set us free from this present evil age, Christ gave himself for our sins, in obedience to the will of our God and Father. 5 To God be the glory forever and ever! Amen. (1.1-5)	

First-century letters, whether Jewish or Greek, usually began with a salutation which included the name of the writer, a reference to the intended readers, and some words of greeting. All of this was usually put in one sentence. In general Paul followed this practice in his letters, but made adjustments to suit his readers and the purpose of each letter.

Paul's letter to the Galatians contains a good example of this practice. He begins with a one-sentence salutation (1.1-5), which includes the usual elements expected at the beginning of a letter: his name, his work (or ministry), his companions when he was writing the letter, the intended readers, and some words of greeting. There are, however, differences between his salutation in this letter and the ways in which he begins his other letters. In verse 1, he not only mentions his work, but he goes to some length to describe how he was called to be an apostle. In verse 4, he includes a statement about the ministry of Christ. Finally, the salutation here is terse compared with others. The usual Pauline practice after the opening greeting is to include a prayer for the recipients of the letters and some words of commendation, leading gradually into the purpose of the letter. Such a pattern would not only follow the normal construction of a first-century letter; it would also satisfy the requirements of Eastern politeness. In this letter, however, he omits any words of commendation or prayer; he does not even include a gradual transition into his statement concerning the purpose of the letter. All of this can be explained by the purpose of the letter and by the mood in which it was written. Paul goes to some length to show the source of his calling as an apostle, because his claim to be an apostle has been questioned. His reference to the Galatians is one short statement, indicating his mood, perhaps not exactly one of anger, but surely one of serious concern. The greeting becomes a theological statement regarding the work of Christ, conveying at once the impression of Paul's authority.

Of primary concern to the translator, of course, is the fact that verses 1 through 5 are one sentence. This form is preserved in some translations (e.g. RSV). TEV, however, along with some other translations (e.g. JB NAB NEB Phps), restructures the passage into two or more sentences in order to produce a better English style.

Though the TEV text does not employ a section heading beginning this letter to the Galatians, in some instances it may be useful because of format arrangements to have such an introductory title. For example, one may employ "Paul greets the Christians in Galatia," "Paul writes to the churches in Galatia," or simply "To the churches in Galatia."

1.1   From Paul, whose call to be an apostle did not come from man or by means of man, but from Jesus Christ and God the Father, who raised him from death.

TEV indicates that this is a genuine letter by beginning with From Paul (see also NEB JB; Phps has "I, Paul"). In a number of languages it is necessary to indicate clearly the author of this letter by the first person singular pronoun "I." Therefore, in some languages the letter may most appropriately begin "I Paul...send greetings to the churches of Galatia."

Paul introduces himself as an apostle. This term usually refers to one who is sent to proclaim an important message, in this instance Christ's message. This term has been described as having both an exclusive and inclusive usage. In the exclusive sense it refers to the original twelve disciples of Jesus (cf. Luke 6.13), but in an inclusive sense it is applied to others who were engaged in the mission and proclamation of the Good News (cf. Acts 14.4; Rom 16.7). In several of his letters Paul uses this term to designate his own ministry (e.g. the Corinthian letters), thereby claiming equal status with the original disciples of Jesus.

One of the issues raised by Paul's opponents is his qualification and right to be an apostle. Not only are his credentials for this office called into question, but the very message which he has proclaimed and continues to proclaim is challenged. Paul meets the challenge head on. The first thing he does is to claim his right to be an apostle (cf. GeCL "Paul, an apostle, writes this letter").

His call, he claims, did not come from man or by means of man (literally, "not from men nor through man"). This means that his apostleship is not derived from any human source ("not from men") or dependent upon any human agency ("nor through man" or by means of man). In the Greek text, Paul switches from the plural "men" when talking about source to the singular "man" when talking about agency; this distinction is retained in some translations (e.g. NAB JB). However, many interpreters understand this change to be simply a matter of style, and therefore do not recommend its retention in translation (cf. NEB "not by human appointment or human commission"; Phps "appointed and commissioned...not by man").

Paul's call to be an apostle is not therefore dependent on human influence of any kind; on the contrary, it is from Jesus Christ and God the Father. The

[4]

emphasis here is twofold; that is, his call is from Jesus Christ as well as from God. In the latter part of this chapter, he expands on this point (see verses 11-24). The Greek preposition in this phrase can be translated "through" (as in RSV); most modern translations, however, understand it as TEV does. Jesus Christ and God are linked to only one preposition, suggesting that for Paul there is no distinction between the calling by Jesus Christ and the calling by God.

Because of the elliptical structure of verse 1 and because of the passive construction, it may be necessary in some languages to restructure this beginning statement rather extensively. For example, in some languages one must say "Jesus Christ and God the Father called me to be an apostle," or "... appointed me to be an apostle." A further difficulty may be involved in the expression God the Father, since in some languages the term Father must always occur with some so-called possessive pronoun indicating the relationship of "Father" to someone else. In general, the most satisfactory expression is "God our Father," and since Paul was here addressing his letter to the Galatians who were presumably believers in God, it would be possible to use "our" in the first person plural inclusive sense for those languages which make a distinction between inclusive and exclusive first person plural.

In translating the verb call, it is important to avoid an expression which would mean "to shout at." The meaning here is "to summon" or "to appoint" or even, as in some languages, "to give a work to."

In a number of languages an apostle is "a sent one" or "one given a special commission." In some languages the term is almost equivalent to "ambassador," that is, an individual who represents another person by carrying a message.

In some languages it is important to state the positive fact before the negative one, and therefore it may be perfectly appropriate to begin in some such form as "Jesus Christ and God our Father called me to be an apostle," followed by the negative contrast, for example, "No man appointed me to be an apostle, and no man was sent in order to appoint me as an apostle." The expression by means of man must refer to secondary agency; that is to say, Jesus Christ and God the Father did not appoint Paul by means of some human intermediary.

Since so much is interspersed between the statement of Paul as the author and his greetings to the churches of Galatia in verse 2, it may be useful to introduce the matter of greetings at two different points, for example, "I, Paul, send greetings to the churches of Galatia. Jesus Christ and God our Father have called me to be an apostle .... All the fellow Christians here join me in sending greetings to you in the churches of Galatia." Only in this way can one do justice to the fact that the letter does begin with both a form of greeting and some defense of Paul's position as an apostle. It must be noted, however, that if the greeting is introduced before the matter of Paul's apostleship is discussed, then the intended emotive impact, which is so basic to the purpose of the letter, may be minimized, if not lost altogether.

The expression who raised him from death is added here without any explanation. It is Paul's practice, when referring to God, to mention something of what he is and what he has done, usually in terms of what he has done in Christ Jesus. Elsewhere in his letters, God's act of raising Jesus from death is taken as proof that Jesus is God's Son (see Rom 1.4). Furthermore, the doctrine of Jesus being raised from death is central to early Christian preaching (see 1 Cor 15.4, 12-20).

The clause who raised him from death must be clearly marked as nonrestrictive; that is to say, it does not specify which God it was who raised Jesus from death. In some languages a nonrestrictive meaning must be set off as a separate sentence, for example, "...God our Father. He raised Jesus from death," "...caused Jesus to live again," or "...come back to life."

1.2   All the brothers who are here join me in sending greetings to the churches of Galatia:

Paul's usual practice is to mention by name those who are with him at the time of writing. Here, however, he mentions no name but only refers to his companions as all the brothers who are here. Brothers usually means "fellow Christians," although it is very possible that here Paul is referring to his fellow missionaries. There has been a great deal of speculation and guesswork as to who these brothers are. One could wish that Paul had named them so that the writing and reception of the letter could be better defined historically and geographically; but they remain anonymous for a very good reason: it is Paul's intention to defend himself against the attacks of his opponents without help from anyone.

In a number of languages the brothers must be rendered as "fellow Christians." If one were to translate brothers literally, the term would have to refer to Paul's own brothers. If, however, one understands brothers in this context to mean "fellow workers," it is then possible to translate the term as "all the persons who are working here together with me for the gospel."

Join me in sending greetings may be rendered in some languages as "are also sending greetings," or "together with me they are sending greetings."

The intended recipients of the letter are now identified: the churches of Galatia. Churches, of course, refers to various local congregations in Galatia. As to the location of Galatia, there are two possibilities: Paul may be referring to the geographical area known as Galatia, or to the political province of the same name. Arguments for both positions abound, and any modern commentary on Galatians will give a summary of the arguments. The weight of scholarly opinion tends to favor the latter view, that is, that Paul wrote to the churches in the Roman province of Galatia in Asia Minor, the towns of which he visited during his first and second missionary journeys (see Acts chapters 13, 14, and 16.1-5).

The question of which Galatia is intended is tied up with the problem of the date of this letter. Many scholars hold the opinion that Galatians was the first letter written by Paul, and they assign to it a date as early as the year 47 or 48 A.D. A later date, however, is suggested by the similarity of this letter to letters of Paul which clearly were written at a later date, particularly Romans and the Corinthian correspondence. The similarity tends to show that all these letters were probably written close to each other. If that is the case, the letter to

the Galatians may have been written either during Paul's second missionary journey or before the start of the third. This also makes it possible to equate Paul's
visit to Jerusalem mentioned in Gal 2 with the visit recorded in Acts 15, when
Paul and Barnabas attended the Jerusalem council.

In some languages it is almost a matter of necessity to indicate the nature
of Galatia. One must translate "the churches in the province of Galatia," or "...
the region of Galatia," depending upon one's interpretation as to which Galatia is
intended.

In selecting a term for <u>churches</u>, it is important to avoid an expression
which will merely refer to buildings. Paul's reference here is to groups of believers or "believers who meet together in various places."

1.3   May God our Father and the Lord Jesus Christ give you grace and
peace.

Verses 3-5 amplify the content of the greeting. Pauline greetings usually
start with <u>grace and peace</u>, continue with a description of what God has done in
Jesus Christ, and conclude with an expression of praise to God.

In the Greek text the greeting starts with "grace to you and peace" at the
beginning of verse 3. <u>Grace</u> is primarily a Christian word, a comprehensive
term which describes God's undeserved love, God's limitless favor towards
man. <u>Peace</u> is essentially a Jewish term, and it connotes total well-being, total
health. Some commentators take these two words in their full theological import.
While this can be justified, it should be borne in mind that what we have here is
a greeting formula which should be considered as a single unit.

The content of verse 3 is essentially a petition or prayer, and in many languages it must be introduced by a corresponding verb of speaking, for example,
"I pray that God our Father and the Lord Jesus Christ may give you grace and
peace," or "I ask God...to give you grace and peace."

In a number of languages one cannot speak of "giving grace and peace."
One can, however, "show kindness to," "be very good to," or even "show undeserved favor to" as an expression of <u>grace</u>. In connection with the term <u>peace</u>,
it may be necessary to use a causative, for example, "cause you to have peace,"
or "cause you to be well in every respect." In some other languages an idiomatic
expression may be employed, for example, "to cause you to sit down in your
hearts." Such an idiom suggests that one is in such a state of well-being that
there is no need for anxiety of any kind.

A comparison between TEV and RSV shows a difference which is caused
by a textual problem. Basically the question is, does the pronoun <u>our</u> go with
<u>Father</u> or with <u>Lord</u>? While the reply does not materially affect the meaning of
the passage, we are still interested in ascertaining what Paul really wrote.
There is much evidence favoring the text followed by the RSV ("God the Father
and our Lord Jesus Christ"), and many translations follow the same reading
(e.g. NEB Phps). However, the textual evidence seems to favor the solution followed by TEV, that the <u>our</u> goes with <u>Father</u> rather than with <u>Lord</u> (see also
NAB).

In place of the appositional construction <u>God our Father</u>, it may be necessary in some languages to use a relative clause, for example, "God who is our Father."

The name <u>Jesus Christ</u> should normally be treated in this type of context as simply a proper name consisting of two parts. Some translators always want to render <u>Christ</u> as "Messiah." In this particular context the focus is not upon Christ's Messiahship, as in some instances in the Synoptic Gospels, but here the term <u>Jesus Christ</u> is used essentially as a proper name.

In a number of languages it is not possible to use a translation of <u>Lord</u> as merely a title in combination with a name such as Jesus Christ. The only satisfactory equivalent may be "Jesus Christ who is our Lord." However, in some languages one cannot use a possessive pronoun with "Lord," for one does not possess a person who controls, and "Lord" may be equivalent to "the one who controls us" or "the one who commands us." Accordingly, <u>the Lord Jesus Christ</u> may be essentially equivalent to "Jesus Christ who commands us."

<u>1.4</u>   In order to set us free from this present evil age, Christ gave
              himself for our sins, in obedience to the will of our God and Father.

Departing from the usual pattern of the greeting, Paul includes a description of the work of Christ, which is one of the issues which he will later discuss at length. There are three elements in this verse: (1) Christ gave himself for our sins, (2) Christ sets us free from this present evil age, and (3) Christ was obedient to the will of God. The ordering of these varies from one translation to another. TEV has the order 2 - 1 - 3, Phps has 3 - 1 - 2, and NEB 1 - 2 - 3. Usually, the order does not matter as long as the relations between the three elements are made clear. In some languages, however, it is necessary to employ an order of means followed by purpose; that is to say, <u>Christ gave himself for our sins</u> must precede the statement of purpose, <u>in order to set us free from this present evil age</u>.

The first affirmation that Paul makes is that <u>Christ gave himself for our sins</u>. The expression <u>gave himself</u> emphasizes Jesus' voluntary self-giving; some translations render this as "sacrificed himself" (e.g. JB NEB). The preposition translated <u>for</u> is usually used in the New Testament to mean "(to do something) on behalf of, in respect to." With this in mind, <u>for our sins</u> could mean "to deliver us from our sins." In a number of languages, however, an expression such as <u>gave himself</u> has little or no meaning. What is meant is that he "gave his life" or "voluntarily died." In some languages one may simply say "Christ died for our sins," but in other languages the voluntary aspect must be expressed as a causative, for example, "Christ caused himself to die."

It is even more difficult in some languages to render appropriately the phrase <u>for our sins</u>. Too often the tendency has been to express <u>for our sins</u> as a reason or cause, for example, "because of our sins," meaning that "our sins caused Christ to die." But that is not the meaning of the passage. It is not "because we sinned Christ died," but rather "Christ died in order to deliver us from sins"; therefore "Christ died on behalf of sins." However, a literal translation of "on behalf of sins" could suggest that "he died in order to increase sins," which would be a complete distortion of the meaning of the passage. Therefore it may be more satisfactory to say "Christ gave his life in order to deliver us from our sins," or "...to free us from our sinning." It is also possible to interpret this as "...in order to take away the guilt of our sins."

The purpose of Christ's giving himself is to set us free from this present evil age. The division between "the present age" and "the age to come" was familiar to every Jew. The present world is described during Paul's time, and echoed in many of the New Testament writings, as a transitory world, a world ruled by evil forces. The position of the adjective evil in the sentence is emphatic, and the phrase could be restructured thus: "this present age with all of its evils" (cf. GeCL "this world ... in which evil rules").

Paul does not define for us what he means by the phrase to set us free. Is he talking about a future deliverance which will come at the end of the age? Or is he talking about being set free from the power of evil forces? Or yet again, is he using the expression "being set free" as a synonym for being justified, that is, being put right with God? We cannot be absolutely certain, but considering the overall purpose of the letter, which is concentrated on the way of being accepted by God in this present life, the second and third of these alternatives are surely closer to Paul's thought than the first.

In many languages it is easy enough to speak of "being set free," but not from the pattern of life suggested by a phrase such as "evil age"; one may be "set free from jail," but not "set free from an age"! In order to convey the essential meaning of this passage, it may be necessary in some languages to say "to set us free so that we do not have to live like people do in this present evil age."

Christ did all this in obedience to the will of our God and Father. It is possible to connect this expression with Christ's giving himself (e.g., in TEV Phps JB), or with his setting us free (as in RSV NEB NAB). Perhaps, however, it is connected with both ideas, that is, it is in obedience to God's will that Christ gave himself in order to rescue us from the present age. In a number of languages it is best to render in obedience to the will of our God and Father as a separate sentence (as in GeCL). This makes it possible to show the connection between the preceding and what follows in such a form as to include both Christ's giving himself and his setting us free, for example, "when Christ did that, he was obedient to what our God and Father wanted," or "in doing that, Christ obeyed what our God and Father desired."

In a number of languages there is a serious problem involved in the phrase our God and Father. If one combines the two nouns with a conjunction such as "and," the suggestion may be that two persons are involved, one God and the other Father. It may therefore be necessary to translate our God and Father as "our God who is our Father," or "our God; he is our Father."

1.5 To God be the glory forever and ever! Amen.

In the Greek, this verse is still part of the one sentence beginning with verse 1. To God is literally "to whom," but it is clear that the pronoun refers to God. Glory is a word with many meanings, but here it probably is used in the sense of "praise," and the whole expression may be equivalent to "May God be praised forever and ever." The word Amen is usually used to end a prayer, and is equivalent to saying "May it be so," or "May it come true."

In a number of languages the closest equivalent to the expression To God be the glory forever and ever! is "Let us praise God forever and ever!", "God deserves praise...!", or "People should praise God...!" The expression forever and ever may, of course, be rendered as "always" or "without ever stopping." A number of languages use a transliteration of the term Amen, but such a transliteration is often misleading in this type of context, since it is generally used at the end of prayers. In this type of context it is usually more appropriate to say "That is the way it should be," "Yes, indeed," or "That is usually true" (referring, of course, to their praise to God).

TEV	RSV
The One Gospel	
6 I am surprised at you! In no time at all you are deserting the one who called you by the grace of Christ,^{a} and are accepting another gospel. 7 Actually, there is no "other gospel," but I say this because there are some people who are upsetting you and trying to change the gospel of Christ. 8 But even if we or an angel from heaven should preach to you a gospel that is different from the one we preached to you, may he be condemned to hell! 9 We have said it before, and now I say it again: if anyone preaches to you a gospel that is different from the one you accepted, may he be condemned to hell!	6 I am astonished that you are so quickly deserting him who called you in the grace of Christ and turning to a different gospel-- 7 not that there is another gospel, but there are some who trouble you and want to pervert the gospel of Christ. 8 But even if we, or an angel from heaven, should preach to you a gospel contrary to that which we preached to you, let him be accursed. 9 As we have said before, so now I say again, If any one is preaching to you a gospel contrary to that which you received, let him be accursed.
10 Does this sound as if I am trying to win man's approval? No indeed! What I want is God's approval! Am I trying to be popular with men? If I were still trying to do so, I would not be a servant of Christ.	10 Am I now seeking the favor of men, or of God? Or am I trying to please men? If I were still pleasing men, I should not be a servant^a of Christ.
	^{a}Or *slave* (1.6-10)
^{a}by the grace of Christ; *some manuscripts have* by his grace.

(1.6-10) | |

The section heading The One Gospel may be rendered in some languages as "There is only one gospel," or "There is no other gospel." In a number of languages, of course, gospel may be rendered as "the message of good news" or simply "good news."

As has already been indicated, one would normally expect here a prayer of thanksgiving for the faith of the Galatian believers. Instead of such kind words, however, one finds strong words expressing surprise, indignation, and concern. It seems that Paul has no time for niceties. The Galatians are in danger of apostasy, and many of them have already given up their earlier beliefs. Paul therefore tackles the problem immediately, wasting neither time nor words, but going right to the heart of the problem. He brands the new teaching which has found its way into the Galatian churches as a new message which is really not the gospel message at all; he warns the Galatians not to believe anyone, not even an angel of God, who preaches a message different from what they heard from him when he was with them.

1.6   I am surprised at you! In no time at all you are deserting the one who called you by the grace of Christ,^{a} and are accepting another gospel.

^{a}by the grace of Christ; *some manuscripts have* by his grace.

The verb translated surprised includes an element of intense unbelief. I am surprised at you is therefore very close to the English expression "I can't believe this of you at all!" In some languages it is difficult to express mere surprise about a person. The more usual equivalent would be "surprise about what a person has done." Therefore, I am surprised at you may be rendered as "I am surprised at what you have done." In other languages "what you have done" constitutes the cause for surprise, and therefore the first sentence of this verse may be rendered as "What you have done causes me to be surprised," "...astonishes me," or "...makes me wonder so that I can scarcely believe it."

Paul's surprise stems from the fact that in no time at all the Galatians are deserting the one who called them. In no time at all translates an expression which may refer to (1) the pace of their desertion after it has begun; (2) the short time between their conversion and their desertion, or (3) the short time between Paul's last visit to them and the writing of this letter. While all three interpretations are possible grammatically, most commentators favor the second of these alternatives.

In no time at all may be rendered in a number of languages as "in such a short time" or "so soon now." In some languages, however, it is almost necessary to indicate more precisely the length of time involved, presumably the time between the conversion of the Galatian believers and the desertion of their faith in the grace of Christ. If one must choose between expressions which would involve a few days, a few weeks, a few months, or a few years, it is probably best to employ the one which would mean "within a few months you are deserting."

The word deserting carries with it the idea of changing one's mind, of a willful forsaking of one's former loyalty and adoption of another. Paul's use of

[11]

the present tense suggests that the process of desertion is still going on, and that it is not yet complete, and therefore it is still possible to check it. In some languages the term deserting may be rendered as "abandoning," "leaving to the side," or even "going off and forgetting."

The object of the desertion is not some doctrine or teaching, but the one who called you, referring not to Paul but to God himself (cf. GeCL "God has called you"). Because it is so easy to understand the phrase the one who called you as a reference to Paul, it may be essential in some languages to say "you are deserting God, who called you."

As the footnote indicates, there is a textual problem involving the phrase by the grace of Christ. In the Greek text there are actually four possible readings: (1) "by grace," (2) "by the grace of Christ," (3) "by the grace of Jesus Christ," and (4) "by the grace of God." The first of these alternatives is probably the original reading of the phrase, and at least one modern translation (NEB) follows it, but most translations follow the second alternative. They follow it, however, primarily for translational reasons, so as to indicate clearly that in this context grace is a reference to God's grace, which comes by means of Jesus Christ.

The expression "by grace" could itself refer either to the purpose of the calling (e.g. "who called you to be in a state of grace") or to the instrument through which the calling was accomplished, i.e. "by grace." While both interpretations are possible, most commentators and translators prefer the second. The whole emphasis of the letter is that the Good News is made possible by the free gift of God through Jesus Christ (which is what grace really is) in contrast with obedience to the Jewish Law. The phrase by the grace of Christ expresses the means by which God had called the believers. This may be expressed in some languages as "by means of Christ being so good to you," "by means of Christ showing you such favor," or "by means of Christ's great kindness to you." If, however, one follows the fourth alternative form of the text, then "God" becomes the active agent of the grace.

The desertion is further explained in the conclusion of the verse: the Galatians are accepting another gospel. The word gospel is the term used to describe the Good News of what God has done in Jesus Christ on behalf of all men. When Paul talks of another gospel, however, he is not talking of this Good News; he is talking about a different message which claims to be the Good News, but really is not (cf. JB "a different version of the Good News" seems to capture accurately Paul's intention). It may be extremely difficult in some languages to speak of another gospel particularly if the term gospel is rendered as "good news." Under such circumstances it would seem to mean something like "more good news," which obviously is not what is intended in this verse. The closest equivalent may be "another message which is said to be good news," "...claims to be good news," or "...is spoken of as good news."

1.7 Actually, there is no "other gospel," but I say this because there are some people who are upsetting you and trying to change the gospel of Christ.

In the previous verse, Paul has just labeled the false teaching as another version of the gospel. Here he is quick to deny that it can even be called that, as he affirms that there is no "other gospel." Literally rendered, this expression is "which is not another" or "not that it is another" (NEB follows the second of these). The apostasy which is affecting the Galatians is simply not another gospel which can be substituted for the gospel which Paul has proclaimed to them. In denying the possibility of "another gospel," one may say in some languages "but there is no other message which is good news," "but what is called good news is really not good news," or "but this other good news really isn't good news."

But I say this because renders the Greek word often translated "except," but in this case it introduces a special factor which needs to be considered, perhaps best introduced by "but I say this only because." Paul is not through minimizing the fact that he described the false teaching as another gospel. The reason for Paul's previous statement is that there are some people who were really at work among the Galatians upsetting them and trying to change the gospel of Christ. This is the first mention of those who are preaching the "other gospel" among the Galatians. (For a brief statement of who they are, see page 1, third paragraph.) The verb for upsetting is in the present tense, indicating perhaps that these people are still in Galatia. The verb itself can mean "to disturb mentally, with excitement, perplexity, or fear" (RSV "trouble," NEB "unsettle your minds," NAB "confuse").

Trying to change the gospel of Christ is literally "want to pervert the gospel of Christ." This indicates that the Galatians have not yet fully succumbed to the influence of the Judaising missionaries. The Greek word for to change is in itself neutral, and simply means to change from one thing into another, or from one state to another, or to an opposite state, but in this context it means to change for the worse (RSV "to pervert," NEB "to distort").

The gospel of Christ is not the gospel belonging to Christ, but the Good News about Christ, hence the Good News with Christ as the content.

There is a serious but subtle problem involved in rendering to change the gospel of Christ since, in fact, to alter the Good News about Christ would be to make it no longer Good News. Therefore, in some languages it may be necessary to say "to take away the good news about Christ and to put in lies," or "to substitute false words for true words in the good news about Christ."

1.8 But even if we or an angel from heaven should preach to you a gospel that is different from the one we preached to you, may he be condemned to hell!

In very strong language Paul now warns the Galatians against the preaching of another version of the good news. But even if we or an angel from heaven would include everyone, and some translations make this explicit (e.g. NEB JB).

We may refer to Paul and the brothers, mentioned in 1.2, but more probably to Paul alone (see also the discussion of we under verse 9). There are instances in Paul's other letters where he has used the plural pronoun to refer to himself (e.g. Romans 1.5).

The hypothetical condition if we ... should preach must be expressed in some languages as a denied condition, e.g. "if we ever preach, but we will not do so."

An angel from heaven gives us a clue as to the Jewish nature of the false teaching. Later in this letter Paul speaks of angels in the giving of the Law as a proof that the Jewish Law is less than what the Jews have made of it (see 3.19-20). The Greek word for angel may refer to any messenger, whether human or celestial, but here the emphasis is on the celestial.

The Greek preposition translated different from can be interpreted in this context as expressing either simply difference (cf. JB, NEB "at variance with," NAB "not in accord with") or contrast (e.g. RSV "contrary to," Mft "that contradicts"). A gospel that is different from the one we preached to you may be rendered in some languages as "good news which is not the same as what we preached to you," "good news which has other meaning from the one we preached to you," or "... says something different from the good news we preached to you."

Condemned to hell translates a Greek word which can be transliterated "anathema" and can refer either to a thing or a person under the curse or the wrath of God and therefore set apart for destruction. Some take anathema to mean in this context "excommunication" (NEB "he shall be held outcast"); it is more likely, however, that this meaning arose much later. The whole expression is a petition to God that the person referred to may be deprived of God's favor and be the object instead of his condemnation. Precisely what Paul has in mind is hard to determine, but may he be condemned to hell! captures the intensity of the original phrase. In some languages the phrase may he be condemned to hell! is rendered as "he will surely suffer in hell," "God will certainly destroy him," or "I ask God to make him suffer."

1.9   We have said it before, and now I say it again: if anyone preaches to you a gospel that is different from the one you accepted, may he be condemned to hell!

It is possible that we have said it before could refer to the statement in verse 8 (NAB "I repeat what I have just said"). Most translators and commentators, however, understand this statement to refer to a previous occasion in the past, when Paul was with the Galatians, in contrast with the present when he is not personally with them but is communicating with them by letter. This previous occasion is probably the initial visit of Paul to Galatia. If one takes the position that Paul is writing to congregations in the Roman province of Galatia, then perhaps a more or less accurate record of this visit can be found in Acts 13.13−14.26. In a number of languages, however, one cannot be ambiguous in the use of the adverb before. One must either choose the immediate reference to what is said in verse 8 or to what was said on a prior occasion. If one chooses the latter, it may be necessary to indicate something of the time lapse of the verb in question. Here, depending on one's understanding of the date for the writing of the letter to the Galatians, one must choose between "several months before" or "a few years before."

The we, as in verse 8, may be understood as referring to Paul himself (NEB NAB JB Phps Mft). An alternative is to understand we as referring not only to Paul but to his missionary companions when he visited the Galatians. This is apparently what TEV prefers, and therefore it preserves the plural form in translation. In languages which would not employ the so-called "editorial we," it may be better to employ the first person singular "I," particularly if one understands that by we Paul is referring to himself alone.

The Greek word for if in the phrase if anyone indicates that Paul is no longer dealing with a supposition or a hypothetical situation (as in v. 8) but with the actual situation of the Galatian churches, and so it may be translated "whoever" or "anyone who." Anyone is general, but the reference is, of course, to the some people of verse 7.

The one you accepted is literally "that which you received." The word "received" contains the element of appropriating something for oneself. The good news had not merely been preached to the Galatians; they had not merely "heard" it (JB Phps), but they had received it and made it their own. The Greek verb used in this context was a technical one in Judaism for "receiving a tradition."

1.10   Does this sound as if I am trying to win man's approval? No indeed! What I want is God's approval! Am I trying to be popular with men? If I were still trying to do so, I would not be a servant of Christ.

Some commentators take verse 10 as an introduction to what follows. Understood in this manner, this verse would echo the accusations of Paul's enemies, i.e., that he is trying to please men. But in talking harshly about those who are preaching another message to the Galatians, Paul has been in effect answering the charge of his enemies that he is more interested in pleasing men than in pleasing God. Paul also answers this accusation by going into many aspects of his life, both before and after his conversion in Damascus.

The first part of this verse is a rhetorical question in the Greek, and TEV makes the implicit answer explicit. Most translations neglect more or less the Greek structure but make the implied answer clear (for example, NEB "Does my language now sound as if I were canvassing for men's support? Whose support do I want but God's alone?"). Does this sound definitely refers to what Paul has just said (cf. NEB) and shows that verse 10 is to be taken with the preceding verse.

In a number of languages it would be impossible to use a rhetorical question such as Does this sound...? The equivalent would be a strong negative statement, for example, "I am obviously not trying to win people's approval," or "By saying that, I am certainly not trying to cause men to approve of me," or "...to cause men to say that I am saying what is right."

What I want is God's approval! may be rendered as "What I want is for God to approve of what I do," or "I want God to say that what I do is right." It may even be possible to say "I want to please God."

Am I trying to be popular with men? has the same thought as the first question, with the emphasis in Greek upon deliberately trying to gain men's approval. This rhetorical question may be immediately answered in some languages by a strong negative, while in other languages, as already stated, it may be impossible to use such a rhetorical question and a strong negative statement may be required, for example, "I am certainly not trying to be popular with men," "...trying to please men," "...trying to make men say that I am fine," or "...cause people to like me."

If I were still trying to do so makes it clear that Paul denies completely the charge laid against him. He might well have been seeking man's approval in the past, that is, before his conversion, but at the time of his preaching to the Galatians that was no longer the case.

If what his opponents were saying was true, then he could not and would not be a servant of Christ. The conditional sentence If I were still trying to do so, I would not be a servant of Christ means first of all that it would be impossible for Paul both to please men and to serve Christ. Second, he is affirming his status and ministry as a servant of Christ. Since he is a servant of Christ, he goes on to discuss the implications of his role and his message, thus providing a link between this second section (1.6-10) and the third section (1.11–2.21).

The word servant is literally "slave," and some commentators advocate translating it literally. It is possible, however, that Paul is using the term with the Old Testament in mind, where the prophets are often known as "the servants of God." The closest equivalent of servant of Christ in some languages is "one who helps Christ" or "one who does what Christ says," in the sense of carrying out the orders of Christ.

<table>
<tr><td align="center">TEV</td><td align="center">RSV</td></tr>
</table>

How Paul Became an Apostle

11 Let me tell you, my brothers, that the gospel I preach is not of human origin. 12 I did not receive it from any man, nor did anyone teach it to me. It was Jesus Christ himself who revealed it to me.

(1.11-12)

11 For I would have you know, brethren, that the gospel which was preached by me is not man's[b] gospel. 12 For I did not receive it from man, nor was I taught it, but it came through a revelation of Jesus Christ.

[b]Greek *according to man*   (1.11-12)

The section heading How Paul Became an Apostle may be somewhat adapted in the form of "How Paul was sent to preach the good news," or "How Paul was given the work of an apostle." In some instances it may be better to employ as a section heading words taken from verse 12, for example, "How Jesus Christ revealed good news to Paul."

Beginning with 1.11 and running through to 2.21, Paul deals with the charge of his opponents that he is not an apostle of Jesus Christ, and that therefore the message that he has been preaching is less than accurate. Paul answers such charges by asserting that the gospel he has been preaching came directly from God, that his call to be an apostle is independent of any human influence, even of the twelve disciples in Jerusalem, and finally that in a private meeting with the leaders of the Jerusalem church his message was approved and his commission as an apostle was recognized.

First of all, then, in verses 11 and 12 Paul claims that the source of his message is not...man but Jesus Christ himself. He resumes the subject which he has introduced in verses 6-9, and which is linked with what follows by the statement about himself in verse 10.

1.11   Let me tell you, my brothers, that the gospel I preach is not of human origin.

Let me tell you may be rendered as "I want you to know," or "I want to make it perfectly clear."

Paul affectionately addresses his readers as my brothers. Among Jews the word "brother" was used for the members of any given family or tribe or sect. Early Christians carried this usage over into their fellowship and addressed each other as "brothers."

The gospel I preach could be understood either as referring to that particular message which Paul preached to the Galatians (NAB "The gospel I proclaimed to you," NEB "the gospel you heard me preach") or as a general reference to the message which Paul continued to proclaim (as in TEV, cf. Mft "The gospel that I preach"). The verb preach is often rendered in a form which indicates habitual action, for example, "the gospel that I customarily preach," or "...announce."

Is not of human origin is literally "is not according to man," and may mean that the gospel (1) is not of human origin, (2) is not dependent on human authority, or (3) is not a human gospel. Some translations (notably NAB NEB, along with TEV) follow the first of these alternatives, while others adhere to the third (e.g. JB "the Good News...is not a human message," Mft "is not a human affair"). The closest equivalent to is not of human origin may be "was not thought out by people," "people did not cause it to be," or "people did not start it."

1.12   I did not receive it from any man, nor did anyone teach it to me. It was Jesus Christ himself who revealed it to me.

Paul expands on his argument by the use of two other negative statements: I did not receive it from any man refers to the initial reception of the gospel, while nor did anyone teach it to me refers to his growing understanding of its contents. The first statement may be rendered as "No man told me this good news," and the second may then be rendered as "and no one taught me what this good news was." The two statements are essentially only two different ways of speaking about the same reality, though the second may be regarded as emphasizing more the fact that Paul was not specifically taught the good news by some qualified teacher.

Finally, Paul informs his readers of the source of his message. The Greek itself is literally "but through a revelation of Jesus Christ"; the "of" could mean either (1) that the revelation was made by Christ to Paul (e.g. TEV, cf. NAB "revelation from Jesus Christ") or (2) that the content of the revelation, which was from God, was Jesus Christ. In view of 1.16, the second of these alternatives is to be preferred, but most translations carry over the ambiguous construction of the Greek. Who revealed it to me may be rendered as "who showed it to me," "who caused me to see it," or even "who caused me to understand the good news."

TEV	RSV
13 You have been told how I used to live when I was devoted to the Jewish religion, how I persecuted without mercy the church of God and did my best to destroy it. 14 I was ahead of most fellow Jews of my age in my practice of the Jewish religion, and was much more devoted to the traditions of our ancestors. (1.13-14)	13 For you have heard of my former life in Judaism, how I persecuted the church of God violently and tried to destroy it; 14 and I advanced in Judaism beyond many of my own age among my people, so extremely zealous was I for the traditions of my fathers. (1.13-14)

In these two verses Paul looks back to his life before his conversion and sees in his experiences the proof of his assertion regarding the divine origin and character of the message he was now proclaiming.

1.13   You have been told how I used to live when I was devoted to the Jewish religion, how I persecuted without mercy the church of God and did my best to destroy it.

You have been told is literally "you heard." The source of information is not mentioned; it is even possible that it was Paul himself who told them. Another possibility which has been suggested is to take "you heard" as reflecting a typical and traditional Eastern way of apologizing before mentioning one's own experiences. This seems to be the sense implied in at least one translation (JB "You must have heard").

How I used to live translates a Greek expression referring to "manner of life," "behavior," "conduct." It may be necessary in some languages to be somewhat more specific than is the English expression used to live. One may say, for example, "how I behaved," "how I acted," or even "what I did."

When I was devoted to the Jewish religion translates a prepositional phrase (literally "in Judaism"). In the New Testament the word "Judaism" is used only here and in the following verse. In the deuterocanonical books of the Maccabees this term is used to refer to the Jewish religion in contrast to other religions, particularly that of the Syrian kings. It is possible that Paul is using it in the same sense here and is contrasting the Jewish set of beliefs with those of the church of God, which in this verse is how he talks about the Christian faith (cf. Phps). But some interpreters, observing that the use of the term "Judaism" in direct contrast to Christianity arose later, that is, at the close of the first century, consider it more likely that what Paul means here is adherence to the total Jewish way of life (so NEB and JB "a practising Jew"). The clause when I was devoted to the Jewish religion may be rendered in some languages as "when I worshiped God as Jews worship God."

With regard to this stage of his life, Paul mentions two things, although they are in reverse chronological order: (1) he was a persecutor of the church, and (2) he was an ardent student of Judaism, both in theory and practice.

Paul's activities as a persecutor of the church are described in the early chapters of Acts (7.58; 8.1; 9.1-2). In this verse, he admits that he persecuted the church without mercy. The Greek word contains the elements of consistency and excess, and various translations try to include either one or both of these elements (RSV "violently," Phps "with fanatical zeal," NEB "savagely," NAB "I went to extremes," JB "merciless," Mft "furiously").

I persecuted...the church of God may be rendered as "I caused groups of believers in God to suffer very much." In many languages it is not possible to use a collective such as the church in this type of context, but one must always use a plural form indicating various groups of believers.

The phrase persecuted without mercy may be rendered as "did everything I could to persecute," "didn't stop at anything in persecuting," "strongly persecuted," or "used violence in making people suffer."

The imperfect tense of the Greek verb translated persecuted suggests that Paul's persecution of the church continued for some time. The force of the imperfect tense may be expressed in some languages as "I kept on persecuting." The imperfect tense of the verb meaning "to destroy" indicates an attempt, as well as an action which continued for a period of time; it may be rendered as "I kept on doing my best to destroy." It is important in employing a verb for destroy to use one which would be applicable to an institution or a group of people and not merely to some building. One may sometimes use a phrase meaning "to cause to come to an end," "to cause to cease," or "to scatter and make disappear."

1.14   I was ahead of most fellow Jews of my age in my practice of the Jewish
         religion, and was much more devoted to the traditions of our ancestors.

Here Paul goes back to his youth, and he has important things to say about himself. First, he was ahead of most fellow Jews of his own age in his practice of the Jewish religion. Concerning the nature of this advancement, we can only speculate. It would certainly include bigger responsibilities within Judaism, particularly within the Pharisaic sect of which Paul was a part (cf. Phil 3.5). Perhaps also it would include achievement in the realm of conduct, that is, in the realm of attaining the ideal way of life in terms of obedience to the Law. As a third alternative it is possible to interpret the following clause as providing the content of this advancement, i.e. devotion to the traditions of his ancestors (NEB "I was outstripping many of my Jewish contemporaries in my boundless devotion to the traditions of my ancestors"), or again, his zeal for the Jewish traditions (NAB "I made progress...in my excess of zeal to live out all the traditions of my ancestors"). Most commentators and translators, however, take Paul's "advancement" and his "zeal" to be two different things.

The phrase in my practice of the Jewish religion may be understood as the means by which Paul outdistanced his fellow Jews of the same age group. Therefore one may translate "by means of the way that I worshiped God as Jews customarily worship God." I was ahead of most fellow Jews of my age may be rendered as "I was superior to most other Jews of my age," "I surpassed most other Jews of my age," "I did even more than most other Jews my age did," "...who were the same age I was," or "...had as many years as I had."

In the last clause the word translated much more devoted is literally "more a zealot." This should not, however, be taken to mean that Paul was a member of the party of the Zealots, but rather as an adjective which means "zealous for" (cf. NEB "boundless devotion to," Phps "greater enthusiasm," Mft "special ardour").

Traditions are teachings which are transmitted from one generation to another over a long period of time and which in the process become authoritative. In the phrase the traditions of our ancestors, it is possible that Paul refers to the particular teachings of his own family (Mft "traditions of my house"), or to the teachings of the sect to which he belonged, the Pharisees. It is more likely, however, that he refers to the traditions of the Jewish nation as a whole.

In some languages it may be difficult to speak of being "devoted to one's traditions." One may say, however, "I tried with all my strength to do what our ancestors had passed on to us," "...had handed down to us," "...what we had heard from many generations of our ancestors," "...what our ancestors kept saying generation after generation," or "...what they kept saying repeatedly from father to son."

TEV	RSV
15 But God in his grace chose me even before I was born, and called me to serve him. And when he decided 16 to reveal his Son to me, so that I might preach the Good News about him to the Gentiles, I did not go to anyone for advice, 17 nor did I go to Jerusalem to see those who were apostles before me. Instead, I went at once to Arabia, and then I returned to Damascus. 18 It was three years later that I went to Jerusalem to obtain information from Peter, and I stayed with him for two weeks. 19 I did not see any other apostle except James,^{b} the Lord's brother.	15 But when he who had set me apart before I was born, and had called me through his grace, 16 was pleased to reveal his Son to^c me, in order that I might preach him among the Gentiles, I did not confer with flesh and blood, 17 nor did I go up to Jerusalem to those who were apostles before me, but I went away into Arabia; and again I returned to Damascus. 18 Then after three years I went up to Jerusalem to visit Cephas, and remained with him fifteen days. 19 But I saw none of the other apostles except James the Lord's

20 What I write is true. God knows that I am not lying!

21 Afterward I went to places in Syria and Cilicia. 22 At that time the members of the churches in Judea did not know me personally. 23 They knew only what others were saying: "The man who used to persecute us is now preaching the faith that he once tried to destroy!" 24 And so they praised God because of me.

*b*any other apostle except James; *or* any other apostle; the only other person I saw was James. (1.15-24)

brother. 20 (In what I am writing to you, before God, I do not lie!) 21 Then I went into the regions of Syria and Cilicia. 22 And I was still not known by sight to the churches of Christ in Judea; 23 they only heard it said, "He who once persecuted us is now preaching the faith he once tried to destroy." 24 And they glorified God because of me.

*c*Greek *in*   (1.15-24)

Having described his previous life as a devoted Jew, Paul proceeds to talk about his call to be an apostle, and the events that immediately followed, with one aim in mind, namely, to show that his apostleship is not dependent on any man, not even on the original twelve apostles, but on God alone.

1.15a   But God in his grace chose me even before I was born, and called me to serve him.

Verse 15 is not a complete sentence in the Greek; it is the beginning of a single long sentence which ends in verse 17. Most modern translators restructure these verses into several sentences, in keeping with the demands of modern language style.

Pursuing his aim to show that his apostleship is dependent on God alone, Paul enumerates several acts of God which were involved in his becoming an apostle. God, he says, chose me, called me, and revealed his Son to me (v.16a).

But shows the contrast of this section with what precedes; it is as if Paul were saying: "Despite all this, when God...."

Most translators relate in his grace to called me, since the phrase immediately follows the verbal expression in the Greek text. TEV, however, understands in his grace as modifying both the choosing and the calling (a perfectly justifiable interpretation), and therefore it moves this phrase to the first part of the sentence. The expression in his grace means that God acted on his own initiative and that his actions were dependent only on his own unconditional and undeserved love, that is, they in no sense involved any merit or lack of merit in Paul. In some languages in his grace must be expressed as a complete clause, for example, "he was good to me," "he showed me great favor," or "he was very kind to me." This may be combined paratactically with what follows, for example, "God was very kind to me; he chose me...." Or God's grace may be looked upon as a reason for his choice of Paul and therefore "because God was so kindly disposed to me, he chose me."

Chose me is literally "set me apart," with the idea of separating one from others for a particular purpose or task. One must be particularly careful in the selection of a term for chose. Frequently the literal meaning "set apart" implies separation of what is bad from that which is good. The emphasis here is upon "selected me in a special way," and the connotation of the term must imply a choice for something good.

Before I was born translates the Hebrew idiom "out of my mother's womb" and can mean either "before birth" (TEV RSV NAB) or "from birth" (NEB Phps cf. Knox "from the day of my birth").

Called has the concepts of both "summon" and "designate." Here Paul refers, of course, to his being summoned as an apostle, or as a servant of Jesus Christ. In a literal translation of called there is a strong tendency to employ a verb which means essentially "to shout at." An expression which means "to summon," "to designate," or "to commission" (cf. v. 1) is much to be preferred for this type of context.

1.15b-16 And when he decided (16) to reveal his Son to me, so that I might preach the Good News about him to the Gentiles, I did not go to anyone for advice,

To reveal his Son to me is literally "to reveal his Son in (or by) me." Does this mean "to reveal his Son to others, by means of me" or "to reveal his Son to me"? While the first of these is possible (a similar construction occurs in 1.24), yet on the basis of the total context and Paul's line of argument, the second alternative is more acceptable. The burden of this passage is how Paul received the gospel, not how he proclaimed it. TEV makes this latter meaning clear (so also NAB and RSV). Most other translations keep the construction "in me," and NEB combines the two ideas ("reveal his Son to me and through me").

It would be possible to render to reveal his Son to me as simply "to show me his Son" or "to cause me to see his Son," but this would scarcely do justice to the fuller implications of the revelation. Some translators prefer an expression meaning "to cause me to know who his Son really is," "to show me who his Son really is," or even "to let me see what I could not see—who his Son really is."

The purpose of this revelation, Paul asserts, is that I might preach the Good News about him. The Greek verb often rendered simply "preach" is more fully "proclaim the good news"; TEV makes this explicit (so also NAB "that I might spread among the Gentiles the good tidings concerning him"; cf. JB).

Gentiles is literally "nations," but Paul, as well as other New Testament writers, uses the word to refer to non-Jews as distinguished from Jews. To the Gentiles could also be "among the Gentiles" (RSV Knox NAB NEB). In a number of languages Gentiles is simply translated as "those who are not Jews"; in other languages the equivalent is "foreigners." But a rendering such as "foreigners" almost inevitably involves complications, since the readers or listeners would normally not think of themselves as "foreigners."

Paul now describes his subsequent actions both negatively (I did not go...
nor did I go...) and positively (Instead, I went).

I did not go to anyone for advice is literally "I conferred not with flesh and blood." "Flesh and blood" is an idiom which simply means a living person. The verb translated "conferred" is used in the New Testament only here and in 2.6; here it means "to hold conference with" or "to communicate with someone" (cf. JB "I did not stop to discuss this with any human being," NEB "without consulting any human being"). One may also render this clause as "I didn't go to talk with anyone about this," "I didn't ask anyone to tell me what all this meant," or "I didn't ask anyone to tell me what to do."

1.17   nor did I go to Jerusalem to see those who were apostles before me. Instead, I went at once to Arabia, and then I returned to Damascus.

Apostles refers to the Twelve, but the term as used here could include others such as James the Lord's brother (v. 19). Paul mentions them here as a special group who would naturally be the first to be consulted by anyone aspiring to become an apostle. In not going to see the apostles, Paul was doing something contrary to natural expectation (cf. Phps "I did not even go to Jerusalem"). When Paul describes the apostles in Jerusalem as apostles before me, he was asserting not only that he recognized the apostleship of the Twelve but that he regarded his own apostleship as being of the same character as that of the Jerusalem apostles. The phrase before me may refer either to time or to status (or precedence), but the temporal interpretation is preferable.

In this context the verb see implies more than merely looking at someone. The equivalent in some languages would be "I did not go to Jerusalem to pay a visit to those who were apostles before me," "...to talk with those who were apostles before me," or "...who had been apostles before I became one."

Having mentioned what he did not do, Paul now asserts two things that he did: (1) He went at once to Arabia, and (2) he returned to Damascus. The purpose of the visit to Arabia is not stated, but apparently it was to seek through meditation a fuller understanding of the meaning of his call. The phrase at once in the Greek comes right before I did not go to anyone for advice. It seems better to take it as modifying, not simply what immediately follows, but the whole sentence; and since the expression itself calls for a positive affirmation, it should be connected with Paul's going to Arabia, rather than with the two prior negative statements (e.g. TEV JB; cf. NEB NAB, where the negative statements are made into dependent clauses: "Immediately, without seeking human advisers, or even going to Jerusalem to see those who were apostles before me, I went off to Arabia"). It may be useful to stipulate Arabia as being a country, for example, "I went off to the country of Arabia," or "...to the region called Arabia."

The mention of "returning to Damascus" is an indirect assertion that the experience of Paul's conversion occurred in Damascus (see Acts 9.1-19 and parallels Acts 22.4-16 and 26.9-18). One may wish to employ a classifier with the word Damascus and translate, for example, "I went back to the city of Damascus."

1.18   It was three years later that I went to Jerusalem to obtain information from Peter, and I stayed with him for two weeks.

In this verse and the next, Paul mentions his first visit to Jerusalem. It was three years later is literally "after three years," but the purpose of this phrase is not merely chronological; rather it is used to put forth the argument that Paul did not establish contacts with the Jerusalem apostles for quite some time (Phps "It was not until three years later"). It is difficult to determine just when these three years began. There are two possibilities: (1) from his return from Arabia or (2) from his conversion. Most commentators favor the latter. In some languages it may be necessary to stipulate the time from which the three years are to be reckoned, and so it may be necessary to say "three years after I returned to Damascus," or "three years after I became a believer." Note, however, that the latter of these alternatives is to be preferred.

To obtain information from Peter involves a verb which can mean either to gather information from him (TEV) or to get acquainted with him (NEB "to get to know Cephas"; Mft "to make the acquaintance of Cephas"). In a number of languages the closest equivalent and most neutral way of expressing the meaning is "to talk with Peter."

Peter is "Cephas" in the Greek; and "Cephas" (meaning "Rock") is the Aramaic equivalent of "Peter."

Two weeks is literally "fifteen days." The emphasis here is on the brevity of the visit; it would have been impossible for Paul to become a disciple of the Jerusalem apostles just by visiting Peter for such a short period of time. In order to emphasize the brevity of the visit and to play down this particular event, it is possible to translate this as "I stayed with him for just two weeks."

1.19   I did not see any other apostle except James,[b] the Lord's brother.

    [b]any other apostle except James; *or* any other apostle; the only other person I saw was James.

Since Paul is here mentioning several items which indicate his very brief contact with the apostles in Jerusalem, it may be useful to begin verse 19 with a conjunction such as "furthermore" or "moreover" ("Furthermore, I did not see...").

Not only did Paul stay in Jerusalem for only a brief time; but also he did not see anyone except Peter and James. As TEV indicates, the phrase except James presents a problem of interpretation. Does Paul mean to include James with the apostles? If that is the case, he is saying that he saw no other apostle except James. Or does Paul exclude James from the apostolic group? In that case he is saying "I did not see any of the other apostles; I only saw James" (as in the TEV footnote and in JB). Either interpretation of the Greek is possible.

James is probably the same person mentioned in Mark 6.3 as Jesus' brother and is referred to simply as James in Gal 2.9, 12; 1 Cor 15.7; Acts 15.13; 21.18. He was known in later tradition as the first bishop of the church in

Jerusalem. He should be distinguished from James the Son of Zebedee and James the son of Alphaeus, who were two of the Twelve (Matt 10.2-3).

Depending upon the interpretation which is adopted, the exception of James may be introduced as "I saw only James," or "the only other apostle was James." One may then introduce the apposition as a separate sentence: "He is the brother of our Lord." In this rendering the Lord is often expressed as "our Lord," since in many languages the relation of people to the Lord must be indicated.

1.20   What I write is true. God knows that I am not lying!

The inclusion of this exclamatory statement is rather typical of Paul (see 1 Thes 2.5; 2 Cor 1.23; 11.31).

What I write can refer either to what immediately precedes or to all that precedes. For the former, see NAB "What I have just written," also JB; for the latter, see Phps "All this that I am telling you."

In order to avoid possible contradiction with the interpretation of 6.11, in which Paul speaks of writing with his own hand, it may be useful in verse 20 to say "what I am telling you." In this way one can avoid the impression that Paul wrote the entire letter personally rather than dictating it, as it is usually understood that he did.

God knows that I am not lying functions here as an oath (cf. Knox "as God sees me," Mft "I swear it before God," Phps "I assure you before God"). What Paul is trying to emphasize is the fact that he is telling the truth. The very fact that he can affirm with an oath that he is telling the truth would indicate to his readers that he is indeed not lying. He can risk a curse (implied by the oath) for he knows God knows that he is not lying. An equivalent expression in some languages is "God can tell you that I am telling the truth."

1.21   Afterward I went to places in Syria and Cilicia.

Paul now notes that he went from Jerusalem to Syria and Cilicia and that because he stayed for only a short time in Judea, the Christians in Jerusalem and Judea had no occasion to get to know him personally (v. 22).

Afterward connects this event with what immediately precedes, namely, Paul's visit to Jerusalem. The phrase Syria and Cilicia probably refers to the Roman province which included both regions. It is not necessary to assume that Paul visited all the places in the province, but only some parts of it (cf. Phps "I visited districts in Syria and Cilicia," also Mft).

1.22   At that time the members of the churches in Judea did not know me
         personally.

The churches in Judea (literally "the churches of Judea in Christ") refers to Christian congregations in that region. Paul states that the members of these congregations did not know him personally in order to indicate clearly that he did not work in any area where the Twelve might have assigned him or where it was possible for him to have contacts with the Twelve, but instead he started an independent mission. The members of the churches in Judea may be expressed in some languages as "the people who belonged to the various groups of believers in Judea." On the other hand, one may use a more general expression such as "the believers in Christ who were in Judea."

Did not know me personally may be rendered as "had not seen me," "had not themselves seen me," or "had not themselves met me."

1.23   They knew only what others were saying: "The man who used to per-
         secute us is now preaching the faith that he once tried to destroy!"

The Christian churches in Judea, however, were not totally ignorant of Paul; they had heard what others were saying about him. The others are probably to be understood primarily as members of churches which had been the special targets of Paul's persecuting activities.

The faith should not be understood as a body of Christian doctrine, but either as a synonym for the good news or as a term referring to the Christian movement in general (cf.v. 13).

The word for "tried to destroy" is the same verb as in verse 13. For a number of languages there are complications involved in the expression is now preaching the faith that he once tried to destroy, since "faith" cannot be the direct object of the customary equivalent expressions for "preaching" and "destroy." One can often speak about "preaching the good news," but what Paul set out to destroy was not the good news but rather those who believed the good news or the Christian movement as such. If one renders faith as "trust," then this must obviously refer to "trust in Christ" or "believing in Christ." One may therefore render is now preaching the faith as "is now telling people how they should trust in Christ." The final clause that he once tried to destroy may then be rendered as "before he was trying to destroy those who trusted in Christ," or "whereas before that he had been trying to stop people believing in Christ."

1.24   And so they praised God because of me.

They praised God because of me is literally "they were glorifying God in me." The preposition "in" is used here as indicating the reason or basis of an action (cf. Knox "They praised God for what he had done in me," Phps "they thanked God for what had happened to me"). Because of me may be understood in terms of "what God had done to me," "what God had done through me," or "what I had done." Since the praise was rendered to God for what Paul was at that time doing, it seems more satisfactory to say "they praised God because of what he had done through me," or "...what God had caused me to do."

TEV	RSV
Paul and the Other Apostles	

1 Fourteen years later I went back to Jerusalem with Barnabas, taking Titus along with me. 2 I went because God revealed to me that I should go. In a private meeting with the leaders I explained the gospel message that I preach to the Gentiles. I did not want my work in the past or in the present to be a failure. 3 My companion Titus, even though he is Greek, was not forced to be circumcised, 4 although some wanted it done. Pretending to be fellow believers, these men slipped into our group as spies, in order to find out about the freedom we have through our union with Christ Jesus. They wanted to make slaves of us, 5 but in order to keep the truth of the gospel safe for you, we did not give in to them for a minute.

6 But those who seemed to be the leaders--I say this because it makes no difference to me what they were; God does not judge by outward appearances--those leaders, I say, made no new suggestions to me. 7 On the contrary, they saw that God had given me the task of preaching the gospel to the Gentiles, just as he had given Peter the task of preaching the gospel to the Jews. 8 For by God's power I was made an apostle to the Gentiles, just as Peter was made an apostle to the Jews. 9 James, Peter, and John, who seemed to be the leaders, recognized that God had given me this special task; so they shook hands with Barnabas and me, as a sign that we were all partners. We agreed that Barnabas and I would work among the Gentiles and they

1 Then after fourteen years I went up again to Jerusalem with Barnabas, taking Titus along with me. 2 I went up by revelation; and I laid before them (but privately before those who were of repute) the gospel which I preach among the Gentiles, lest somehow I should be running or had run in vain. 3 But even Titus, who was with me, was not compelled to be circumcised, though he was a Greek. 4 But because of false brethren secretly brought in, who slipped in to spy out our freedom which we have in Christ Jesus, that they might bring us into bondage-- 5 to them we did not yield submission even for a moment, that the truth of the gospel might be preserved for you. 6 And from those who were reputed to be something (what they were makes no difference to me; God shows no partiality)--those, I say, who were of repute added nothing to me; 7 but on the contrary, when they saw that I had been entrusted with the gospel to the uncircumcised, just as Peter had been entrusted with the gospel to the circumcised 8 (for he who worked through Peter for the mission to the circumcised worked through me also for the Gentiles), 9 and when they perceived the grace that was given to me, James and Cephas and John, who were reputed to be pillars, gave to me and Barnabas the right hand of fellowship, that we should go to the Gentiles and they

among the Jews. 10 All they asked was that we should remember the needy in their group, which is the very thing I have^c been eager to do.

to the circumcised; 10 only they would have us remember the poor, which very thing I was eager to do.

(2.1-10)

^{c}have; *or* had.   (2.1-10)

Paul now goes into a description of his second visit to Jerusalem, in which he relates two incidents which would prove to his readers the validity of the message he was proclaiming. The first of these is the case of Titus, who accompanied Paul to Jerusalem (vv. 1, 3-5). The fact that Titus was a Greek among Jews provided Paul with an excuse for introducing the subject of Christian freedom. The second incident (vv. 2, 6-10) is Paul's private meetings with the leaders of the Jerusalem church, during which they not only approved the message he was proclaiming, but they also accepted him as a coworker, assigned to proclaim the good news primarily to the Gentiles.

The section heading, Paul and the Other Apostles, if translated literally, can be somewhat confusing, since in some languages it might imply that Paul and the other apostles were joined together in some common work or activity. It may be better to employ at this point a section heading such as "Paul's relation to the other apostles," "The other apostles accept Paul," or "The other apostles agree to Paul's ministry."

2.1   Fourteen years later I went back to Jerusalem with Barnabas, taking Titus along with me.

Fourteen years later. Again, Paul leaves us guessing as to the beginning of what he mentions as a specific period of time. Do the fourteen years date from his conversion or from his last visit to Jerusalem? Either interpretation is possible, but most commentators favor the latter. The emphasis here is on how long Paul stayed away from the other apostles. In many languages it is obligatory to indicate the reference point for a temporal phrase such as fourteen years later. In this instance one is perhaps best advised to employ an expression such as "fourteen years after I had visited Jerusalem," "... after my earlier visit to Jerusalem," "... after Jesus revealed himself to me," or "... after I became a believer," depending upon which interpretation is followed.

With Barnabas is to be understood as Barnabas accompanying Paul rather than vice versa. Barnabas is mentioned as Paul's companion in his first missionary journey (Acts 13.1-3) and as accompanying him to Jerusalem on the occasion of the Jerusalem council (Acts 15.2 ff.). In order to indicate the proper relationship between Paul and Barnabas, it may be best to say "I went along with Barnabas."

Titus was a Greek, that is, a non-Jew. He played an important role in the correspondence between Paul and the church at Corinth. (See 2 Cor 2.13; 7.6; and other places. Some persons have thought that "Silas" in the book of Acts is another name for Titus.) In translating taking Titus along with me, it is impor-

[28]

tant to avoid an expression for <u>taking</u> which would suggest "lead" (as one would lead a small child). An equivalent of this expression in some languages is "I had Titus go along with me." However, since Barnabas has already been mentioned as accompanying Paul, it may be necessary to say "... along with us," in order to indicate clearly that three persons were involved.

<u>2.2</u>   I went because God revealed to me that I should go. In a private meeting with the leaders I explained the gospel message that I preach to the Gentiles. I did not want my work in the past or in the present to be a failure.

<u>Because God revealed to me that I should go</u> is literally "in accordance with a revelation." The word "revelation" usually describes God's act of making himself or his will known, and the preposition "in accordance with" is better understood here as "because of" (cf. NEB, also Phps "My visit on this occasion was by divine command"). How and when this revelation took place, Paul does not say. For this type of context the most appropriate equivalent of <u>revealed</u> is in many languages "told," for example, "because God told me that I should go." If, however, one can use a more general expression such as "showed" or "made me to understand," that may be better, rather than to suggest some direct verbal communication between God and Paul.

It is possible to put verse 1 and the first part of verse 2 together, to make the meaning much clearer, e.g. "fourteen years later, I returned to Jerusalem at the Lord's direction."

<u>In a private meeting with the leaders I explained</u> can be literally rendered "I laid before them, but privately before those who were of repute." "Those of repute" is an expression describing men of good and high standing in the fellowship, hence the TEV rendering <u>leaders</u> (JB "the leading men," Phps "church leaders").

<u>In a private meeting with the leaders</u> may be expressed in some languages as "in a meeting just with the leaders." It is also possible to be somewhat more specific and say "in a meeting with the leaders and without other people present." The introductory prepositional expression may also be rendered as a temporal clause, for example, "when I met with just the leaders." In a number of languages, when speaking of leaders, it may be necessary to indicate who or what is led. In such a case one may say "the leaders of the church." An equivalent expression in some languages is "the most important people in the church," or "those in the church who made the decisions."

When Paul says "I laid before them," whom does he mean by "them"? Are they to be taken as referring to the whole Christian community in Jerusalem or as synonymous with "the men of repute"? Most translators favor the second alternative, and TEV restructures the sentence to make this understanding clear. TEV makes the private meeting with the leaders a prepositional clause and places it at the beginning of the sentence (cf. JB "privately I laid before the leading men the Good News"; NAB "I laid out for their scrutiny the gospel... all this in private conference with the leaders").

The gospel message (literally "the gospel") refers to that particular version of the Good News which Paul has been preaching.

To the Gentiles can also be "among the Gentiles" (Phps Knox, cf. NAB JB) referring to people who live in Gentile lands (note this expression in 1.16).

In some languages it may be necessary to indicate quite clearly the tense or aspect of the verb preach. Since Paul is here referring to his habitual practice or customary manner of preaching to the Gentiles (or "non-Jews"), one may say "I explained the good news that I have customarily been preaching to the Gentiles."

I did not want my work in the past or in the present to be a failure translates an idiom which expresses apprehension (literally "lest somehow I should be running or had run in vain," RSV). What is the meaning of this idiom? It should not be understood to mean that Paul had any doubts about the truth of the gospel which he was preaching or of the course he was pursuing, an idea which seems to be implicit in some translations. Rather, Paul was presenting his message to the Jewish authorities at Jerusalem because he saw the danger of his work both past and present being rendered ineffectual if those authorities disapproved of it. Some translations therefore focus on the fear that the Jewish authorities might not see the validity of what Paul was doing (JB "I did so for fear the course I was adopting or had already adopted would not be allowed"; NAB "to make sure the course I was pursuing, or had pursued, was not useless"; Phps "to make sure that what I had done and proposed doing was acceptable to them"). Other translations (e.g. TEV) focus on the result of such disapproval.

My work in the past or in the present may be rendered as "what I had been doing or what I was continuing to do," or "what I had done in the past or what I would continue to do." The expression to be a failure translates a phrase referring to something being "empty," "fruitless," "ineffective," or "in vain." It may be rendered in some languages as "to result in nothing" or "to produce nothing." It is possible that Paul was fearful that disapproval by the authorities in Jerusalem would result in people rejecting the truth that he had been proclaiming.

2.3   My companion Titus, even though he is Greek, was not forced to be circumcised,

The Greek text starts with a "but" (as in RSV, cf. NEB "yet"; JB "and what happened?"), indicating that, contrary to his worst fears, Paul's views prevailed. He cites two incidents to illustrate this: (1) the case of Titus (vv. 3-5) and (2) the attitude of the Jerusalem leaders toward himself and his message (vv. 6-10).

Titus is already noted in verse 1. He is described as a Greek, a term used here in its broad sense of "Gentile" or non-Jew (see Rom 1.16; 2.9, 10). As a non-Jew, Titus had not been circumcised, circumcision being practiced only by the Jews.

My companion Titus may be expressed in some languages as "Titus, who had come with me," or "Titus, who had accompanied me."

Even though he is Greek expresses what is referred to as a "concession."

That is to say, one would expect that a Greek would be forced to be circumcised if he was to accompany Jews such as Paul or Barnabas and to associate with Jews, especially in his contacts in Jerusalem. However, contrary to such expectation, he was not required to be circumcised. A concessive clause may involve an additional feature of adversative expression, for example, "My companion Titus was a Greek, but nevertheless he was not forced to be circumcised." In some languages there may be difficulty involved in the passive expression was... forced to be circumcised, for the causative agent in forced is not specified nor is the causative agent in the passive expression to be circumcised indicated clearly. Such agents may, of course, be indicated, for example, "The leaders of the church did not require that some person circumcise Titus." Note that obviously there is here a contrast between the requirements made by the church leaders and the insistence of some persons who did want to have Titus circumcised.

The phrase was not forced to be circumcised is in itself ambiguous. Some scholars understand this to mean that Titus was circumcised, but his circumcision was not a result of compulsion (e.g. Knox). Most, however, interpret the verb form meaning "was not forced" in a resultative sense: that is, what is denied is not the pressure, but the result. This would mean that Titus was not circumcised at all. TEV makes this clear in verse 4: although some wanted it done, that is, to have him circumcised.

In languages used by people who normally do practice circumcision, there is no difficulty involved in finding a term for the practice which will be acceptable on a so-called formal level of discourse, that is, in language appropriate for a document to be read in church. There are almost always other ways of talking about circumcision, many of which are rather crude or vulgar, and these, of course, must be avoided. For languages spoken by people who have no knowledge of circumcision or who regard it as a wholly inappropriate custom, it may be difficult to find a satisfactory term to designate this kind of religious rite. In most societies in which circumcision is practiced it is actually one of the so-called "rites of passage," that is to say, rites related to certain important crises in life. Circumcision is frequently associated with puberty and sexual maturity, and it is not religious and ethnic identity as in the case of the Jewish practice performed on male infants eight days of age. In some languages translators have attempted to indicate the meaning of circumcision by translating literally "cutting away the foreskin of the penis," but this type of expression is often regarded as vulgar and uncouth. As a result, other translators have simply used the expression "ritual cutting," and still others a somewhat obscure expression such as "cutting around." It is even possible in some languages to use a phrase such as "a mark of cutting." What is important is that some expression be employed which will designate this ritual of circumcision in an appropriate way, without introducing connotations which may render the expression inappropriate. If a vague or obscure expression is used, it may be important to have a satisfactory definition or description of circumcision in a glossary.

2.4   although some wanted it done. Pretending to be fellow believers, these men slipped into our group as spies, in order to find out about the freedom we have through our union with Christ Jesus. They wanted to make slaves of us,

Rather than translating literally <u>wanted it done</u>, it may be better to indicate what <u>it done</u> refers to. These persons, who were simply the causative agents, not the actual agents of the circumcision, "wanted to have him circumcised" or "wanted to cause someone to circumcise him."

This verse is an incomplete sentence in the Greek. How does it connect with what precedes and what follows? Did Paul mean to say that, because of the false brothers, he did have Titus circumcised? Or did the suggestion for Titus' circumcision arise out of the presence of these false brothers (JB NEB)? Or again, did the false brothers themselves urge the circumcision of Titus, an idea which Paul rejected (TEV)? The interpretation of verse 4 is closely linked with the interpretation of verse 3, particularly as to the question of whether Titus was circumcised or not. TEV introduces the clause <u>although some wanted it done</u> as a means of helping to resolve at least certain aspects of the ambiguity in this passage.

<u>Pretending to be fellow believers, these men</u> is literally "the false brothers" (see RSV). It may be that they themselves claimed to be a part of the fellowship, even if they were not. (This sense is captured by RSV, cf. NAB "Certain false claimants to the title of brother.") It could mean, however, that this represents Paul's own judgment; in other words, that the "false brethren" were really members of the fellowship, but in Paul's judgment they should not have been (so Phps "for the presence of some pseudo-Christians," NEB "certain sham-Christians"). <u>Pretending to be fellow believers, these men</u> may be expressed in some languages as "some men who said they were fellow believers but were not," or "some men who falsely claimed to be believers."

<u>Slipped into our group</u> translates a combination of a verb and a verbal adjective (see below) which could be interpreted either in a passive sense, implying that these false brothers were brought in (NAB "certain false claimants to the title of brothers were smuggled in"); or in an active sense, which would mean that it was through their own initiative that they came in (TEV, cf. NEB "interlopers who had stolen in"; JB "have furtively crept in"; Phps "who wormed their way into our meeting"). In some languages the expression <u>slipped into our group</u> may be expressed as "insisted that they were also part of the group," "...part of the believers," or "...one with the other believers."

<u>Slipped into our group as spies</u> is a metaphorical expression, the figure being that of a spy who infiltrates an enemy camp. The expression consists of two Greek verbs, the first one meaning "to come in" but usually implying secrecy and stealth, and the second (literally "to spy out") with the associated idea of hostile intent and with the purpose of destruction. Various translations endeavor to recapture the intensity of the metaphor (e.g. NAB "they wormed their way into the group to spy on"; JB "who...have furtively crept in to spy"; Mft "who had crept in to spy out"). It may also be possible to say "they came in

without people realizing what had happened, and they were just like spies."

Freedom here is the Christian's freedom from the bondage of the Jewish Law, of which circumcision is a key example. Paul characterizes this freedom as the freedom we have through our union with Christ Jesus. The Greek itself (literally "which we have in Christ Jesus") allows three possible meanings: (1) a causal relation, with Jesus being the cause of the freedom; (2) a relation of association, "in union with," that is, describing a relationship with Jesus Christ characterized by close fellowship and communion (this is followed by most translations, e.g. NEB "the liberty we enjoy in the fellowship of Christ Jesus," NAB "the freedom we enjoy in Christ Jesus"; so also Mft JB Phps Knox); and (3) a combination of the first and second meanings, as in TEV.

To find out about the freedom we have may be expressed in some languages as "to find out how free we are," "...how we have been delivered," or "...how we have become free." In this context to find out should imply more than mere gathering of information. There is definite hostile intent.

The combined meaning of cause and fellowship may be expressed in some languages as "because we are united with Christ Jesus," "...are one with Christ Jesus," or "...are joined to Christ Jesus."

Make slaves of us means "make us slaves to the Jewish Law." The "us" may refer either to Paul and his companions or to Christians in general, including the Galatian Christians. If understood in the former sense, "us" would be translated in its exclusive form; but if in the latter sense, the inclusive form would be used.

The sentence They wanted to make slaves of us is essentially a metaphor. What these false brethren wished to do was to enslave believers to the system of Jewish ritual. The metaphorical usage may be indicated by shifting into the form of a simile, for example, "They wanted to make us just like slaves." It may also be necessary in some instances to indicate precisely what kind of servitude is involved, for example, "They wanted us to be just like slaves in having to do exactly what the law said we must do," or "...what the Jewish law prescribed."

2.5   but in order to keep the truth of the gospel safe for you, we did not give in to them for a minute.

The truth of the gospel refers to the truth either (1) contained in or belonging to the gospel or (2) consisting of the gospel (an appositional relation). The gospel here is either good news about Jesus Christ or the good news which Christ has brought. In some languages the truth of the gospel may be expressed as "the true words of the good news." In other instances it may be necessary to say "the good news which is true." Obviously, the phrase the truth of the gospel should not be translated in such a way as to indicate that the gospel contained both truth and falsehood and that only the truth was to be kept safe.

To keep...safe for you is literally "may abide with you." Some translations take this to mean "continue" (NEB "should be maintained for you"; cf. NAB "might survive intact for your benefit"). To keep the truth of the gospel safe for you may be rendered as "to keep the truth of the good news without being distorted," "...without being changed," or "...without being made false."

We did not give in means that Paul did not give in to the pressure or demand for Titus' circumcision. We did not give in to them may be rendered in some languages simply as "We did not agree with their demands," or "We did not say yes to what they said we must do."

For a minute translates a Greek phrase (literally "for an hour") which is used to designate a relatively short time (NEB "for one moment"). The phrase for a minute, combined with the negative of the same sentence, may be expressed more satisfactorily in some languages as "never," for example, "We never gave in to them."

With a negative statement such as we did not give in to them, it may be necessary to express the purpose in order to keep the truth of the gospel safe for you as a matter of intent or reason for not having given in, for example, "We did not give in to them for a minute, for we wanted to keep the truth of the gospel safe for you."

2.6   But those who seemed to be the leaders—I say this because it makes no difference to me what they were; God does not judge by outward appearances—those leaders, I say, made no new suggestions to me.

Paul now cites a second incident (already mentioned in v. 2), that of his meeting with the Jerusalem leaders, during which his message was accepted and he himself was recognized as a missionary to the Gentiles.

Some understand those who seemed to be the leaders to be equivalent to the expression in 2.2 (NEB "men of high reputation," JB "these people who are acknowledged leaders," Phps "the leaders of the conference," GeCL "who were considered to be authorities"). Others, however, take this as a deprecatory statement against the authorities mentioned, or if not of the authorities, at least of the arrogant claims which Paul's opponents had apparently made about them. While no irony is involved in verse 2, there may be some kind of irony here, and it seems to be preserved in TEV (cf. RSV). It may be possible to translate those who seemed to be the leaders as simply "those who appeared to be the leaders among the believers." However, in some languages it is more natural to speak of "those who were said to be the leaders," "those whom others regarded as the leaders," or "those who had the reputation of being the leaders."

The phrase I say this is added in TEV to indicate the connection between the previous clause and the expression of cause which follows. The pronoun this refers to the entire preceding clause.

It makes no difference to me may be expressed as "as far as I am concerned, it's all the same," or "I do not make any distinction," or "it doesn't concern me." One may say, for example, "I say this because what they were does not concern me."

What translates a Greek qualitative word meaning "of what kind." In what they were the reference is probably not to their present standing (as in NEB and

JB), but to the status which they gained by their former association with Jesus (as in most translations). The Greek supports the latter interpretation by its use of the word meaning "once," "formerly," or "at some time or other," not specifically translated in TEV. One may also say in some languages "what kinds of persons they were," or "what their positions were," with a term such as "positions" referring to social status.

God does not judge by outward appearances translates an idiom which literally rendered is "God does not accept the face of a man." To accept the face of someone is to judge him and his actions on the basis of external circumstances, such as wealth, social standing, or rank. In this particular case, the externals are related to what they were in the past. In some languages God does not judge by outward appearances may be best expressed as "God does not judge a man by what he looks like." In some languages this expression is more or less idiomatic, for example, "God doesn't judge a man by the kind of clothes he wears," or "God doesn't call a man good or bad just because he is tall or short."

After the parenthetical statement in which he asserts that he is not impressed by outward appearances, Paul begins his statement anew, and now he refers to the Jerusalem authorities as those leaders, using the same type of phrase as in verse 2.

Made no new suggestions translates the same verb found in 1.16, where it means "to submit for consideration, to confer with." NEB takes it in the same sense here ("did not prolong the consultation"). Most translations, including TEV, take it to mean here "to impart something" or to "impose something" (Phps "they had nothing to add to my gospel"). The implication is clear: the Jerusalem authorities were completely satisfied with what Paul was doing. Made no new suggestions to me may be expressed as "didn't tell me to do anything different," "said to me, We have nothing else to add," or "did not ask me to make any changes in the good news which I was preaching."

2.7   On the contrary, they saw that God had given me the task of preaching the gospel to the Gentiles, just as he had given Peter the task of preaching the gospel to the Jews.

This verse in Greek is an involved participial phrase with an included clause (in fact, verses 6-10 are one long sentence). Furthermore, the construction of the phrase is passive, with God as the implicit agent. While most translations retain the Greek form, TEV restructures the phrase in two ways: (1) it makes it an independent sentence, and (2) it makes the passive construction active, with God as the explicit agent.

The phrase on the contrary may be rendered as "but instead of making new suggestions to me," or "but rather than adding something new to what I had said."

The verb saw in the expression they saw that God had given me the task must be rendered in a number of languages as "realized" (GeCL), since there was nothing actually for the leaders of the churches to "see," that is, to look at.

Had given me the task is the Greek verb often translated "believe," but

here it occurs with the special meaning of "entrust" (RSV cf. JB "commissioned"), that is, to give the task to proclaim or to preach the gospel.

Gentiles is literally "the uncircumcision," used here as a term signifying
non-Jews. In the same manner, the Jews is literally "the circumcision."

In translating the two phrases gospel to the Gentiles and gospel to the Jews,
one must be careful to avoid giving the impression that there are two gospels,
one for the Jews and another for the Gentiles. Some translations indeed can be
understood in this manner (NEB "that I had been entrusted with the Gospel for
Gentiles as surely as Peter had been entrusted with the Gospel for Jews"; also
Phps "the Gospel for the uncircumcised was as much my commission as the
Gospel for the circumcised was Peter's"). To avoid this misunderstanding, one
should make it clear that both Paul and Peter are entrusted with proclaiming one
gospel, except that Paul is to proclaim it to Gentiles and Peter to the Jews (JB
"they recognized that I had been commissioned to preach the Good News to the
uncircumcised just as Peter had been commissioned to preach it to the circumcised"; NAB "I had been entrusted with the gospel for the uncircumcised, just as
Peter was for the circumcised"). The essential unity of the gospel may be preserved in some languages by translating "they realized that God had given both
me and Peter the task of preaching the gospel. I was to preach to the Gentiles,
and Peter was to preach to the Jews."

2.8   For by God's power I was made an apostle to the Gentiles, just as
           Peter was made an apostle to the Jews.

Verse 8 is a parenthetical statement and can be literally translated "for he
who worked in Peter into apostleship to the circumcision worked also in me to
the Gentiles." The "he" may refer to Christ, but more likely it refers to God,
for it is Paul's practice to speak of God as the source of his apostleship and
Christ as the agent or mediator. Accordingly, God is mentioned as the agent
in TEV (but see also NEB, which explicitly makes God the subject).

Instead of mentioning God as the agent in a phrase such as by God's power,
it is possible to introduce God as the causative subject, for example, "God made
me an apostle to the Gentiles." And the last clause of this verse may be rendered
as "in the same way that he made Peter an apostle to the Jews." In some languages, however, it may be difficult to speak of "making an apostle," and therefore one may say "caused me to become an apostle," or "sent me as a special
messenger to the Gentiles."

The expression "worked in" could be understood in two ways: (1) It could
refer to the inner experience by which Peter and Paul were commissioned for
their work, that is, their experience of being called to be apostles, or (2) it
could refer to the known results of their apostleship, that is, God's working
through both of them and making their mission successful. The first interpretation is followed by TEV (JB "the same person whose action had made Peter the
apostle of the circumcised had given me a similar mission to the pagans"; NEB
"For God whose action made Peter an apostle to the Jews, also made me an apostle to the Gentiles"). The second alternative is preferred by NAB ("for he who

worked through Peter as his apostle among the Jews had been at work in me for the Gentiles"; cf. Phps "for the God who had done such great work in Peter's ministry for the Jews was plainly doing the same in my ministry for the Gentiles").

2.9   James, Peter, and John, who seemed to be the leaders, recognized that God had given me this special task; so they shook hands with Barnabas and me, as a sign that we were all partners. We agreed that Barnabas and I would work among the Gentiles and they among the Jews.

The leaders are finally identified as James, Peter, and John. James is probably the same as the one identified as the Lord's brother in 1.19. John is probably the Apostle of that name, the brother of another James (Acts 12.1-2), one of the sons of Zebedee. The order of their names probably suggests their position in the Jerusalem church.

These three men are described as those who seemed to be the leaders (literally, a figurative expression "who are reputed to be pillars"), a description which most commentaries interpret as synonymous with similar expressions in 2.2 and 2.6. "Pillars" is a designation of those upon whom responsibility rests; it was used by Jews in speaking of the great teachers of the Law.

Recognized that God had given me this special task is literally "when they perceived the grace that was given to me." Many interpreters understand this to be essentially synonymous with "I had been entrusted with the gospel" in verse 7. Others, however, understand "grace" to mean the favor or privilege which God has given to Paul in making him an apostle (cf. Rom 1.5). The implicit subject of the expression (God) is made explicit in TEV and other translations (e.g. Phps NEB). Had given me this special task may be rendered as "had caused me to have this special work," "had told me that this was my work to do," or "had assigned me to this special work."

It is particularly important to make clear the relation between the first part of this verse and what follows, namely, the fact that the leaders extended the hand of fellowship to Barnabas and Paul. This result is indicated by the conjunction so. In some languages it may be necessary to say "because of this," "as a result of this," or even "because they recognized this."

They shook hands with Barnabas and me, as a sign that we were all partners is literally "they gave me and Barnabas the right hand of fellowship." The whole action means entering into a covenant, a binding agreement between two parties, a pledge that they will abide by what is agreed upon. "Fellowship" introduces the idea of partnership. While many translations retain the original expression, others restructure it to express its meaning more clearly (NEB "accepted Barnabas and myself as partners, and shook hands upon it"; JB "shook hands with Barnabas and me as a sign of partnership"). In a number of languages, however, the fact of shaking hands does not necessarily indicate agreement. In fact, it may suggest merely that Paul and Barnabas were at the point of leaving. A more appropriate equivalent in some languages may be "they showed that they were in agreement with Barnabas and me," "they showed that they agreed with us by shaking hands with us," or "they made us partners by shaking hands with us."

Partners may be expressed as "persons who were working together," "persons who shared work," or even "persons who saw that one another's work was also good."

The agreement itself involved a division of labor. Barnabas and I would work among the Gentiles and they among the Jews is literally "that we to the Gentiles and they to the circumcision." The implicit action may be "go" (as in most translations), "preach," or the more inclusive expression (as in TEV), work among.

It is not clear whether the division here described is territorial or racial. The problem is particularly complex because Jews were scattered in the so-called Gentile lands and there were many Gentiles living in Palestine. Does "Gentiles" mean Gentile lands or Gentile people, and does "circumcised" mean Jewish lands or Jewish people? It is possible that what is meant here is people and that the division is racial rather than territorial. But it is more likely that the meaning is that Paul would preach the gospel in Gentile lands, but to Gentiles and Jews, while Peter would work in the Jewish homeland, Palestine. In order to indicate the regional meaning involved, one may translate "we would work where the Gentiles mainly lived, and they where the Jews mainly lived."

2.10   All they asked was that we should remember the needy in their group, which is the very thing I have^c been eager to do.

    ^chave; *or* had.

There is only one condition appended to the agreement: that Paul and Barnabas should remember the poor and needy (see Acts 11.30 and 2 Cor 9.1). These are the poor Christians in Jerusalem, a fact made clear by TEV (cf. NEB "their poor"). The needy in their group must be made somewhat more specific in some languages: "the poor people among the believers there in Jerusalem," or "the poor people who belonged to their group of believers."

The word translated eager in the clause the very thing I have been eager to do does not simply refer to one's state of mind, but primarily to one's activity. It could therefore be translated "worked hard at." Some translations tend to put emphasis on the former (TEV, also JB "I was anxious to do," Phps "only too ready to agree"). Most translations, however, capture the spirit of the clause, being divided only as to whether this refers to a subsequent action and/ or attitude of the apostle (as it seems to be in Knox) or to a previous action and/ or attitude which continued up to the time of this letter (NAB "the one thing that I was making every effort to do"). In order to indicate clearly the continuous nature of Paul's activity on behalf of the poor believers in Jerusalem, one may say "and I have always been eager to do just that." Note, however, that in this context the verb remember does not imply necessarily that the poor had been forgotten. The meaning here is that "we should continue to think about," or "should constantly be concerned for."

TEV | RSV

Paul Rebukes Peter at Antioch

11 But when Peter came to Antioch, I opposed him in public, because he was clearly wrong. 12 Before some men who had been sent by James arrived there, Peter had been eating with the Gentile brothers. But after these men arrived, he drew back and would not eat with the Gentiles, because he was afraid of those who were in favor of circumcising them. 13 The other Jewish brothers also started acting like cowards along with Peter; and even Barnabas was swept along by their cowardly action. 14 When I saw that they were not walking a straight path in line with the truth of the gospel, I said to Peter in front of them all, "You are a Jew, yet you have been living like a Gentile, not like a Jew. How, then, can you try to force Gentiles to live like Jews?"

(2.11-14)

11 But when Cephas came to Antioch I opposed him to his face, because he stood condemned. 12 For before certain men came from James, he ate with the Gentiles; but when they came he drew back and separated himself, fearing the circumcision party. 13 And with him the rest of the Jews acted insincerely, so that even Barnabas was carried away by their insincerity. 14 But when I saw that they were not straightforward about the truth of the gospel, I said to Cephas before them all, "If you, though a Jew, live like a Gentile and not like a Jew, how can you compel the Gentiles to live like Jews?"

(2.11-14)

The section heading Paul Rebukes Peter at Antioch should be translated in such a way so as to avoid the suggestion of "scolding." This is done in some languages as "At Antioch Paul says that Peter was wrong," or "...had not done what was right." One may also say "Paul speaks against Peter at Antioch."

2.11 But when Peter came to Antioch, I opposed him in public, because he was clearly wrong.

Paul now relates the incident of Peter's visit to Antioch as a further proof of his independence from the other apostles.

We are not sure when Peter visited Antioch, but it certainly was after Paul's second visit to Jerusalem. Antioch is the major city in Syria, and the book of Acts informs us that it was from there that Paul started his first missionary journey (13.1-3). The membership of the church in Antioch consisted of both Jews and Gentiles, and apparently this had not caused any problems within the fellowship.

In rendering the clause when Peter came to Antioch, it is important to indicate that this was merely a visit and not a permanent change of residence.

I opposed him may be rendered as "I spoke against him," or "I spoke against what he did."

In public is literally "to the face," a current idiom during Paul's day. Some understand this to mean a face-to-face confrontation (NAB "I directly withstood

[39]

him"). Others see an open public encounter as the main component (cf. Phps "I had to oppose him publicly," thus connecting v. 11 with v. 14). In order to make clear that the phrase in public refers to the group of Christians and not to the people of the city in general, one may say "I opposed him with all the believers listening," or "...in front of all the believers."

He was clearly wrong may be rendered as "he stood condemned" (RSV), here having the force of "guilty." What Paul means is that it was obvious from Peter's own actions that he was wrong (Knox "he stood self-condemned"). Since the mistake that Peter had made was not one of words but of actions, it may be important to translate "because what he did was wrong," or "because it was clear that what he had done was not right."

2.12   Before some men who had been sent by James arrived there, Peter had been eating with the Gentile brothers. But after these men arrived, he drew back and would not eat with the Gentiles, because he was afraid of those who were in favor of circumcising them.

This verse and the following explain what Peter did that led to Paul's public denunciation of him. When Peter first arrived, he had no difficulty joining in the mixed fellowship, but afterwards, at the instigation of, or for fear of, some men, he refused to have anything to do with the Gentiles.

One of the principal difficulties involved in the translation of this verse results from the temporal relations as reflected in the various tense forms and temporal conjunctions, for example, before, had been sent, arrived, had been eating, after, drew back, and would not eat. A special complication occurs in the first sentence of this verse in which the conjunction before goes with the verb arrived, while there is an embedded relative clause of prior time, who had been sent by James. It may, therefore, be necessary to restructure the order and arrangement of elements within this verse, for example, "James had sent some men to Antioch, but before they arrived there Peter had been making it a practice to eat with the Gentile believers. But after these men arrived there, he refused to continue eating with them. He did this because he was afraid of those who said that the Gentiles should be circumcised."

Had been eating is in the imperfect tense in the Greek, indicating that Peter did this not only once, but regularly. The phrase itself may refer either to regular meals, or to the fellowship meals, that is, the meals which were part of the sacrament of the Lord's Supper. In either case, the Jews would have some problems in a mixed group, since the Jewish law forbade Jews to eat with Gentiles because of the danger of eating food declared by the Law to be unclean, that is, forbidden because it made one impure before God. In Antioch, Peter went against this particular regulation and regularly joined the Gentile Christians in their meals. Some languages have a so-called repetitive form of verbs, and this would fit in well in this context, that is to say, "he had been repeatedly eating with believers who were not Jews."

Gentile brothers (literally "Gentiles") are Gentile members of the congregation. TEV makes explicit the fact that Peter did not eat with all the Gen-

tiles, as a literal translation might suggest, but only with Gentile Christians.
The occasion for Peter's withdrawal is the arrival of some men who had been sent by James (literally "some men from James"). The Greek of this phrase is ambiguous. What is clear is that these men were connected in some way with James, but it is not clear whether they were sent by James (as understood by TEV, also Mft "emissaries of James") or were simply members of the Jerusalem church but whose visit to Antioch was not ordered by James (JB "certain friends of James arrived"; Phps "the arrival of some of James' companions").

He drew back and would not eat with the Gentiles is literally "he was drawing back and separating himself." Because of the imperfect tense of the two verbs in the Greek text, some commentaries understand this to represent a process: Peter did not take this step all at once, but gradually (Knox "he began to draw back," also Mft). Furthermore, some commentaries understand "was separating himself" in the general sense of Peter's withdrawal from associating with the Gentiles (JB "kept away from them altogether," NEB "he drew back and began to hold aloof"). Some, however, interpret this separation in a more specific sense, that is, referring back to the eating of meals just mentioned (so TEV, cf. Phps "he withdrew and ate separately from the gentiles"). In some languages the equivalent of drew back would be expressed negatively, for example, "he did not continue to associate with" or "he refused to continue association with." In certain languages the relation is expressed somewhat idiomatically, for example, "he put a distance between himself and the Gentile believers."

Those who were in favor of circumcising them translates what is literally "those of (the) circumcision." While this could be interpreted as meaning simply "those who were circumcised" (NAB), that is, the Jews (Phps "out of sheer fear of what the Jews might think"), it could refer to a party within the Christian community at Antioch which favored the circumcision of Gentile Christians but more likely to those Jewish Christians who had been sent by James (JB "for fear of the group that insisted on circumcision"; NEB "he was afraid of the advocates of circumcision"). In some instances one may also translate "those who said, The Gentile believers must be circumcised," or "...Someone must circumcise the Gentile believers."

2.13   The other Jewish brothers also started acting like cowards along with Peter; and even Barnabas was swept along by their cowardly action.

The effect of Peter's withdrawal is now mentioned: the other Jewish members of the congregation, and even Barnabas, likewise began to dissociate themselves from the Gentile members.

The words translated acting like cowards and cowardly action come from a Greek root usually rendered as "hypocrisy," "pretense," or "make believe"; it means hiding one's real self through actions that would convey a different impression (Phps "deception," JB "pretense," Knox "insincerity," NEB "showed the same lack of principle"). The use of this word to describe Peter's action and that of the rest of the Jewish Christians in Antioch implies that Paul still believed that they knew what was right, but that they were acting against their own con-

victions in the matter. Failure to act in accordance with one's convictions because of fear of what some persons might say certainly is "to act like a coward."
In this sense the rendering of TEV is justified. Nevertheless, the focus seems
to be primarily upon the failure of one to act according to his own principles.
Therefore one may translate the first clause of this verse as "the other Jewish
believers also started to behave in the way they knew they shouldn't," or "...in
a way that they knew was not right." The phrase along with Peter may be rendered as "they did the same thing that Peter was doing," or "they acted in the
same way Peter was acting."

The clause Barnabas was swept along by their cowardly action means that
Barnabas not only felt pressured to join, but that he actually did join the rest of
the Jewish Christians in separating themselves from the Gentile believers (NEB
"Barnabas was carried away and played false like the rest," JB "Barnabas felt
himself obliged to copy their behavior"). One may also say "even Barnabas felt
that he must do the same," "...act in the same way they did," "...imitate them
in doing what he knew he shouldn't do," or "...in doing what he knew was not
right."

2.14   When I saw that they were not walking a straight path in line with the
        truth of the gospel, I said to Peter in front of them all, "You are a
        Jew, yet you have been living like a Gentile, not like a Jew. How, then,
        can you try to force Gentiles to live like Jews?"

Paul now tells us what happened when he opposed Peter in public, as he has
already mentioned in verse 11. Paul did not take a position of open opposition to
Peter immediately, but only after the events narrated in verses 12 and 13 had
taken place.

Walking a straight path translates a Greek verb which occurs in the New
Testament only here and which usually means "to make a straight path," referring either to one's attitude or to one's conduct, but it is extremely difficult to
distinguish between these. Some translations seem to focus on the attitude (JB
"they were not respecting the true meaning of the Good News"; NAB "they were
not being straightforward about the truth of the gospel"). The focus on conduct,
however, is preferred by most translations (NEB "their conduct did not square
with the truth of the Gospel"; Phps "this behavior was a contradiction of the
truth of the Gospel"). This verbal phrase can also mean to progress or to ad-
vance in the direction of something, and therefore it is possible to translate this
clause as "they were not on the right road toward the truth of the gospel" (NEB
margin "not making progress towards...").

Though in a number of languages the metaphor of walking a straight path is
quite acceptable, it may be relatively meaningless in other languages. One may
express the same idea in such languages as "not doing what they should do," "not
behaving as they should," or "not living as they should," for example, "When I
saw that they were not living as they should live, in accordance with the true
words of the good news, I said to Peter...," or "When I saw that they were not

conforming their actions to what the true words of the good news had said, I said to Peter...."

For the truth of the gospel, see 2.5.

In front of them all means in the presence of all the members of the Christian congregation in Antioch.

The quotation that follows is a conditional sentence in the Greek ("If...then..."), and this form is followed in most translations. The conditional clause refers not, however, to a hypothetical case, but to something which is true because it is borne out by the facts. TEV makes this clear by changing the conditional clause into a simple statement of fact (cf. JB "In spite of being a Jew, you live like the pagans and not like the Jews, so you have no right to make the pagans copy Jewish ways").

Living like a Gentile and (living) like a Jew translate Greek words which suggest adhering to Gentile and Jewish customs respectively, particularly in the matter of food. Paul is saying that in eating with the Gentiles Peter disregarded Jewish laws, and therefore was living like a Gentile. This may frequently be expressed as "following the customs of the Gentiles," or "doing what Gentiles do."

Similarly, (living) not like a Jew may be expressed as "and you have not been following the customs of the Jews," or "you have not been doing what Jews customarily do."

Try to force Gentiles to live like Jews has reference to the fact that by drawing back Peter was actually forcing the Gentile Christians to find ways to be acceptable to the Jewish Christians, and that way could very well be by following the Jewish Law, which in effect would make them live like Jews. The verb force may be rendered as a causative, for example, "How can you try to cause the Gentiles to live like Jews?" or "...to follow the customs of the Jews?" It is also possible to express the causative sense by a statement of direct discourse involving some verb of "require" or "insist," for example, "How can you try to insist, Gentiles must live like Jews live?"

TEV	RSV
Jews and Gentiles Are Saved by Faith	
15 Indeed, we are Jews by birth and not "Gentile sinners," as they are called. 16 Yet we know that a person is put right with God only through faith in Jesus Christ, never by doing what the Law requires. We, too, have believed in Christ Jesus in order to be put right with God through our faith in Christ, and not by doing what the Law requires. For no one is put right with God by doing what the Law requires. 17 If, then, as we try to be put right with God by our union	15 We ourselves, who are Jews by birth and not Gentile sinners, 16 yet who know that a man is not justified[d] by works of the law but through faith in Jesus Christ, even we have believed in Christ Jesus, in order to be justified by faith in Christ, and not by works of the law, because by works of the law shall no one be justified. 17 But if, in our endeavor to be justified

with Christ, we are found to be
sinners, as much as the Gentiles
are--does this mean that Christ is
serving the cause of sin? By no
means! 18 If I start to rebuild
the system of Law that I tore down,
then I show myself to be someone
who breaks the Law.   (2.15-18)

in Christ, we ourselves were found
to be sinners, is Christ then an
agent of sin? Certainly not!
18 But if I build up again those
things which I tore down, then I
prove myself a transgressor.

^dOr *reckoned righteous;* and so
elsewhere   (2.15-18)

These verses do not seem to be addressed to Peter alone, but to a wider
audience. Their main burden is the question of how the Galatian believers have
been put into a right relationship with God. Paul's answer is that this has happened, not by their following the Law, but by their faith in Jesus Christ.

A problem that is hard to resolve is the translation of the first person
plural pronoun "we" in these verses. Should it take the exclusive or the inclusive
form? The solution of this problem is tied up with the relation of this section to
the quotation in verse 14. If one regards verses 15 ff. to be part of the quotation
(that is, Paul is still speaking publicly to Peter and to the Jewish Christians in
Antioch), then the pronouns will take the inclusive form. If, however, one re-
stricts the quotation to verse 14 and believes that Paul is no longer talking only
to Jewish Christians, then the exclusive form should be used. English translations usually do not bother about this problem, because there is no inclusive-
exclusive distinction in this language (but note Phps, where it is made clear that
the exclusive form should be read: "And then I went on to explain that we, who
are Jews by birth," etc.). It is also possible to interpret this paragraph as being
addressed not to the wider audience in Antioch but as a commentary by Paul to
the people in Galatia to whom he was writing. Under these circumstances the
form of "we" would also be exclusive. There is clearly a shift to the Galatians
in the mind of Paul, since at the beginning of chapter 3 he specifically addresses
them. To imply that the contents of verses 15-18 were directed to Peter would
seem to be overdoing the matter. A shift of audience can be introduced, and in
fact it is necessary in some languages, by the introduction of a verb of speaking
in a different tense form, for example, "Indeed I say to you who are...."

There are two translational difficulties involved in the section heading Jews
and Gentiles Are Saved by Faith. In the first place, it may be necessary to indicate who is the agent of the salvation and, accordingly, "God" must be made explicit. Secondly, one may be required to specify the object of faith or trust and
this is, of course, "Jesus Christ." Accordingly, the section heading would then
be rendered as "God saves both the Jews and the Gentiles because of their trusting in Jesus Christ," or "...by means of their trusting in Jesus Christ."

2.15   Indeed, we are Jews by birth and not "Gentile sinners," as they
          are called.

The expression Jews by birth accents the Jew's claim to privilege by
virtue of his being born a Jew. We are Jews by birth must be expressed in

some languages as "our parents were Jews," or "our forefathers were Jews."

In this context <u>sinners</u> refers not to persons who have committed sin or wrong, but to those who are outside the Law. The term is therefore used by Jews as synonymous with "Gentiles." Jews regarded the Gentiles as inherently sinful, since they were born outside of the Law. But literal translation of <u>not Gentile sinners</u> without some indication of this being a quotation can be quite misleading, for it might be understood to mean "not Gentiles, who are sinners," thus declaring that all Gentiles were evil people, rather than indicating their position outside the Law. Since the expression <u>"Gentile sinners"</u> was a more or less traditional name used by Jews to refer to Gentiles, it may be possible to indicate this fact by translating "and not so-called 'Gentile sinners,'" or "and not what Jews speak of as 'Gentile sinners'." This would mean that the phrase would be then interpreted as a way in which Jews spoke of Gentiles rather than as a description of all Gentiles.

2.16   Yet we know that a person is put right with God only through faith in Jesus Christ, never by doing what the Law requires. We, too, have believed in Christ Jesus in order to be put right with God through our faith in Christ, and not by doing what the Law requires. For no one is put right with God by doing what the Law requires.

The whole point of this verse is that being put right with God, even for Jews, is not by doing what the Law requires, but by faith in Jesus Christ. Paul starts his argument by a general statement (<u>a person</u>), continues with a reference to Jewish Christians alone (<u>we, too</u>), and ends with another general statement encompassing both Jews and Gentiles (<u>no one</u>).

<u>Put right with God</u> is literally "justified." For Paul, "to justify" (and the nominal form "righteousness") when applied to God, refers to an activity of God in which he rights a wrong or vindicates, the goal of such "righting" being man. "Righteousness" is therefore better translated "God's act of putting man right with himself" (i.e. with God) or "God's activity in restoring man to a right relationship with him." Rather than the passive expression <u>a person is put right with God,</u> it may be necessary in some languages to use an active form, for example, "God puts a man right." However, the man is put right with God, not merely put right with himself as a person. Therefore it is essential that the person with whom a man is put right is clearly identified as being God. In some languages this concept of being put right with God is expressed idiomatically as "God leads a man back to himself," or even "God ties a man to himself," as an expression of the renewal of a proper relationship.

<u>Faith in Jesus Christ</u> includes not only believing the message about Jesus Christ, but also trust in and commitment of oneself to him. <u>Only through faith in Jesus Christ</u> expresses the means by which a man is put right with God. But since <u>faith</u> must often be expressed as a verb meaning "to trust," it may be necessary to express this means in some languages as cause, for example, "only because a man trusts in Jesus Christ," or "...puts his confidence in Jesus Christ."

[45]

Doing what the Law requires is literally "works of law," and Paul means by it the obeying of certain rules and regulations in the Law in order to win God's approval. The Law here probably refers to the Jewish Law, the Torah, although it can also be understood as referring to any law (NAB "legal observance"), especially if a person is interpreted as referring to any person, rather than to Jewish Christians alone.

It is possible to interpret the Greek to mean that obeying the Law is not enough to put man in a right relationship with God, and that therefore it needs to be accompanied or supplemented by faith, but that is not what Paul means. What he does mean is that "faith in Jesus Christ" and "works of law" are two different ways: the first one is valid, and the second one is not. It is only by faith that one is put right with God, not by anything else. TEV makes this clear: never by doing what the Law requires (cf. NEB "no man is ever justified by doing what the law demands, but only through faith in Christ Jesus"). In some languages one may render this clause as "he never gets in a right relation with God by doing what the Law says he must do." There is, however, a very serious complication involved at this point in the translation of Law. In some languages it is simply impossible to use a singular form even with some graphic symbolization such as the use of capital letters to indicate the Law of Moses. Since the Law of the Old Testament actually consisted of many different regulations, one can only refer to the Law as "laws." However, Paul is obviously not referring here to the laws of any society but only to the laws handed down through Moses. Since the Law is often referred to in the New Testament as "the Law of Moses" or "the Law given through Moses," it may be appropriate in this instance also to speak of "the laws which came by means of Moses," or "...through Moses." Some translators prefer to use an expression such as "the laws of the old covenant," "...the old agreement," or "...the former agreement."

We, too, is emphatic in the Greek, the idea behind it being that "although we are Jews, yet we also have believed." For translating we, refer to previous discussion at the beginning of this section. In at least one translation, the exclusive form is used (JB "We had to become believers in Christ Jesus no less than you had"). In some languages it may be useful to introduce this sentence as "Even we have believed in Christ Jesus."

For no one is put right with God by doing what the Law requires seems to be a quotation from Psalm 143.2, following the Septuagint. That is, the Septuagint reads "each one who lives" whereas Paul has "all flesh." Also, the Old Testament verse does not have the phrase "works of Law" but instead has "before you." No one is literally "no flesh," with "flesh" equivalent to "human being."

2.17   If, then, as we try to be put right with God by our union with Christ, we are found to be "sinners," as much as the Gentiles are—does this mean that Christ is serving the cause of sin? By no means!

This verse is apparently an answer to the assertion of Paul's opponents that his message of being put right with God by faith in Jesus Christ amounts to making Christ a minister of sin, since those who put themselves "outside of the law" (by not obeying its demands) would be regarded by Jews as being "sinners."

To be put right with God by our union with Christ is literally "to be justified in Christ." Many interpret the clause to mean that Christ is the active agent of justification (JB "looking to Christ to justify us"), while others see this to mean that Christ is the means of our justification. A literal translation would, of course, be ambiguous. TEV understands God to be the primary source or causative agent of justification, and therefore the implicit subject of the passive verb, and the phrase "in Christ" to refer to means (as in 2.4), namely, the intimate fellowship between Christ and the Christian. One may also translate this expression as "to get into the right relationship with God because we are joined to Christ," "...because we have become one with Christ," or "...by means of our being so closely associated with Christ." It is rare that one can use in a receptor language a literal rendering of "in Christ."

Try is literally "seek," and it should be rendered in such a way that it does not mean simply attempting or striving without any assurance of success, but rather desiring fervently or hoping (RSV "endeavor," Knox "putting our hopes of justification in Christ").

We are found is a literal translation, but the difficulty with keeping the literal form is that in many cases the agent of a passive verb has to be made explicit. Here, however, the expression is simply equivalent to "to become" (cf. NEB "turn out to be"). In some languages we are found to be may be rendered as "it happens that we are."

One of the complications involved in understanding the first part of this verse is the embedding of a clause of attendant circumstances (as we try to be put right with God by our union with Christ) within a conditional clause (if...we are found to be "sinners"). It may be better in some languages to eliminate this embedding of one clause within another. One may translate "We endeavor to be put right with God by our being joined with Christ. But if as we do this we are found to be...."

Sinners could mean either in the ethical sense (wrongdoers, evildoers) or, as in verse 15, a term to designate those who are outside the Law. Most probably the latter is meant here, and therefore one may translate the expression as "to be so-called 'sinners' as much as the Gentiles are." It may even be possible in some instances, in order to make the meaning quite clear, to say "to be so-called 'sinners' (as far as the Law is concerned) as much as the Gentiles are."

Does this mean that Christ is serving the cause of sin? is literally "Is Christ therefore a minister of sin?" A "minister of sin" is one who furthers the interests or cause of sin, who promotes and encourages it (Phps "makes us sinners," JB "induced us to sin," NAB "is encouraging sin," NEB "an abettor of sin").

The whole verse may be understood in the following way: Paul is saying that to be put right with God by faith, Jewish Christians have to abandon the Law. By abandoning the Law, they have become sinners, that is, outside the Law. Can it therefore be deduced from this that they have made Christ a minister of sin? To this, Paul answers: By no means. The expression is emphatic, expressing complete negation of the premise of a question which has just been asked (cf. Phps "of course not"; NAB "unthinkable"). In some instances one may translate "that is certainly not true," or "in fact, the opposite is true."

2.18   If I start to rebuild the system of Law that I tore down, then I show
         myself to be someone who breaks the Law.

Rebuild and tore down are figures of speech derived from the construction of buildings, but the Greek text does not specify what is being rebuilt or what was previously torn down. The reference may be (1) to the statutes of the Law which Paul had declared as no longer valid for the Christian (NAB "If...I were to build up the very things I had demolished"); (2) to the whole system of man being put right with God by means of obedience to the Law (NEB "If I start building up again a system which I have pulled down"; Phps "But if I attempt to build again the whole structure of justification by the law"); or (3) to one's favorable attitude toward the Jewish idea of being put right with God by means of law (JB "If I were to return to a position I had already abandoned").

Breaks the Law translates a Greek word which literally means "transgressor" or "law-breaker," here used in its moral sense, one who disobeys the moral spirit of the law, and therefore practically equivalent to "wrongdoer," "evildoer," or "sinner" in the ethical sense. In order to emphasize the ethical sense of "transgressor" in this context, one may say "I really am doing what is wrong," or "I am really then a sinner." This will serve to contrast actual sin from the sin mentioned in verse 17.

The point of Paul here is that contrary to the assertion that Christ is made an agent of sin, it is only when a person returns to the old Jewish system of works of law that he becomes a sinner in terms of the Law.

TEV	RSV
19 So far as the Law is concerned, however, I am dead--killed by the Law itself--in order that I might live for God. I have been put to death with Christ on his cross, 20 so that it is no longer I who live, but it is Christ who lives in me. This life that I live now, I live by faith in the Son of God, who loved me and gave his life for me. 21 I refuse to reject the grace of God. But if a person is put right with God through the Law, it means that Christ died for nothing! (2.19-21)	19 For I through the law died to the law, that I might live to God. 20 I have been crucified with Christ; it is no longer I who live, but Christ who lives in me; and the life I now live in the flesh I live by faith in the Son of God, who loved me and gave himself for me. 21 I do not nullify the grace of God; for if justification[e] were through the law, then Christ died to no purpose.

*e*Or *righteousness*   (2.19-21) |

Beginning with the last half of the previous verse and continuing on to the end of the chapter, Paul becomes very personal and uses exalted language to describe his own experience with regard to the Law, and more especially with regard to Christ.

2.19   So far as the Law is concerned, however, I am dead—killed by the Law itself—in order that I might live for God. I have been put to death with Christ on his cross,

So far as the Law is concerned, however, I am dead—killed by the Law itself is literally "For I through the Law died to the Law." "Dying" to something means primarily to be rescued from its domination and control. "Dying to the Law" therefore means that Paul no longer considers the Law as controlling him, as important in his life; he has given up the Law as a valid instrument through which one is put right with God.

I am dead must be understood figuratively, and a shift from metaphor to simile may be required in some languages, for example, "I am just the same as dead," or "I am like as though I were dead." However, it is fairly possible that this figurative language, even in the form of a simile, would be completely mis-understood in the sense that it was the Law which condemned Paul to death. It may be important in this instance to indicate by a marginal note that "dying to the Law" would, in this context, mean "no longer being under the control of the Law." It may also be necessary, because of the completely wrong meaning associated with "death" or "being killed," that the implications of I am dead be included within the text, for example, "I am as it were dead and therefore not controlled by the Law," or "I am as it were dead and thus not under the Law." The expression killed by the Law itself may then be rendered as "the Law itself did this to me," or "the Law itself caused me to be this way."

The phrase "through the Law" identifies the instrument of Paul's death as the Law itself. It was his experience under the Law that in the light of God's revelation in Christ had led him to the conclusion of the Law's ineffectiveness (see Phil 3.2-11).

In order that I might live for God expresses the purpose of Paul's dying to the Law. To live for God is to live in accordance with God's will; here it is practically synonymous with being put right with God. To live for God is to have a right relationship with him. This purpose may be expressed in some languages as "that I might live to serve God."

It is important, however, that the purpose expressed in the clause in order that I might live for God not be connected immediately with the preceding clause killed by the Law itself. Paul was not killed by the Law itself in order that he might live for God (that is, the Law had no such prior intent), but what happened in his life turned out to have the purpose of his living for God. One may therefore introduce this purpose as "all this happened so that I might live for God."

Paul carries further the figure of dying: I have been put to death with Christ on his cross (literally, "I have been crucified with Christ"). This is a figure of speech which cannot be interpreted literally. Here the Law is implicitly identi-fied as that which put Christ to death on the cross, since in the previous verse the Law is explicitly referred to as putting Paul to death. Elsewhere in his letters, Paul expresses the idea that Christ's death brings to an end the reign of the Law (e.g. Rom 7.4; 10.4; Col 2.14) and that the Christian is free from the Law by participating in Christ's death (e.g. Col 2.20; Gal 3.13). Paul may be expressing the same thought here.

There is a certain complication involved in the passive expression I have been put to death with Christ on his cross. The implication is that this is the result of the Law, but it may be impossible to say in some languages "the Law put me to death," since only an active animate agent could inflict literal death. The closest equivalent, therefore, may be "I died with Christ on his cross," "it was as if I died with Christ on his cross," or "I died, so to speak, with Christ when he died on the cross."

2.20   so that it is no longer I who live, but it is Christ who lives in me. This life that I live now, I live by faith in the Son of God, who loved me and gave his life for me.

So that translates a Greek connective which could be rendered either as "but" or as "and." Most translators take the connective to be continuative, indicating that what follows is a further explanation of the previous verse, and not adversative to it (for the adversative, cf. KJV "nevertheless, I live," Knox "and yet I am alive").

In it is no longer I who live, Paul may be saying that under the old system of the Law, the "I" was prominent, it was the "I" that lived. To depend on the Law is to put emphasis on one's own powers to do what it requires. Instead of that, it is now Christ who lives in him. "Christ in me" is as intimate as the converse expression "in Christ." Many languages do not have a so-called expletive such as it which may occur at the beginning of a clause and refer to something occurring later in the same clause. However, the same idea may be expressed as "the one who is living is no longer I," or "I am not the one who is still living, but Christ is the one who is living in me."

It is impossible in some languages to speak of "living a life," and therefore one cannot translate literally this life that I live now. One may, however, translate as "the way I live now," "the manner in which I live," or "how I am now living."

The next statement makes the previous one much clearer: Paul's new life is based on faith in the Son of God. The Son of God is one of the titles which the early Christians used to refer to Jesus Christ. Again, faith is trust in and commitment to Christ. By faith in the Son of God may be rendered as "by trusting in God's Son," or "by putting my confidence in God's Son."

Paul mentions two acts of Christ: (1) who loved me and (2) gave his life for me. The word for "love" here suggests unmerited, undeserved, self-giving love, while the word for "give" suggests Christ's voluntary surrender of himself to die on the cross (cf. Phps "sacrificed himself for me," NEB "gave himself up for me"). This dying is now identified as a dying for me, i.e., Christ's act on the cross is intensely personal; it is as if he died for Paul alone, but there is nothing self-centered in Paul's statement.

In some languages it is quite impossible to speak of "giving one's life."
One can, however, "willingly die" or "willingly suffer death."

For me may be indicated as a benefactive in a number of languages, for
example, "for my benefit." But in other instances it may be necessary to translate as "in order to help me."

2.21   I refuse to reject the grace of God. But if a person is put right with
        God through the Law, it means that Christ died for nothing!

Some commentaries understand the grace of God to refer to the Law itself
as God's gift to Israel. Elsewhere, Paul has affirmed that the Law has a function,
but he has denied vehemently that the Law was intended to be the instrument by
which God puts man right with himself. Here he is affirming that he is not rejecting the Law, but that he understands the Law's function to be quite different
from what the Jews have made it to be.

On the other hand, it is possible to interpret the grace of God as referring
to God's gift in Jesus Christ, i.e., God's gift of new life. This interpretation has
the merit of connecting this sentence with what precedes and also what immediately follows.

In a number of languages grace in the sense of the grace of God may be
expressed as "loving kindness" or "love which expresses itself in kind deeds."
Accordingly, one may translate I refuse to reject the grace of God as "I do not
throw away God's loving kindness to men," or even "...the way in which God
loves and is kind to men."

A person is put right with God translates the word "righteousness"; it
should be taken in the same sense as the verb "to justify" (see 2.16-17).

The phrase through the Law as an expression of means for justification
must be somewhat amplified in a number of languages, for it is not the Law as
a set of regulations but obedience to such regulations which would constitute a
presumed means of one's being justified. Therefore the condition in this sentence may be rendered as "If a person can get right with God by means of doing
what the Law says, he must do."

For nothing translates a word which could mean "freely," "without pay-
ment," or "undeservedly," but here it has the meaning of "uselessly," "needless-
ly," or "without purpose" (cf. Knox "Christ's death was needless," NAB "Christ
died to no purpose!").

What Paul is saying in this verse is that he is not rejecting God's grace by
rejecting the Law as an instrument of justification. Indeed, if the Law could
function as such, then Christ died for nothing. The implication is that the fault
lies with those who assign such a function to the Law, who in effect are rejecting
God's grace, and who cannot see any purpose in Christ's death. Understood this
way, this verse serves as a good summary of Paul's discussion in the entire
second chapter, and it constitutes a prelude to his subsequent arguments in the
next two chapters.

CHAPTER 3

In the first two chapters of Galatians, Paul's main concerns have been the defense of his commission as an apostle and of the good news that he has proclaimed to the Galatian churches. In the next two chapters, Paul carries the battle to the camp of the enemy, and there he defends the doctrine that people become acceptable to God through their faith rather than through anything that they do. In this defense he uses Old Testament Scripture extensively, since he is directing his arguments primarily to those who had evidently been influenced by ideas based on Old Testament texts. His main argument is that it is those who believe God and trust in him who are the real descendants of Abraham.

TEV

RSV

Law or Faith

1 You foolish Galatians! Who put a spell on you? Before your very eyes you had a clear description of the death of Jesus Christ on the cross! 2 Tell me this one thing: did you receive God's Spirit by doing what the Law requires or by hearing the gospel and believing it? 3 How can you be so foolish! You began by God's Spirit; do you now want to finish by your own power? 4 Did all your experience mean nothing at all? Surely it meant something! 5 Does God give you the Spirit and work miracles among you because you do what the Law requires or because you hear the gospel and believe it?
(3.1-5)

1 O foolish Galatians! Who has bewitched you, before whose eyes Jesus Christ was publicly portrayed as crucified? 2 Let me ask you only this: Did you receive the Spirit by works of the law, or by hearing with faith? 3 Are you so foolish? Having begun with the Spirit, are you now ending with the flesh? 4 Did you experience so many things in vain?--if it really is in vain. 5 Does he who supplies the Spirit to you and works miracles among you do so by works of the law, or by hearing with faith?
(3.1-5)

In this section Paul addresses the Galatians directly, reminding them of their spiritual experiences, which in themselves are arguments for the truth and validity of the message which Paul has proclaimed to them.

The section heading Law or Faith is quite effective, but in some languages it is necessary to introduce verbal expressions, for example, "Obeying the Law or believing in Jesus Christ," or "Doing what the laws say or trusting Christ."

Throughout this section there are various translational problems due primarily to the introduction of exclamations and rhetorical questions. Most of these questions are not answered specifically, but their implications are suggested by their forms. This means that the connections between the thoughts are often elliptical, and this may require considerable restructuring in some languages.

3.1   You foolish Galatians! Who put a spell on you? Before your very eyes you had a clear description of the death of Jesus Christ on the cross!

The tone of the whole verse—and of the whole section, for that matter—is one of unbelief. It is unthinkable to Paul that the Galatians have changed so quickly. The only explanation possible is that they have gone out of their minds!

Foolish (NAB "senseless," NEB "stupid," JB "mad") puts the emphasis not on natural stupidity but on failure to use one's mental and spiritual powers.

A vocative expression such as You foolish Galatians! may be both grammatically awkward and misleading in sense. It might mean, for example, that all the people in Galatia were stupid, which, of course, is not what Paul means. He is addressing particular Galatians and he is saying that they are "not using their heads" or "not thinking right." It may be necessary, therefore, to say in some languages "You Galatians are not thinking right," or "...not using your minds as you should." In some languages the meaning of foolish is expressed idiomatically, for example, "you have lost your heads," "your minds have left you," or "your heads are empty."

Who put a spell on you? (literally, "who has bewitched you?") is a rhetorical question, and the "who" probably refers to the same people spoken of in 1.7. The emphasis here, however, is not on who did the bewitching, but on the fact that the Galatians are indeed bewitched (NEB "You must have been bewitched"). The word "bewitched" itself suggests the use of magic, particularly the casting of a spell through the use of the evil eye. The belief that one person could cast a spell over another is common in many parts of the world, but one must not deduce from this statement that Paul believed in magic. He is more likely using "bewitched" in a metaphorical sense, and he probably means by it "to pervert," "to lead astray," or "to confuse the mind." The form of the question Who put a spell on you? might seem to focus attention upon the individual responsible for bewitching the Galatians. Since, however, the focus is upon the condition of the Galatians and not upon who caused the trouble, it may be better to change the question into a statement, for example, "You are indeed bewitched," "You certainly must have been bewitched," or "Someone must have certainly put a spell upon you."

Before your very eyes is a part of a dependent clause in the Greek, and while most translations retain the original form, TEV makes the clause into a separate sentence. The whole expression is metaphorical and describes the familiar practice of making public announcements by means of bills or posters. In this case the announcement is "the death of Jesus Christ on the cross."

The final sentence in this verse is related to the preceding as a reason for Paul's having concluded that the Galatians had been bewitched. It may be important in some languages to indicate this connection by rendering the final sentence as "How could this have happened, since before your very eyes you had a clear description...?"

It may, however, be quite difficult to employ a more or less literal translation of this final sentence in verse 1, for it is rare that one can speak of "having a clear description." Since it was Paul himself who had described the death of Jesus Christ, it may be better to say "since I described to you so clearly how Jesus Christ died on the cross." The form of the Greek participle referring to the death of Jesus Christ is perfective; it indicates something which took place in the past but which has present implications. One may therefore wish to use some such form as "how Jesus Christ has died on the cross." In some languages, however, the cross must be interpreted not simply as the location of Christ's death but as the means of it. Therefore one may need to say "how Jesus died by means of the cross," or "how people caused Jesus Christ to die by means of a cross."

Whether one employs a definite or indefinite article to go with the term corresponding to cross depends largely upon the syntactic requirements of the receptor language in question. In some languages it may be necessary to say "a cross." However, since this letter is part of a much larger text (the entire New Testament), it may seem quite appropriate in other languages to use a definite article and therefore translate "the cross," in the sense that the particular cross on which Jesus Christ dies is identified by the larger context.

3.2   Tell me this one thing: did you receive God's Spirit by doing what the Law requires or by hearing the gospel and believing it?

Verse 2 is also in the form of a rhetorical question, directed at the experience of the Galatians. If one retains this rhetorical question in translation, then tell me this one thing must sometimes be rendered as "answer this one question." On the other hand, in languages which do not permit rhetorical questions (since Paul is obviously not really asking for information), it may be necessary to transform this verse into a conditional statement, for example, "If you tell me how you received God's Spirit, then you will obviously say it was by hearing the gospel and believing it and not by doing what the Law requires you to do." In this way the force of the rhetorical question is retained without loss of essential content. In other languages it may be possible to retain the rhetorical question, but the answer must be given immediately following the question. Therefore, one must insert an answer such as "Obviously you received God's Spirit by hearing the good news and believing it."

God's Spirit is literally, "the Spirit," but undoubtedly refers both to their initiation into the Christian faith and to their reception of the gifts of the Spirit, the outward signs of his presence, such as speaking with tongues and prophesying. In some languages it is impossible to say literally receive God's Spirit. This would suggest that God's Spirit was some kind of a thing which could be handled and accepted as one could do with a material gift. An equivalent may be "did God's Spirit come into your life because you did what the law said you should do?" or "did God's Spirit take control of you...?" or "...rule your heart...?"

Doing what the Law requires (literally "works of law") and hearing the gospel and believing it (literally "hearing of faith") express the leading antithesis of the whole letter. (On "works of law," see 2.16.) The assumed answer to the rhetorical question is, of course, "hearing of faith." This particular phrase primarily means the act of listening to the Good News, with the result of believing and accepting it (cf. Phps "believing the message of the Gospel," JB "you believed what was preached to you," NEB "believing the gospel message").

The two participial clauses by doing what the Law requires and by hearing the gospel and believing it express means, but in some languages this is most effectively conveyed by an expression of cause, for example, "Did you receive God's Spirit because you did what the Law tells you to do or because you heard the Good News and believed it?"

3.3   How can you be so foolish! You began by God's Spirit; do you now want to finish by your own power?

How can you be so foolish expresses unbelief on the part of Paul. He finds it difficult to believe that the Galatians can be that foolish (cf. Phps "Surely you can't be so idiotic"; NEB "Can it be that you are so stupid?"). In place of an exclamatory question How can you be so foolish!, it may be necessary in some languages to use a strong negative expression, for example, "You surely cannot be so foolish!" or, idiomatically, "Certainly your minds must not have left you so completely!"

You began by God's Spirit; do you now want to finish by your own power? is literally "Having begun with (in, by) the Spirit, with (in, by) the flesh are you now finishing?" Here Paul presents a twofold contrast: beginning/finishing, God's Spirit/flesh. As in the previous verse, "Spirit" here again refers to the Spirit of God. "Flesh" could be interpreted in many ways. It could mean the "body," that is, a reference to what is circumcised. Or it could refer to the natural powers of men apart from the divine Spirit, hence the ΓEV rendering by your own power. Again, "flesh" could refer to outward observances such as the Jewish rite of circumcision and other requirements of the Law (JB "Are you foolish enough to end in outward observances what you began in the Spirit?"; Phps "reverting to outward observances"; but see NEB, where the antithesis is between the "material" and the "spiritual": "You started with the spiritual; do you now look to the material...?").

One of the serious complications involved in this contrast between God's Spirit and a person's own power is the fact that the verb began occurs without any verbal complement. In a number of languages one simply cannot use a verb such as began without indicating what began. In some languages one can say "You began your new life by means of God's Spirit," or "God's Spirit caused you to begin to live in a new way." It is also possible to speak of "your new relation to God."

In place of the question do you now want to finish by your own power?, one may employ a statement for languages which would not use a rhetorical question. One may say, for example, "you certainly do not want to complete your life by just what you can do for yourself." However, one may wish to restructure the relations rather extensively, for example, "how do you think that you are strong enough to complete the life that you have begun?", or "how do you think that you can continue living to the end by your own strength?"

3.4   Did all your experience mean nothing at all? Surely it meant something!

Your experience translates a verb which is ambiguous, since it could be
understood either negatively or positively. Negatively, it could be understood
as "suffering" and therefore could refer to the persecutions that the Galatian
Christians had gone through (Phps "Has all your painful experience brought you
nowhere?"; Knox "Was it to no purpose that you went through so much?"). Positively, it could refer to the spiritual experiences of the Galatians as a result of
their reception of the Holy Spirit (JB "Have all the favours you received been
wasted?"; NAB "Have you had such remarkable experiences all to no purpose
...?"; NEB "Have all your great experiences been in vain...?").

The Galatian Christians would probably have known the specific experience
referred to in Paul's words, but unfortunately we do not. Our choice therefore
is either to select one of the above renderings or to retain the ambiguity of the
Greek verb, as indeed TEV does. This ambiguity may be retained in some languages by translating "Did all that happened to you mean nothing at all?" In some
languages this type of question may be retained since it is answered in the immediately following statement, Surely it meant something! In general, however, it
is difficult to find a strictly neutral term with regard to experience, and therefore one is normally obliged to select an expression which means either "to suffer" or "to enjoy benefits."

Surely it meant something! is literally "if it be really in vain" (RSV). The
expression once again indicates that Paul finds it hard to believe that everything
the Galatians have experienced has not meant a thing to them (Phps "I simply
cannot believe it of you!"). It may be difficult, however, in some languages to
speak of an experience as "meaning something." It may be possible to speak of
"words meaning something," but an experience often belongs to quite a different
semantic domain. However, one can sometimes say "Did what happened to you
not cause you to think about it?" Similarly, Surely it meant something! may be
rendered as "Certainly what happened to you must have made you think how important the happening was."

3.5   Does God give you the Spirit and work miracles among you because
you do what the Law requires or because you hear the gospel and believe it?

This verse is a repetition of verse 2, but with a slight shift of focus. It
summarizes Paul's appeal to the experience of the Galatians. Again, as in the
case of the question in verse 2, it may be necessary to shift this rhetorical question into the form of a statement, for example, "God does not give you the Spirit
and cause miracles to happen among you because you do what the Law requires;
rather, he gives you the Spirit and causes miracles to happen among you because you hear the good news and believe it." It is possible in a number of receptor languages to eliminate some of the redundancy in this type of statement
by employing appropriate pronouns to refer to the giving of the Spirit and the
working of miracles.

Does God give you the Spirit is literally "He that supplies the Spirit to you." The pronoun obviously refers to God, and this is made explicit in most translations. The verb for give expresses the idea of "supply abundantly," "giving freely and liberally." Paul's use of the present tense form indicates that, for him, the experience of receiving the Spirit is not merely an experience in the past but can be thought of as being in progress, even up to the time of his writing this letter. The continuity in God's giving his Spirit may be expressed in some languages as "he constantly gives the Spirit," "he continually gives the Spirit," or "he is always supplying the Spirit."

Miracles refers to what are often spoken of as the charismatic manifestations of the Spirit. Among you may also be understood as "in you," but most translations understand it in the same sense as TEV. In a number of languages miracles are spoken of as "wonderful events" or "unexpected happenings," while in other languages they may be referred to by idiomatic expressions, for example, "longnecked things" (referring to the fact that people stretch their necks to watch miracles) or "mouth-opening happenings" (since in surprise people are supposed to open their mouths).

What the Law requires and hear the gospel and believe it are to be understood in the same sense as in verse 2. For the Law it may be necessary to use a plural form as a collective, namely, "laws," and, in some instances, to specify that these are "the laws that came through Moses." Otherwise, the reference would imply merely local government regulations. Similarly, it may be necessary to indicate the object of the "Good News," since in some languages one cannot simply speak of "Good News" without indicating what the Good News is about. In this instance it would be "the Good News about Jesus Christ."

TEV	RSV
6 Consider the experience of Abraham; as the scripture says, "He believed God, and because of his faith God accepted him as righteous." 7 You should realize, then, that the real descendants of Abraham are the people who have faith. 8 The scripture predicted that God would put the Gentiles right with himself through faith. And so the scripture announced the Good News to Abraham: "Through you God will bless all mankind." 9 Abraham believed and was blessed; so all who believe are blessed as he was. (3.6-9)	6 Thus Abraham "believed God, and it was reckoned to him as righteousness." 7 So you see that it is men of faith who are the sons of Abraham. 8 And the scripture, foreseeing that God would justify the Gentiles by faith, preached the gospel beforehand to Abraham, saying, "In you shall all the nations be blessed." 9 So then, those who are men of faith are blessed with Abraham who had faith. (3.6-9)

In these verses Paul affirms his fundamental contention that Abraham was put right with God by faith and that those who are put right with God in the same manner are Abraham's true descendants. A difficulty of this paragraph is that the scripture is spoken of as doing various things: says (v. 6), predicted (v. 8),

3.6

and announced the Good News (v. 8). Finding terms to translate these expressions adequately and smoothly may be a problem in a number of languages.

<u>3.6</u>   Consider the experience of Abraham; as the scripture says, "He believed God, and because of his faith God accepted him as righteous."

The Greek word used to introduce this section (RSV "thus") could be taken either (1) as introducing a subordinate clause which is dependent on the preceding section, (2) or as introducing a new topic. The latter interpretation seems to be preferred. In the previous verses (1-5), Paul has been appealing to the experience of the Galatians. Now he brings in the case of Abraham, and from this point until the end of chapter 4, Paul affirms his fundamental contention that Abraham was put right with God by faith, and that therefore those who are put right with God in the same manner are the true descendants of Abraham.

Some translations smooth out the rather abrupt introduction of a new topic in order to bring in the case of Abraham more naturally (JB "Take Abraham for example," NAB "Consider the case of Abraham," NEB "Look at Abraham"). It is also possible to begin this paragraph by a phrase such as "Now think about Abraham," "And now we should consider what happened to Abraham," or "What happened to Abraham is here important."

As the scripture says is not in the text; it is added in TEV to signal to the reader that what follows is a quotation from the Old Testament. The quotation itself is from Gen 15.6 and follows the Septuagint rather than the Hebrew version. In a number of languages one cannot speak of "the scripture saying" or "...speaking"; it is only people who say things. One can, however, use some such phrase as "as one may read in the Scriptures," or "...in a passage of the Scriptures."

Abraham is considered the father of the Jewish nation. An appeal to his experience would be an effective argument against the Judaizers, that is, those who insisted that conformance to the Law was necessary for salvation.

He believed God indicates more than mental assent. It describes Abraham's willing and unreserved surrender to God, his humble and utter dependence on him, and his confident trust in his word. This meaning is frequently expressed in translations as "Abraham trusted God," or "Abraham put his confidence in God." In some languages trust is expressed idiomatically, for example, "Abraham leaned his weight upon God," or "Abraham hung onto God with his heart."

Because of his faith God accepted him as righteous is literally "It was reckoned to him as righteousness." "It" is, of course, his faith, and the implicit agent of "was reckoned" is God. The phrase "reckoned to him as righteousness" can be interpreted either to mean that God recognized Abraham as having acted rightly, or that it was Abraham's faith that was accounted as the ground of his being accepted by God. "Righteousness" in the latter case would have the primary element of being put right with God or being put into a right relationship with him.

The phrase because of his faith may be rendered as "because he trusted God."

God accepted him as righteous may be rendered as "God received him as one who is righteous," or "...who had done what was right." However, if "righteousness" is to be understood in terms of being put right with God or being placed in a right relation to God, one may say in some languages "God joined him to himself in the right way."

3.7   You should realize, then, that the real descendants of Abraham are the people who have faith.

The people who have faith (literally, "those from faith") are those who, like Abraham, believe and trust in God and whose life and character are determined by that faith. In a number of languages one must always indicate the goal of faith, and therefore it may be necessary to say "the people who have faith in God," or "those who trust God." It is these people who are the real descendants of Abraham. This is, literally, "sons of Abraham," but "sons" is not used here in a genealogical sense, but rather as denoting people who show the same characteristics as the one they are compared with. The "sons of Abraham" are those who, like Abraham, rely on faith. The real descendants of Abraham are not those who have descended from him physically, but those who share a spiritual kinship with him.

A literal translation of the real descendants of Abraham might imply the biological offspring of Abraham, the very opposite of what is intended, and so in this context the word real may be misleading. However, it can sometimes be employed in a restructured context, for example, "more really the descendants of Abraham than are his actual offspring."

3.8   The scripture predicted that God would put the Gentiles right with himself through faith. And so the scripture announced the Good News to Abraham: "Through you God will bless all mankind."

This verse is one sentence in the Greek: a participial phrase and a main clause, with two embedded so-called substantive clauses. This form is retained in most translations, but TEV restructures it into two sentences. The basic argument that Paul sets forth here, obviously in response to his opponents' assertions, is that the blessing of the nations through Abraham is not achieved by either physical descent or by the legal rite of circumcision. Rather, it is given by God in the same way that it was given to Abraham, namely, through faith.

The scripture usually denotes a particular passage of the Old Testament. Here the quotation is from Gen 12.3 and follows the rendering in the Septuagint but with some slight differences. The translator must translate the quotation as Paul quoted it, rather than try to render it from its Old Testament Hebrew form.

In this passage, the scripture is personified, and most translations keep the personified form. It is possible, however, to translate in such a way that the emphasis is not on scripture personified, but on the particular passage being referred to (Knox "There is a passage in Scripture"). In many languages it is impossible to personify a passage of scripture and to say "the scripture predicted." But it may be possible to say "One may read in a passage of scripture that God would put the Gentiles right...."

As personified, scripture predicted, that is, saw or declared ahead of time, long before the coming of the Good News in Jesus Christ. What had scripture foreseen? That God would put the Gentiles right with himself through faith— literally,"that God would justify the Gentiles by faith." The word "justify" means God's act of putting people in the right, or, more correctly, in putting people in proper relationship with himself. Through faith has reference not to God's faith, but to the attitude of the Gentiles, an attitude characterized by faith and trust in God.

Continuing the personification of scripture, Paul now asserts that it announced the Good News. Good News has reference to God's act of putting man right with himself.

In a number of languages it is almost meaningless to say that the scripture announced the Good News, since only a person can engage in such an activity. It is sometimes possible to speak of "words telling about," and one may be able to render the second sentence of verse 8 as "And so in the Scriptures there are words about how the good news was told to Abraham even before what was talked about took place."

As already indicated, the quotation is from Gen 12.3. Paul quotes it in a passive form: "all nations shall be blessed." The implicit subject is God, and TEV makes this explicit: God will bless. "Nations" refers not to political states, but to peoples, hence the TEV rendering: all mankind.

A phrase such as through you in some languages must be understood as a secondary agent in a causative expression. The corresponding rendering is "God will cause you to bless all mankind." This makes God the primary causative agent and Abraham the secondary agent. In other languages the same relations are expressed by a formula such as "God will use you to bless all the people on earth," or "You will be the means by which God will bless all the people on earth."

In this type of context bless is often rendered as "to cause kindness to," "to show favor to," or "to cause goodness to come to."

3.9   Abraham believed and was blessed; so all who believe are blessed as he was.

Verse 9 literally rendered is "so that (or therefore) those of faith are blessed with the faithful (or believing) Abraham." Two ideas are expressed: (1) Abraham believed and was blessed; (2) all who believe are blessed as he was. The source of the blessing in each case is God himself. Here again, belief is not simply mental assent, but trust and confidence in God.

Abraham believed and was blessed must be expanded in some languages to read "Abraham trusted God, and God blessed him." What Abraham did, however, may be best considered as cause in some languages and therefore "Because Abraham trusted God, God blessed him." Similarly, the resulting clause so all who believe are blessed as he was may be rendered as "therefore God blesses all those who believe in him, just as he blessed Abraham."

TEV

10 Those who depend on obeying the Law live under a curse. For the scripture says, "Whoever does not always obey everything that is written in the book of the Law is under God's curse!" 11 Now, it is clear that no one is put right with God by means of the Law, because the scripture says, "Only the person who is put right with God through faith shall live."*d* 12 But the Law has nothing to do with faith. Instead, as the scripture says, "Whoever *does* everything the Law requires will live."

13 But by becoming a curse for us Christ has redeemed us from the curse that the Law brings; for the scripture says, "Anyone who is hanged on a tree is under God's curse." 14 Christ did this in order that the blessing which God promised to Abraham might be given to the Gentiles by means of Christ Jesus, so that through faith we might receive the Spirit promised by God.

*d*put right with God through faith shall live; *or* put right with God shall live through faith. (3.10-14)

RSV

10 For all who rely on works of the law are under a curse; for it is written, "Cursed be every one who does not abide by all things written in the book of the law, and do them." 11 Now it is evident that no man is justified before God by the law; for "He who through faith is righteous shall live";*f* 12 but the law does not rest on faith, for "He who does them shall live by them." 13 Christ redeemed us from the curse of the law, having become a curse for us--for it is written, "Cursed be every one who hangs on a tree"--14 that in Christ Jesus the blessing of Abraham might come upon the Gentiles, that we might receive the promise of the Spirit through faith.

*f*Or *the righteous shall live by faith* (3.10-14)

In these verses the apostle introduces new arguments against his opponents. In the preceding section, Paul has spoken of "those of faith," i.e., those who believe and trust God and on this basis are accepted by him. Here, in deliberate contrast, Paul speaks of "those out of works of law," and shows God's attitude towards them. Instead of receiving the blessings of God, these people are in fact under God's curse.

3.10   Those who depend on obeying the Law live under a curse. For the scripture says, "Whoever does not always obey everything that is written in the book of the Law is under God's curse!"

Those who depend on obeying the Law is literally "as many as are out of works of law" (RSV "who rely on works of the law"). Although law can mean any law, since the Greek speaks of "law" and not of "the Law," most translators and commentators take "law" here to refer to the Jewish Law, since it was the Jewish Law whose role as an instrument in putting man in a right relationship with God is now in question. It is this same Jewish Law that the Galatians are being urged by the false teachers to accept.

"Works of law" means here, as it does in 3.2, "doing what the law requires." The whole expression, then, "as many as are out of works of law" means those who depend on obeying the Law as the means by which they may be put in a right relationship with God, or those who seek to please God by following specific regulations in the Law.

The expression those who depend on obeying the Law involves considerable semantic ellipsis, since the purpose of the dependence has been omitted; in other words, these are people who depend on obeying the Law in order to be put right with God. Furthermore, in a number of languages it makes very little sense to say depend on obeying the Law unless one indicates the purpose for such an action. Therefore, it may be necessary to translate this initial clause as "those who think they will be received by God because they obey what the laws say," or "those who think they will get right with God because they obey what the laws say they must do."

Curse is in this verse contrasted with "blessing" in verses 8 and 9. A curse is a wish or a prayer for evil to befall someone. In treaties and contracts, the curse was directed at any party who in the future might dare to violate the provisions agreed upon. In verse 10, the curse is defined more fully in the quotation which follows. Therefore, while it is possible to say "under a curse from God" or "under the curse of God," it is better in the present case to retain the original form "under a curse," so that it can clearly be seen as a reference to the quotation which follows.

The phrase live under a curse may be extremely difficult to render in such a way as really to communicate the meaning of the Greek text. In many languages a literal translation of this expression would mean "to continue living after someone has already cursed you." This, of course, is not the meaning. It is rather the threat of condemnation which continues for any person who thinks that he can become right with God by obeying the Law. Therefore, one may translate live under a curse as "continue under threat of being condemned," or "live all the time knowing that God will condemn them."

In some languages it may be perfectly appropriate to use a technical term for curse, but in other languages this would not be advisable since a "curse" is regarded only as an instrument of evil, and anyone putting a curse on another would be doing something entirely wrong. Such an interpretation would, of course, not be satisfactory for the scripture quotation which speaks of God's curse.

The quotation "whoever does not..." is from Deut 27.26 and follows the Septuagint, with some variations.

The implied premise of the whole verse is twofold: (1) that in order for one to gain God's approval through the Law, he must obey everything that is provided therein; and (2) that no one can follow everything that is written in the book of the Law. Since, therefore, anyone who does not follow everything in the Law is under God's curse, and no one is able to follow everything in the Law, then everyone who depends on obeying the Law lives under a curse.

The phrase <u>for the scripture says</u> must sometimes be rendered "as one may read in the Scriptures," or "according to the words of the Scriptures."

The indefinite relative clause <u>"whoever does not always obey everything that is written in the book of the Law"</u> must be reinterpreted in some languages as a condition, for example, "if someone does not always obey everything that is written in the book of the Law." In place of the passive expression <u>everything that is written in the book of the Law</u>, it is possible in some cases to use "all the words of the book of the laws."

Since in this context the term <u>book</u> refers simply to the listing, it may be preferable not to employ a term which would imply that all the laws were contained within a single book. It may be better to say "obey all the regulations of the laws," or "obey all the regulations listed in the laws."

<u>Under God's curse</u> is literally "cursed," with the implied agent being God, hence "cursed by God." Accordingly, <u>is under God's curse</u>, may be rendered as "is exposed to God's condemnation." On the other hand, the entire sentence may be restructured to read as "God condemns anyone who does not always obey all that is written in the book of the Law." It may be necessary to indicate here that <u>the Law</u> refers to "the laws coming through Moses," or "... given by means of Moses."

3.11-12   Now, it is clear that no one is put right with God by means of the Law, because the scripture says, "Only the person who is put right with God through faith shall live."<i>d</i> (12) But the Law has nothing to do with faith. Instead, as the scripture says, "Whoever <u>does</u> everything the Law requires will live."

dput right with God through faith shall live; or put right with God shall live through faith.

In these two verses, Paul expands the contrast between faith and law. His argument is as follows: since he who is put right with God through faith shall live, and since the Law demands "doing" rather than "faith," therefore it is very clear that no man is put right with God by means of the Law.

<u>It is clear</u> is literally "it is evident." The Greek construction suggests the introduction of additional argument for Paul's position as expressed in verse 10 (Phps "it is made still plainer," NAB "it should be obvious," Twentieth Century "again, it is evident"). This may be rendered in some languages as "anyone can see," or "surely one can realize."

<u>Put right with God</u> is literally "justified." Here, as in other letters of Paul, this expression has as its main component God's activity in putting man into a right relationship with himself. The passive expression <u>no one is put right with God</u> may be changed into an active form by saying "God puts no one right with himself." It must be made clear that the reflexive "himself" refers to God, not to the person.

<u>By means of the Law</u> is an expression of means, but in a number of languages the Law itself cannot be the means of performing this kind of activity. It may be necessary to expand this phrase into a clause of cause and to introduce

the verb "obey," since it is really not the Law itself but obedience to the Law which is the means Paul is speaking about. Accordingly, one may say, "No one is put right with God because he does what the Law requires."

The scripture says is not in the Greek text, but since the quotation that follows is from scripture, TEV marks it accordingly (cf. NEB "we read," JB "we are told"). There are two ways of rendering the quotation: either "the just shall live by faith" (TEV margin, NAB JB Phps), or "the just through faith shall live" (TEV text, NEB RSV). The quotation is from Hab 2.4 (quoted by Paul also in Rom 1.17).

The person who is put right with God translates a noun (literally, "the righteous one"). Some translations take this in an ethical sense (NAB "the just man," various versions "the righteous man"), while others, including TEV, interpret it in the sense of the Greek verb "justify," and therefore understand Paul to be referring to a man who has been put right with God, rather than to a morally upright person.

In the same way that by means of the Law must often be expanded to mean "because one obeys the laws," it may also be necessary to amplify the phrase through faith as "because one trusts in God."

The phrase shall live should not be rendered in such a way as to mean mere continued existence. It is important to employ a verb here which will suggest a higher quality of life. In some languages this may be equivalent to "shall really live."

But expresses the contrast between the Law and faith. Has nothing to do with faith is literally "is not of faith." Accordingly, there are various ways of rendering it. Some translations take it as saying that one does not need faith in order to follow the Law or that the law does not depend on faith (cf. NAB; also RSV "the law does not rest on faith," Mft "the law is not based on faith"). Other translations interpret it as referring to the definite distinction between the Law and faith, their complete dissimilarity and lack of relation to each other, as does TEV (also Phps "the law is not a matter of faith," NEB "now law is not at all a matter of having faith").

The statement But the Law has nothing to do with faith is very succinct, for the Law in this context refers not primarily to regulations as such but to a person's obedience to the Law. Similarly, faith is not to be understood as an abstract term, but must be related to one's actual trust and confidence in God. This sentence, therefore, may be rendered as "But when a person obeys the Law, that is not at all the same as when one trusts God." One may even say, in some instances, "But obeying the Law is not related to trusting God."

As the scripture says is once again added to signal to the reader that what follows is a quotation from the Old Testament. It is from Lev 18.5 (quoted by Paul also in Rom 10.5) and is taken to be antithetical to the quotation from Hab 2.4. The two quotations spell out the two ways of obtaining life, one by faith and the other by doing. The former is primarily an attitude of trust and confidence in God; the latter is not concerned with attitudes, but simply with performance or the lack of it.

Does everything the Law requires is literally "does them." It is clear that "them" refers not to the Law in general (<u>Law</u> in the first part of the verse is singular), but to the requirements of the Law (JB "the man who practises these precepts"; Knox "the man who carries out the commandments"). <u>Everything the</u> <u>Law requires</u> may be rendered as "everything the laws talk about," or "every-thing the laws say that a person must do."

The final phrase in the Greek text of this verse, namely, "by them," is in a sense a duplication of the thought of the clause <u>whoever does . . . requires.</u>

<u>3.13</u>   But by becoming a curse for us Christ has redeemed us from the curse that the Law brings; for the scripture says, "Anyone who is hanged on a tree is under God's curse."

Verse 13 is introduced very abruptly in the Greek, without any connective. It is clear, however, from the context, that this verse provides the answer to the problem of the curse of the Law in the preceding verses (10-12). Accord-ingly, while most translations retain the abruptness, TEV introduces the verse with <u>but</u> (cf. Phps "now Christ" and especially Knox "from this curse invoked by the Law Christ has ransomed us"). Whereas the Greek begins immediately with the statement of Christ's act of redemption, followed by the means thereof, TEV rearranges the clauses and starts by explaining the means by which Christ ac-complished this deliverance from the curse of the Law, namely, <u>by becoming a</u> <u>curse for us.</u> The Greek follows this explanation of means by reference to the Old Testament passage in which Paul finds support for the surprising view that Christ became <u>a curse,</u> but TEV separates this participial phrase from its scrip-tural support. In light of that Old Testament passage (<u>anyone who is hanged . . .</u>), the unexpressed premise here is that when Christ was hanged on the cross, he became accursed by God (cf. Phps "by himself becoming a curse for us when he was crucified"). Therefore, <u>becoming a curse for us</u> should be understood pri-marily in the sense that for our sake Jesus Christ suffered on the cross as one who was accursed by God, rather than in terms of any particular doctrine of atonement in which the phrase may be thought to defend. Again, the expression of means may be most effectively indicated in some languages as cause, for ex-ample, "But because he was condemned on our behalf . . . ."

The verb translated <u>redeemed</u> (literally, "to buy up") has here the pri-mary meaning of "to effect deliverance" or "to secure the release of someone," at some cost to the person who secures it in terms of effort, suffering, or loss. Again, it would seem much more profitable to put primary emphasis on this main component, that is, that by his death Christ has secured our release, or has set us free from the curse of the Law, rather than attempting to draw from this verse support for different doctrines of the atonement, and answers to such questions as "How much did Christ pay?" and "To whom did he pay it?"

For this type of context, <u>Christ has redeemed us from</u> may be expressed effectively as "Christ has caused us to be free from," "Christ has delivered us from," or "Christ has caused us no longer to be under (the condemnation) of."

<u>The curse that the Law brings</u> is, of course, connected with verses 10-12; it is the curse that the Law brings to those who try to live by its precepts but

who in fact cannot fulfill everything that it requires. It may be necessary to use a term such as "condemnation" rather than curse, since the latter term may carry connotations which go beyond the meaning of the Greek text itself. The curse that the Law brings may therefore be rendered as "the condemnation in accordance with the laws," "condemnation resulting from the laws," or "... from not obeying the laws."

The quotation from the Old Testament that follows (Deut 21.23) gives, as indicated above, the reason why Christ's hanging on the cross can be interpreted as his becoming accursed. In its original context the verse refers to the practice of hanging the bodies of criminals on trees and leaving them there; the Jews believed that to do so would defile their land. One can see how easy it was to include in the reference of this text those who later were put to death by means of the Roman practice of crucifixion, including Christ himself.

In rendering anyone who is hanged on a tree, it is important to avoid a wording which will suggest that Jesus himself was put to death by a rope being put around his neck. It may be necessary to modify this expression so as to read "anyone who is executed on a tree," or "anyone who was executed and whose body was hung on a tree."

It is not necessary to render tree by a term which will mean a live tree. The Greek term may refer simply to a "post," and it may be more appropriate to employ a term which would also be applicable to a cross. To use an expression which must refer to a live tree would introduce an unnecessary inconsistency.

As in the case of verse 10, the phrase under God's curse may be rendered as "condemned by God."

3.14   Christ did this in order that the blessing which God promised to Abraham might be given to the Gentiles by means of Christ Jesus, so that through faith we might receive the Spirit promised by God.

Verse 14 is composed, in the Greek, of two dependent clauses, each introduced by a conjunction meaning either "so that" or "in order that"; that is, they are either purpose or result clauses. The first of these clauses depends on the main clause of verse 13 (Christ has redeemed us). The second could do the same, or it could depend on the first clause of verse 14. TEV makes clear the connection of the first clause with verse 13 by adding the words Christ did this, thereby also making verse 14 a separate sentence (cf. NAB "this has happened so that..."; NEB "and the purpose of it all was that..."; for a slightly different way of connecting the two verses, cf. Phps "God's purpose is therefore plain...").

The blessing which God promised to Abraham is literally "the blessing of Abraham." It is possible to interpret this as "the blessing which Abraham has received from God" (NAB "the blessing bestowed on Abraham"; Twentieth Century "the blessing given to Abraham"). More likely, however, it refers to the blessing promised to Abraham. In a sense, however, both aspects of the blessing may be present in Paul's thought. The blessing itself, in the light of verses 8-9, is God's activity in putting the Gentiles into a right relationship with himself. The blessing which God promised to Abraham may be rendered in some languages as "the good that God promised to Abraham that he would do," or "the favor that God said to Abraham he would be giving."

Might be given to the Gentiles may be transformed from passive to active by saying "God might give this to the Gentiles."

By means of Jesus Christ is literally "in Christ Jesus." The same construction appears in 2.4, 17. Some interpreters take the expression to be used in the sense of "fellowship with" or "union with" Christ Jesus. Many others, however, including TEV, understand this phrase to be used here with the meaning of agency (cf. Phps "through Jesus Christ"; NAB "in Jesus Christ").

In some languages it may be necessary to reorder the elements in the first purpose clause of this verse, for example, "In order that by means of what Christ Jesus did God would give to the Gentiles the blessing that he had promised to Abraham." It is important in the rendering of this clause, and especially the expression "promised to Abraham," to avoid an implication that God was going to take away the promise he had given to Abraham and give it instead to other people. The promise is that recorded in verse 8, that through Abraham God was going to bless all the people on earth. It may be necessary, in speaking of "what God had promised to Abraham," to say "what God had said to Abraham that he would do."

The second clause, as indicated above, can be understood as either dependent on or coordinate with the first clause. TEV leans toward the dependent relationship (also NAB "thereby making it possible"; cf. NEB); while some other translations favor the coordinate relationship (JB "and so that"; Phps "that the blessing promised to Abraham might reach the Gentiles through Jesus Christ, and the promise of the Spirit might become ours by faith").

The phrase through faith may be rendered as "by our trusting God," or "by our trusting in Jesus Christ." In some languages this expression of means may be more appropriately indicated as cause, for example, "because we trusted in God."

We should be understood not as "we Jews," in contrast to Gentiles in the first clause, but as "we Christians," including both Jews and Gentiles (Phps "to us all").

Might receive the Spirit is expressed in some languages as "might have the Spirit come upon us," "... come into us," or "might be controlled by the Spirit." In a number of languages, however, it is not sufficient simply to speak of "the Spirit"; it may be necessary to indicate clearly that this is "God's Spirit" or "the Holy Spirit."

The Spirit promised by God is literally "the promise of the Spirit," but it is understood as "the promised Spirit." This may be understood either as equivalent to "the blessing of Abraham" (in which case the content of the blessing of Abraham would be the giving of the Spirit), or, as in most translations, a second result of Christ's act of redeeming us from the curse of the Law. Understood in the latter way, there are two results of Christ's act of redemption: (1) the blessing which consists in God's acceptance of Gentiles by means of Christ Jesus, and (2) the receiving of the Spirit by all who believe.

TEV	RSV

The Law and the Promise

15 My brothers, I am going to use an everyday example: When two people agree on a matter and sign an agreement, no one can break it or add anything to it. 16 Now, God made his promises to Abraham and to his descendant. The scripture does not use the plural "descendants," meaning many people, but the singular "descendant," meaning one person only, namely, Christ. 17 What I mean is that God made a covenant with Abraham and promised to keep it. The Law, which was given four hundred and thirty years later, cannot break that covenant and cancel God's promise. 18 For if God's gift depends on the Law, then it no longer depends on his promise. However, it was because of his promise that God gave that gift to Abraham.
(3.15-18)

15 To give a human example, brethren: no one annuls even a man's will,^{g} or adds to it, once it has been ratified. 16 Now the promises were made to Abraham and to his offspring. It does not say, "And to offsprings," referring to many; but, referring to one, "And to your offspring," which is Christ. 17 This is what I mean: the law, which came four hundred and thirty years afterward, does not annul a covenant previously ratified by God, so as to make the promise void. 18 For if the inheritance is by the law, it is no longer by promise; but God gave it to Abraham by a promise.

^{g}Or *covenant* (as in verse 17)
(3.15-18)

In these verses Paul uses as an illustration something which was commonly known, namely, that once contracts are agreed upon they cannot be altered, changed, or annulled. From this he draws the conclusion that God's covenant with Abraham cannot be modified or altered by the Law which was given many years later.

A literal translation of the section heading The Law and the Promise might be misleading, since it would suggest that in some way or other the Law and the promise did something together or were in some way mutually related. A section heading such as "The differences between the Law and the promise" would suggest more clearly the intent of Paul's argument. One may be even more specific and say "A law cannot change a promise," "A later regulation cannot change an earlier promise," or "God's promise cannot be changed by a later law."

3.15   My brothers, I am going to use an everyday example: when two people agree on a matter and sign an agreement, no one can break it or add anything to it.

The term brothers in this context should be understood as "fellow Christians" or "fellow believers in Christ."

I am going to use an everyday example is literally "I speak according to man" or "as men do." The meaning here is simply that Paul is going to talk about something that is of common knowledge to his readers (JB "compare this with

what happens in ordinary life"; NEB "let me give you an illustration. Even in
ordinary life...". One may also translate as "I'm going to compare God's
promise with something that happens all the time," or "What I have been talking
about is similar to what you yourselves know about."

When two people agree on a matter and sign an agreement represents the
Greek "a covenant (or, a will) once ratified, though it be man's....". The differences in various translations stem from the problem of how to translate the
term which TEV renders here as "agreement," since it is the more natural word
in this context; but in verse 17 TEV renders the same word as "covenant," since
it is the more natural word in that context. Does this word mean "will" ("testament") and involve only one man (RSV "a man's will," JB "a will," NEB "a man's
will and testament")? Or does the word get its meaning from the Hebrew concept
of "covenant" ("contract") and accordingly involve two participants (cf. Phps
"once a contract has been properly drawn up and signed...")? The biblical usage
of the term and the overall context favor the latter alternative. It is true that in
classical Greek, and in some later Jewish writers like Josephus, the term is used
in the sense of "will" or "testament." Furthermore, the use of "inheritance" in
verses 18 ff. seems to suggest this meaning. However, these arguments are offset by stronger ones in favor of "covenant." The biblical usage of the term is in
the sense of an agreement between two parties, sometimes between two men or
two nations, but in most cases, between God on the one hand and a person, group
of persons, or a nation on the other. Furthermore, in the Septuagint, the Hebrew
word for covenant is rendered with the same Greek word here in question. There
is little doubt that even in the New Testament, with one or two exceptions, the
word used is equivalent to the Hebrew word for "covenant." Still further, the
same word is used in verse 17, and there it clearly means "covenant," since to
translate it "testament" or "will" would imply the death of God before the testament goes into effect! Regarding the argument that wills were irrevocable during those days, the evidence is inconclusive as to whether Greek wills could be
included in this category. To the argument that Paul's Gentile readers would
understand the term to mean "will" and nothing more, it should be noted that
Paul is here arguing against Jewish Christian adversaries, and therefore Paul
used terminology which was familiar to them. It is likely that the terminology
was also familiar to the Gentile Christians in Galatia because of the raging con-
troversy in which they were involved.

Agree and sign render a Greek legal word which could be translated "ratified" (RSV) or whatever is done to an agreement in order to give it legal force
(NAB "legally validated," NEB "duly executed," Phps "properly drawn up and
signed"). Expressions such as agree and sign in reference to an agreement,
covenant, or contract may be expressed in a number of different ways, some
quite idiomatic, for example, "tie themselves together," "cut an agreement,"
"snap fingers together," "touch one another concerning," or "eat with one
another about."

No one could be understood either as referring to an outside party (Phps
"can neither be disregarded nor modified by a third party") or to anyone, in-

cluding the parties to the agreement. Mutual agreement for either annulment or amendment is, of course, always possible, but is not important to the force of the illustration. In order to emphasize the fact that one person on his own initiative cannot alter such an agreement, one may say "no one alone can break the agreement," or "no one person just because he wants to can break the agreement."

Break is to "violate" or "disregard" (Phps JB) or to "set aside" (Knox NAB NEB). The Greek word, however, can also mean "annul" (RSV), that is, to declare it legally not binding. To break an agreement or covenant may be expressed in a number of different ways, for example, "to throw an agreement away," "to forget an agreement," "to wipe out a covenant," or "to say that a covenant has become nothing."

Add anything to it translates a Greek word which is used in the New Testament only here. It means "to make additional prescriptions." This may be rendered as "add other words to it" or "make more requirements in it."

3.16   Now, God made his promises to Abraham and to his descendant. The
        scripture does not use the plural "descendants," meaning many peo-
        ple, but the singular "descendant," meaning one person only, namely,
        Christ.

The transitional adverb now, which begins this verse, must not be understood in a temporal sense. It is equivalent in some languages to "but note that."

Verse 16 is judged by some as a parenthetical elaboration of verse 15, since verse 15 can be connected in a natural manner with verse 17. What connects verse 16 with verse 15 is the word "promises," which now supplants the word "covenant." Since God's covenant with Abraham consisted of promises, this substitution is appropriate (see Eph 2.12).

Promises is plural in the Greek, the reference apparently being to the repeated occasions on which the promise was made to Abraham, and the various forms in which it was expressed (Gen 12.2 ff.; 13.14 ff.; 15.1, 5, 18; 17.2 ff.). Elsewhere Paul uses the singular form (e.g. in vv. 17, 18, 22, 29; Rom 4.13, 14, 16, 20), and it seems that to him there is no marked difference of meaning between the singular and the plural. It is in this light that some translators (e.g. Phps) render "promises" in the singular. It is even possible to avoid the problem of number altogether by converting the noun into a verb: "God promised...." Or one may introduce something of the plural meaning by translating "God promised on various occasions," or "... repeatedly."

It is important in this first sentence of verse 16 to employ a form which will clearly identify only one of Abraham's descendants. This is necessary if Paul's interpretation of the scripture passage is to be meaningful. Therefore, one may have to translate "God repeatedly promised to Abraham blessing to him and to one of his descendants." In some languages it would be impossible to say "promised to Abraham and to one of his descendants," since the promise was made specifically to Abraham and the blessing simply applied to one of his descendants. The promise itself was not made specifically to one of the descendants since the descendant had not been born at the time that the promise was made.

The scripture does not use is literally "(it) does not say" (the subject is missing in the Greek). It is even possible to understand "God" as the subject. Most translators and commentators, however, understand "scripture" as the implicit subject of the sentence (see JB NAB Phps).

The real exegetical problem in this verse is in Paul's use of "descendant" and "descendants" (literally, "seed" and "seeds"). Although he was certainly aware that the Hebrew and Greek forms of the word "seed" are singular in form but collective in meaning, yet he goes on to distinguish between the singular and the plural in order to prove his point, namely, that the promises of God were given to Abraham and one descendant, not many; and that one descendant is Christ. Some scholars have found rabbinical parallels to Paul's exegetical method in this verse, and other interpreters have used ingenious ways to justify Paul's reasoning here. Fortunately, the translator does not have to hold to a particular position regarding these verses in order to translate them accurately.

In some languages it may be necessary to render the second sentence of this verse as "The scripture does not have the words 'and to your descendants' (that is, talking about many people)." Likewise, the following sentence may have to begin "but the scripture has the words 'and to your descendant.'" However, in some other languages there is a problem in the expression "and to your descendant," since this might imply that Abraham had only one descendant. For that reason it may be necessary to say "and to one of your descendants." Accordingly, the final explanation in this verse may be rendered as "these words refer to only one person, and that person is Christ."

3.17-18   What I mean is that God made a covenant with Abraham and promised to keep it. The Law, which was given four hundred and thirty years later, cannot break that covenant and cancel God's promise. (18) For if God's gift depends on the Law, then it no longer depends on his promise. However, it was because of his promise that God gave that gift to Abraham.

In these two verses Paul continues his argument started in verse 15 and applies the illustration he gave there. Accordingly, what I mean is goes back as far as verse 15. The Greek expression itself is used to further argue and explain a thought already expressed. What Paul illustrated in verse 15, using an ordinary human example, is now applied to the covenant between God and Abraham. In some languages what I mean is may be rendered as "what I am trying to say is," "the words that I spoke add up to," or "this is really what my words mean."

The Greek of these two verses is rather complicated; it may be interpreted as one sentence with a number of embedded clauses. TEV simplifies the Greek construction, making the verse much easier for the English reader to understand.

God made a covenant with Abraham and promised to keep it translates the Greek clause "a covenant previously ratified by God." TEV expands "ratified" into two major components: (1) God making a covenant and (2) God promising to keep it. In some languages it is necessary to specify both parties involved in a covenant or agreement, and therefore it may be necessary to supply the other party, as TEV does, and to add the phrase with Abraham. The phrase promised to keep it may be expressed in some languages as direct discourse, for example, "and said, I will do what I have promised," or "and promised, I will do it."

Four hundred and thirty years is derived by Paul from the Hebrew text of Exodus 12.40, where it denotes the number of years the people of Israel spent in exile in Egypt. In Gen 15.13 (which Stephen uses in Acts 7.6) the period of Israel's sojourn in Egypt is designated as four hundred years. The Septuagint text of Exodus 12.40 designates four hundred and thirty years as the length of Israel's stay in Canaan and exile in Egypt. The important point, however, is not whether Paul is correct in his arithmetic, or how he got his figures, but that the Law was given some four hundred years after the covenant, and during all those years before the Law God's promise to Abraham had been in effect.

In verse 18, there is a direct contrast between Law and promise. Paul strongly asserts that if God's blessing depended on following the Law, then it cannot depend on God's promises. (The converse is also true: if what God gives depended on his promises, then it cannot depend on the Law.) What happened in Abraham's case is clear: God bestowed his blessing on Abraham because he promised it.

The passive construction the Law, which was given can be changed to an active construction, with "God" indicated as the agent, for example, "God gave the laws." Also the relative clause which was given...later can be made into an independent clause. The second sentence of verse 17 may then be translated as "God gave (or, God instituted) the laws four hundred and thirty years later, but the laws cannot do away with the covenant and cancel God's promise." However, the expression cancel God's promise may be rendered as "make God's promise as though it were nothing," or "destroy what God has promised."

God's gift is literally "the inheritance," but here Paul is obviously using it, not in a literal sense, but figuratively. To a Jew, the word "inheritance" would be a reminder of the promise of God to Israel concerning the possession of Canaan, the promised land, and of what God had done in order to fulfill that promise. Therefore, the word "inheritance" came to be used figuratively to refer to spiritual favors and blessings from God. In Paul's thought it may refer more specifically to the content of God's promise to Abraham, namely, the gift of a right relationship with God (v.6).

It may be very difficult in some languages to speak of God's gift as "depending on the Law." The relation is more likely to be interpreted as causal, and therefore one may say "if what God gives is caused by the laws," or "if God gives because of the laws." However, as in a number of other similar contexts, it is not the Law itself which determines God's gift, but obedience to the Law which is here in focus. It may therefore be necessary to say in some languages "For if what God gives comes to one because he has obeyed the Law, then it does not come because of what God has promised he would do." Such a translation would prepare the way for the conclusion to this paragraph at the end of this verse.

The last part of verse 18 can be rendered literally "but to Abraham God gave (it) by promise" (see RSV). The "it," of course, refers to the "inheritance" in the first part of the verse. The Greek word for "gave" is a verbal form of the word "grace"; it emphasizes the fact that what God gives he gives freely, even if those for whom the gift is intended do not deserve it. The force of the argument is that God's blessing was given to Abraham, not because Abraham did anything to deserve it, but by virtue of God's promise alone. The relation of reason to result in the last sentence of verse 18 must be made more specific in some languages, for example, "but because God had promised the blessing to Abraham, that was the reason why he gave it to Abraham."

TEV	RSV
19 What, then, was the purpose of the Law? It was added in order to show what wrongdoing is, and it was meant to last until the coming of Abraham's descendant, to whom the promise was made. The Law was handed down by angels, with a man acting as a go-between. 20 But a go-between is not needed when only one person is involved; and God is one.*e*	19 Why then the law? It was added because of transgressions, till the offspring should come to whom the promise had been made; and it was ordained by angels through an intermediary. 20 Now an intermediary implies more than one; but God is one. (3.19-20)

*e*and God is one; *or* and God acts
 alone.   (3.19-20)

In the next few verses, Paul states clearly the function and purpose of the Law. He has already stated that the Galatians had received God's Spirit not by doing what the Law requires, but by believing the gospel (vv. 2-5). Furthermore, he has contended that those who depend on the Law are under a curse, the curse of the Law (vv. 10-14), and that God's blessings are given not because of the Law but because of God's promise. If all this is true, then why does one bother with the Law at all? Has the Law not lost its reason for being?

3.19   What, then, was the purpose of the Law? It was added in order
        to show what wrongdoing is, and it was meant to last until the coming
        of Abraham's descendant, to whom the promise was made. The Law
        was handed down by angels, with a man acting as a go-between.

It is quite logical, therefore, to ask, What, then, was the purpose of the Law? The literal form "What then (is) the Law?" or "Why then the law?" (RSV) can be understood as a question regarding the nature of the Law. Primarily, however, it is a question about the law's purpose (TEV Knox JB), its function (NEB "then what of the law?), its relevance (NAB), and its significance.

In order to indicate purpose, it is necessary in some languages to indicate what is to be accomplished, for example, "Then what could the Law accomplish?", or "What were the laws given by Moses supposed to do?" There is, however, a difficulty in some languages with this type of rhetorical question, since there is no specific answer to it except through an expression of purpose, as in TEV, joined to the statement concerning the Law having been added. For languages in which such a rhetorical statement would be either misleading or awkward, it may be possible to change the question into a statement, for example, "But the Law did have a purpose," or "But the Law did accomplish something."

It was added is intended to show the position of the law in relation to the covenant: it is both supplementary and subordinate to it. It is impossible in some languages to speak of something being "added" without indicating to what it is added, and so one must make clear that the Law was added to the covenant. This may be stated in some languages as "the Law was given in addition to the covenant in order to show that...."

Furthermore, the Law was added for a specific purpose, to show what wrongdoing is. This particular expression (literally, "on account of transgressions," or "because of transgressions") is not easy to interpret, and the difficulty is reflected in the various ways of rendering it in modern translations (some examples: JB "to specify crimes," Knox "to make room for transgression," NAB "in view of transgressions," NEB "to make wrongdoing a legal offence," Phps "to underline the existence and extent of sin," Mft "for the purpose of producing transgressions").

We have two clues as to the interpretation of this expression. First, the expression literally rendered "on account" or "because of" is sometimes used to show cause or purpose. If we take cause as primary (because people were sinning), then the clause may mean that the Law's function was to check, correct, or restrain transgressions. This meaning may be expressed in some languages as "to keep people from sinning," or "to stop people from doing what was bad." If "purpose" is primary, it could mean that the Law's immediate function is to define transgression, to show its real nature, or even to produce and multiply it, by specifying the reality of guilt. This interpretation of purpose (which is far more common) may be expressed as "in order to show people what sin really is," "in order to tell people that they were really doing wrong by doing certain things," or "in order to show that the bad things people were doing were really sin."

A second clue comes from the word literally rendered "transgressions," which means not simply wrongdoing (TEV), but wrongdoing as a result of willfully violating an existing law. If this is the case, before the Law was given there could not have been any transgressions. There were, of course, wrongdoings or evil deeds, but these were not in violation of any law, since the Law did not exist. The Law, therefore, made it possible for these wrongdoings to be recognized as "transgressions," thereby exposing their sinful character.

The statement that the Law was meant to last until the coming of Abraham's descendant involves some rather subtle problems for the translator. The verb to last must be understood in the sense of "to remain valid" or "to remain in force." For one thing, it must not be understood merely in the sense that the paper on which the laws were written continued to the time of Jesus. A more difficult expression, however, is involved in the passive form <u>was meant</u>. Often this must be changed into an active expression, for example, "God purposed the Law to continue in force," "God designed the Law so that it would remain valid until...," or "...would say what people could or could not do until...."

The phrase <u>until the coming of Abraham's descendant</u> must be made more specific in some languages: "until the time that Abraham's descendant would come." This is a specific reference to Christ, and in some languages it is necessary to say "that special descendant of Abraham," or "that descendant of Abraham already mentioned."

The final clause of this sentence, <u>to whom the promise was made</u>, must be made a completely new sentence in some languages, for example, "God had made the promise to that descendant," or "God had promised that descendant." This is, of course, a reference to the <u>descendant</u> mentioned in verse 16. Since in the same verse he is specifically identified as Christ, it may be necessary even in verse 19 to employ some appositional expression, for example, "until the time that Christ, the descendant of Abraham, would come; it was about that descendant that God made the promise." In translating the clause <u>to whom the promise was made</u>, it is important not to rule out what has already been said in verse 16, namely, that God made his promises to both Abraham and his descendant.

The last part of verse 19 along with verse 20 shows the inferiority of the Law in terms of the way it was given and administered: it did not come directly from God, but it <u>was handed down by angels</u> and <u>with a man acting as a go-between</u>. That the angels played a part in the giving of the Law is part of Jewish tradition, and recorded in Scripture (Deut 33.2 [LXX]; Heb 2.2; Acts 7.38, 52 f.). The go-between (literally "mediator") is evidently Moses.

In translating <u>the Law was handed down by angels</u>, it is important to indicate clearly that the angels were only secondary agents; they were not the source of the Law. This may be expressed in some languages as "the Law was handed down with the help of angels," or even "God used angels in passing on the Law to Moses."

The phrase <u>with a man acting as a go-between</u> must be expressed in some languages as "and a man acted as a mediator between God and the people." It is often essential to indicate clearly the role of a mediator, especially since in the immediately preceding clause the angels have been mentioned.

In some languages there may be a problem involved in the indefinite use of the phrase <u>a man</u>, since it might be interpreted as simply "any man." That may be particularly so in this context, since it may already have been necessary to indicate that the Law related in some way to Moses in some such phrase as "the Law given to Moses," or "the Law given by means of Moses." Hence, one may be required to render this last phrase of verse 19 as "while the man Moses acted as a go-between."

3.20   But a go-between is not needed when only one person is involved; and
        God is one.*e*

*e*and God is one; *or* and God acts alone.

Literally, this is "but the mediator is not of one, but God is one." The
phrase "of one" most probably refers to the parties in a given transaction. Paul
is therefore saying that unless there are two parties, a mediator is not needed
(cf. JB "now there can only be an intermediary between two parties"; NAB "there
can be no mediator when only one person is involved"; NEB "an intermediary is
not needed for one party acting alone"). Rather than the negative form a go-
between is not needed when only one person is involved, it is often better to use
a positive statement, for example, "a go-between is only needed when there are
two parties," or "...two persons involved." The implication is that a go-between
is required when two parties have different interests in a particular solution, and
therefore some compromise position needs to be worked out.

The theological implications of the verse are difficult to understand. Here
Paul again uses rabbinical methods to drive home his point. His point here is
the superiority of the promise over the Law. What he has in mind all along is
that the promise was not given through a go-between, but came directly from
God. It is really difficult to make sense of the final statement in this verse,
God is one. It reflects an Old Testament declaration, but its application to this
particular context is certainly not clear. In some languages one cannot say literally "God is one." It is, of course, possible to say "God is one God," but this
would appear to be repetitious and meaningless. Apparently the thought behind
the expression employed by Paul is that "God acted directly," or "God acted as
one person without a go-between," and in some instances this may be the only
legitimate way to communicate the intent of this rather obscure expression.

TEV	RSV
The Purpose of the Law	
21 Does this mean that the Law is against God's promises? No, not at all! For if mankind had received a law that could bring life, then everyone could be put right with God by obeying it. 22 But the scripture says that the whole world is under the power of sin; and so the gift which is promised on the basis of faith in Jesus Christ is given to those who believe. (3.21-22)	21 Is the law then against the promises of God? Certainly not; for if a law had been given which could make alive, then righteousness would indeed be by the law. 22 But the scripture consigned all things to sin, that what was promised to faith in Jesus Christ might be given to those who believe. (3.21-22)

The section heading The Purpose of the Law may be rendered in some languages as "What the Law was designed to accomplish," or "What God meant the
Law to do." Or the expression employed at the beginning of verse 19 ("What was
the purpose of the Law?") may be adapted as a title for this section.

[76]

3.21   Does this mean that the Law is against God's promises? No, not at all! For if mankind had received a law that could bring life, then everyone could be put right with God by obeying it.

Once more Paul asks a question which logically follows from his previous statements. If there is such a distinction between the Law and the promise, and if there is such a clear superiority of the promise over the Law, then does this mean that the Law is against God's promises? This rhetorical question is immediately answered with a strong negative statement. The presence of this statement makes it possible in a number of languages to retain the rhetorical question. However, in some languages one may need to transform the question itself into a positive statement, for example, "The Law is certainly not against God's promises." This statement can then be followed by a further strong negative, "No, indeed."

It may, however, be difficult in some languages to speak of a law being "against promises." One can, however, often say "Does this mean that what the Law says is against what God has promised?", or "...that the words of the Law are against the promises of God?"

Against means "contrary to." Is against must be expressed in some languages as "say the opposite," "speak against," or "say something different from," for example, "Do the words of the Law say something different from what God has promised?" This question may be introduced in some languages as "Is it true that the words of the Law are against God's promises?"

For the plural form of "promises," see verse 16. The expected answer, in the light of everything Paul has said so far, is in the affirmative. But Paul answers in the negative: No, not at all! (Phps "certainly not"; JB "of course not"; NAB "unthinkable!"; NEB "no, never!"). For this expression, see 2.17.

Paul is able to give a negative answer to this question because he not only allows that the Law has a function, but that function is even related to the fulfillment of God's promise. Already he has said that the Law functions as showing what wrongdoing is (v.19), and later he takes up other functions of the Law: as teacher (vv.23-25) and as guardian (4.1 ff.). But the function of the Law is not the same as the function of the promise. The function of the promise is to bring life. If the Law could do that, then it would be competing with the promise. But the Law cannot bring life, because it was not given for such a purpose.

Some interpreters understand law in the clause for if mankind had received a law to refer to the Torah or the Jewish law (NAB JB "if the Law we were given"). However, since in the Greek "law" is not preceded by the article, many exegetes have argued that Paul is here referring to any law, and particularly, as the context shows, any divine law (cf. Phps RSV Knox). The expression if mankind had received a law may need to be made more specific in a number of languages, for example, "If God had given mankind a law." However, it is essential to pay careful attention to the rendering of a law, for if this is to be understood in the sense of any divine law rather than merely any specific regulation, then it is perhaps necessary to use in some languages a phrase which would be essentially equivalent to "some special kind of law" or "some set of laws."

Most translations simply render the expression <u>bring life</u> in the way TEV does, without making the meaning of "life" clear in this passage. Basically there are two possible ways of interpreting the expression to <u>bring life</u>:

(1) "Life" may be interpreted as "eternal life," "spiritual life," or "moral life," as opposed to physical existence. This kind of life is made possible by man being in a right relationship with God. What Paul is saying, then, is: If there is a law that could put men right with God, then eternal life could be achieved through law. In this sense one may often translate as "could cause men really to live," or "could cause men to share the life that comes from God" (as a reference to "spiritual life").

(2) "Life" may be interpreted simply as a state brought about by a right relationship with God. Previously, Paul has used "to live" as synonymous with "to be put right with God" (see v.12), and here he may be doing the same thing. If this is the case, then "to bring life" could be understood as another way of saying "to be put right with God."

<u>Be put right with God</u> is one word in the Greek, literally, "righteousness." Many commentators and translators understand this to have the same meaning as its verb form "to justify" (cf. JB) and primarily refers to right relationship with God, acceptance by God. Another possible translation is "God would accept people in a right relationship to himself."

The phrase <u>by obeying it</u> must often be expressed as "by doing what the law says people must do." However, in this context the term "law" must refer back specifically to <u>law</u> mentioned in the beginning of this same sentence. If, for example, one has used at the beginning of the verse "a certain set of laws," then at the end of the verse one may refer to "such a set of laws."

<u>3.22</u> But the scripture says that the whole world is under the power of sin; and so the gift which is promised on the basis of faith in Jesus Christ is given to those who believe.

The first part of this verse may be translated literally as "But the scripture shut up all things under sin."

The word <u>scripture</u> is generally used by Paul to refer to a passage of the Old Testament, but there is no single passage that can fit this context. The closest parallels are Deut 27.26 and Psalm 143.2, which Paul has already quoted (2.16; 3.10). Again, as in verse 8, scripture is personified, and here it is assigned the function of jailer. But since the reference is to a passage of scripture (even though we are not sure what that passage is), TEV is right in rendering it <u>the scripture says</u> (JB "scripture makes no exceptions when it says"; NEB "scripture has declared the whole world to be prisoners"). As in many instances, it may be necessary to modify a statement such as <u>the scripture says</u> to read "a person may read in a passage of scripture," or "some words of the scripture indicate."

The clause "shut up all things under sin" (literal rendering) presents many translation problems. "Shut up" is a technical term used in reference to prisoners, hence "to confine" or "to imprison."

The whole world (TEV NEB; JB "everywhere") is used elsewhere by Paul to mean the whole universe. While this is probably correct, it is possible to interpret this expression to refer only to people (Phps "all men").

"Under sin" may be interpreted in the light of verse 10, and parallel to "under a curse," and therefore will mean under the power of sin (Knox "under the bondage of sin," NEB "in subjection to sin," NAB "under the constraint of sin").

The whole expression "shut up under sin" thus means being under the power and bondage of sin, with no possibility of escape. It is possible to drop the metaphor, as TEV does. Some translations, however, still retain it (NEB "the whole world to be prisoners in subjection to sin").

In a number of languages it is practically impossible to personify sin. Sin refers to events in which people themselves participate, that is, "people sin," and therefore it is extremely difficult to speak of sin as being a person-like agent that would have power to control the whole world or all people. The closest equivalent to the power of sin is in many languages "the desire to sin" or "the strong desire to sin." Therefore, the whole world is under the power of sin may be rendered in some instances as "everybody in the world is controlled by his strong desire to sin," "strong desires to sin command everyone," "...tell people what they must do," or "...order them about." In these expressions it is the desire which is personified and not the sin itself.

The purpose of the whole world being under the power of sin is expressed in the latter half of the verse (literally, "in order that the promise out of faith in Jesus Christ may be given to those who believe"). "The promise" is the promise given to Abraham, and, as in verse 14, the reference is not to the promise itself, but to its content, hence the rendering of TEV the gift which is promised (RSV "what was promised," NEB "the promised blessing"). Whether this refers to the gift of the Holy Spirit or to the gift of right relationship with God is hard to ascertain.

"Out of faith" expresses the ground on which the giving takes place, therefore on the basis of faith in Jesus Christ (NEB "so that faith in Jesus Christ may be the ground on which the promised blessing is given").

To those who believe is in contrast to the whole world. It is possible to interpret this as a technical term, namely, "the believers," the Christians. However, more likely Paul is not using it here in this sense but in the sense of anyone who trusts God or Jesus Christ.

In some languages it may be necessary for this verse not only to restructure what may be interpreted as a final purpose clause (though TEV treats this clause as result), but even to break the purpose clause into two sentences. For example, one may translate "so that God could give to those who believe in Jesus Christ what he promised. What he promised comes to them only by their trusting in Jesus Christ." In other languages it may be best to express on the basis of as being a condition, for example, "what God promised if they trusted in Jesus Christ," or "what God promised to give them if they put their trust in Jesus Christ."

TEV	RSV
23 But before the time for faith came, the Law kept us all locked up as prisoners until this coming faith should be revealed. 24 And so the Law was in charge of us until Christ came, in order that we might then be put right with God through faith. 25 Now that the time for faith is here, the Law is no longer in charge of us. (3.23-25)	23 Now before faith came, we were confined under the law, kept under restraint until faith should be revealed. 24 So that the law was our custodian until Christ came, that we might be justified by faith. 25 But now that faith has come, we are no longer under a custodian; (3.23-25)

In these verses Paul expands the theme of the inferiority of the Law over the promise by talking of the condition of people while they were under the Law and their condition afterwards when they are under faith. He describes the Law as a jailer (v. 23) and a custodian or tutor (v. 24) and asserts that now that the time of faith has come, the Law no longer exercises these functions.

3.23   But before the time for faith came, the Law kept us all locked up as prisoners until this coming faith should be revealed.

Before the time for faith came (literally, "before the faith came") is Paul's way of talking of the time of the reign of the Law. Faith here (literally, "the faith") refers to what Paul mentioned in the previous verse, namely, faith in Jesus Christ. Some translations indicate this relationship (e.g. NEB Mft "before this faith came").

In a number of languages faith must be expressed as a verb, and therefore a certain amount of restructuring may be required, for example, "before it was time that people could trust in Jesus Christ," or "before people could be related to God by trusting in Jesus Christ." However, the focus here is upon the extent of time involved, and it may be important to say in some languages "up to the time that people could put their trust in Jesus Christ."

Kept us all locked up as prisoners translates two Greek verbs. The first may be rendered "kept us guarded," with the purpose not of protection but of restriction. The second is the same word used in verse 22, but here it has the present participle form, indicating continuous action, and therefore can be translated "being held in confinement," or "being imprisoned." What Paul is trying to picture to us is that the Law is like a stern jailer who not only has imprisoned us, but who has made sure that we remain imprisoned by stationing himself on the outside where he can guard us.

The Law is here once again the Jewish law, and not any law as in verse 21b. It is often impossible to personify the Law, and it may even be necessary, as in some other contexts, to speak of the Law as "the laws given by Moses." One can often say "the laws given by Moses were just like guards who kept us locked up in prison," "... stood guarding us in prison," or "... stood guarding us while we were prisoners locked up in jail, so to speak." Because of the figurative meaning involved, it may be essential in some languages to employ an expression such as "so to speak" or "as it were" in order to identify the figurative interpretation.

Until this coming faith should be revealed presents the translator with several difficulties in understanding and interpreting the passage. The Greek word for until (literally "into") may be either temporal (TEV and some other translations) or purposive; that is, an event introduced by "into" can be the purpose of the immediately preceding and related event. In this particular passage, the Law's act of confinement and imprisonment may be said to have as its purpose preparation for embracing and accepting the faith when it is finally revealed. This latter interpretation is followed by some translations (e.g. Mft "with the prospect of the faith that was to be revealed").

In this coming faith should be revealed it is important to understand "coming" (literally,"about to be") as modifying not faith but the revelation of it. Faith here is the same faith referred to at the beginning of the verse, namely, faith in Jesus Christ.

From the Greek text of verse 25, it is clear that at the time of writing the revelation is already past, and therefore faith has already been revealed. The time of the coming of faith is future only in relation to the time of the Law, and not in relation to the time when Paul was writing this letter.

The clause until this coming faith should be revealed poses problems for the translator. In the first place, this coming faith is extremely difficult to render in some languages. One may say in some cases "this trusting in Jesus which people would do," or "this trusting in Jesus which would happen later." Moreover, the passive expression should be revealed may need to be made active, with God as the agent, for example, "until the time that God would show." However, if this final clause is to be understood as purpose, then one may say "so that God would show."

3.24   And so the Law was in charge of us until Christ came, in order that
        we might then be put right with God through faith.

Paul introduces another metaphor in verse 24, but his use of the connective and so (NEB "thus") indicates that he apparently wants it connected with the metaphor of the jailer in the previous verse. The Law, he says, was our "pedagogue." The difficulty of translating this term is shown by the various ways of rendering it (TEV in charge of us, RSV "our custodian," Phps "like a strict governess," JB "our guardian," NAB "our monitor," Knox "our tutor," NEB "a kind of tutor in charge of us"). In Paul's time the "pedagogue" was a slave employed in Greek and Roman families whose job was to supervise a minor child (ages six through sixteen) both within and outside the home. Although the Greek word may suggest instruction, his main duty was not teaching (and therefore to translate it "tutor" as Knox and NEB do would be misleading), but rather enforcement of discipline and moral supervision of conduct. As a strict enforcer of rules and regulations and a watchful supervisor, the pedagogue would be an appropriate symbol of the Law and logically connected to the jailer of verse 23 in terms of function, namely, strict supervision.

3.25

Personification of the Law is not possible in some languages except as the Law may be likened to a person, for example, "The Law was like a person who made us behave until the time Christ came," or "...tried to make us do what was right...," or "...tried to keep us from doing bad...." If, however, one translates in charge of us as "keeping us from doing what is bad," it may be necessary to alter the order of the clause until Christ came, since the latter clause might then be too closely connected with "doing bad." One may alter the first part of this verse to read "So, until the time that Christ came, the Law was like a person who was making us behave."

The Law, then, was in charge of us until Christ came (literally, "into Christ"). Some understand this to be purposive, that is, that the Law functioned as a pedagogue in order to lead us to Christ (e.g. Knox "so the law was our tutor, bringing us to Christ"). Others, however, understand the expression simply as temporal, that is, as a designation of time (TEV Phps JB NEB and many others).

The last clause in this verse, in order that we might then be put right with God through faith, is connected by some with until Christ came (NAB "until Christ came to bring about our justification through faith"). Most commentators, however, prefer to relate the purpose to the Law was in charge of us, that is, that the purpose of the Law being a "pedagogue" is that through faith we might be put in a right relationship with God. This purpose may be most conveniently rendered in some languages as a separate sentence introduced by a partial repetition of the preceding statement, for example, "The Law did this so that we would be put right with God through our believing," or "...by means of our believing in Christ."

3.25   Now that the time for faith is here, the Law is no longer in charge of us.

Paul asserts that the Law has now served its intended function and is no longer in charge, because the time for faith is here. Faith (literally "the faith") should again be understood as "faith in Jesus Christ," and as almost always in Paul's writings, it contains an element of trust and dependence. The phrase the time for faith must be understood in this context as a period of time, not merely an occasion, and therefore it may be necessary in some languages to translate the first part of this verse as "but since it is now the period of time when people should believe in Christ," or "but since now we are able to trust in Christ."

The final clause, the Law is no longer in charge of us, should be translated in such a way as to reflect what has been said positively at the beginning of verse 24.

TEV	RSV
26 It is through faith that all of you are God's sons in union with Christ Jesus. 27 You were baptized into union with Christ, and now you are clothed, so to speak, with the	26 for in Christ Jesus you are all sons of God, through faith. 27 For as many of you as were baptized into Christ have put on Christ.

life of Christ himself. 28 So there is no difference between Jews and Gentiles, between slaves and free men, between men and women; you are all in union with Christ Jesus. 29 If you belong to Christ, then you are the descendants of Abraham and will receive what God has promised. (3.26-29)

28 There is neither Jew nor Greek, there is neither slave nor free, there is neither male nor female; for you are all one in Christ Jesus. 29 And if you are Christ's, then you are Abraham's offspring, heirs according to promise. (3.26-29)

In the remainder of the chapter, Paul focuses attention on his Galatian audience. By using the second person pronoun, he emphasizes the implication of what he has been saying to them and their problem.

3.26   It is through faith that all of you are God's sons in union with Christ Jesus.

All of you is emphatic and may mean either "all of you Gentiles" (Galatians and other non-Jewish Christians) or "all of you Galatians" (both Jews and Gentiles in the Galatian churches).

You are God's sons carries through the metaphor of verse 25. In contrast to the minor child under the supervision of a pedagogue, God's sons have reached the age of maturity, and therefore now enjoy the privileges and rights of mature men.

An exegetical problem in this verse is the connection between the phrases through faith and in union with Christ Jesus. Literally, this is rendered simply "through faith in Christ Jesus." It is possible to interpret Paul as saying that "it is through faith in Christ Jesus that you are God's sons" (Phps "for now that you have faith in Christ you are all sons of God"; JB "you...are sons of God through faith in Christ Jesus..."; NAB "each one of you is a son of God because of your faith in Christ Jesus"). However, most commentators interpret the verse in much the same way that TEV does. It is through faith that one becomes a son of God. The expression "in Christ Jesus" should therefore be taken as an appositive to the whole statement and should be interpreted in the way that Paul uses the formula elsewhere, that is, implying close communion with Christ and incorporation into his fellowship.

Through faith is expressed in most languages as means, for example, "by means of your faith" or "...your trust in Christ." Means, however, is expressed in some languages as cause, for example, "because you trust in Christ." Since being God's sons involves an actual change of state (that is, the believers were previously not God's sons), it may be necessary to render are as "become" or "have become," for example, "by means of your trusting Christ, you have become God's sons." The final appositional character of the phrase in union with Christ Jesus may then be interpreted as a kind of explanation of what has previously been said, for example, "that is to say, you are closely joined to Christ Jesus," or "this means that you are closely joined to Christ Jesus."

[83]

3.27   You were baptized into union with Christ, and now you are clothed,
so to speak, with the life of Christ himself.

You goes back to "all of you" of verse 26. A literal rendering (RSV "for
as many of you as ...") would be misleading, for it tends to suggest that it is
only part of the "all of you" that Paul is talking about, which is not his intention
at all.
Baptized into union with Christ is literally "baptized into Christ." Some
take this expression as equivalent to "baptized in the name of Christ" (Knox "you
have been baptized in Christ's name"). Most translators, however, render the
expression as implying fellowship with Christ and incorporation into Christ,
hence into union with Christ.
You were baptized into union with Christ involves essentially a change of
state signaled by the rite of baptism. This relation may be expressed as a type
of result in some languages, for example, "You were baptized and thus are in
union with Christ." Rather than change were baptized into an active form, which
would require a specific agent, for example, "someone baptized you," it may be
better to use a kind of pseudopassive, for example, "You experienced baptism,"
or "You experienced the rite of baptism."
You are clothed, so to speak, with the life of Christ himself translates a
metaphorical expression (literally "you have put on Christ"). The expression
"to put on" when used figuratively means "to take on the character or standing"
of the person referred to, or "to become as" the person referred to. To put on
Christ is to become as Christ, to take upon oneself his character, his standing
before God (as God's Son). Most translations retain the figure of speech, as
TEV does (JB "you have all clothed yourselves in Christ"; NAB "you...have
clothed yourselves with him"; NEB "you have all put on Christ as a garment").
It is generally difficult, however, to preserve the figurative expression "putting
on Christ" or "clothing yourself in Christ." It may be necessary, therefore, to
drop the metaphorical expression and to say, for example, "you have taken upon
yourselves the qualities of Christ," or to employ a simile, for example, "you
have put on Christ as though he were a garment." But even this often results in
a wrong meaning, implying that Christ is some type of article of clothing which
can be put on or off depending on circumstances. It may be better to simply say
"you have become like Christ himself," or "you have determined to be just like
Christ himself."

3.28   So there is no difference between Jews and Gentiles, between slaves
and free men, between men and women; you are all one in union with
Christ Jesus.

The mention of baptism in the previous verse may suggest the corresponding issue of circumcision, the rite which, as interpreted by the Jews, separated
them from Gentiles and symbolized their difference. But here, in the light of
what he has said about faith and about baptism, Paul goes on to assert that the
distinctions created by circumcision are no longer valid or existent. It is not

that the distinctions between Jews and Gentiles, slaves and free men, male and female no longer exist, as a literal rendering might suggest (RSV NAB NEB), but that in union with Christ Jesus, those who are baptized are all one, and that there is no difference between them because of their nationality, their social standing, or even their sex. In other words, the distinctions which exist are no longer important and present no impediment to any of these persons becoming children of God. The distinction between Jews and Gentiles is, of course, the main issue here, but Paul gets so carried away with the message of faith that he applies it to two other distinctions prominent in those days, namely, slaves and free men and men and women.

A literal rendering of so there is no difference between Jews and Gentiles, between slaves and free men, between men and women may be quite misleading. In a sense the phrase in union with Christ Jesus applies not only to the "oneness" but also to the basis for difference. It may, therefore, be important in some languages to say "so as far as your being joined to Christ Jesus is concerned, there is no difference between how this takes place for Jews and Gentiles, for slaves and free men, for men and women; you are all just like one person in being joined closely to Christ Jesus," or "...you are all the same in being closely tied to Christ Jesus."

The emphasis of you are all one (NEB "all one person") is on being united in the fellowship of Christ.

In union with Christ Jesus is literally "in Christ Jesus." It is used the same way as in verse 26.

3.29   If you belong to Christ, then you are the descendants of Abraham and will receive what God has promised.

This verse functions not only as the climax of Paul's argument in this section, but picks up again the theme started in verse 7 and referred to again in verses 9, 14, and 16, namely, the question of who are the real descendants of Abraham. The condition for becoming a descendant of Abraham is here stated differently, but the meaning is the same: if you belong to Christ. The if does not introduce a mere hypothesis, but it suggests that what follows is true and certain (cf. JB "merely by belonging to Christ"). Since this condition does imply an actual fact, it may be expressed more accurately as a condition of cause, for example, "because you belong to Christ, then you are the descendants of Abraham," or "...belong to the lineage of Abraham."

Will receive what God has promised is literally "heirs according to the promise." As in verse 18, the inheritance implied in the word "heirs" is the gift of God, the content of God's promise, and therefore the "heirs" are the recipients of God's promised gift. It may, moreover, be necessary to specify those to whom the promise was made, for example, "will receive what God has promised to you as descendants of Abraham," or "will receive what God has promised Abraham's descendants," or even "...Abraham and his descendants."

CHAPTER 4

TEV	RSV
1 But now to continue--the son who will receive his father's property is treated just like a slave while he is young, even though he really owns everything. 2 While he is young, there are men who take care of him and manage his affairs until the time set by his father. (4.1-2)	1 I mean that the heir, as long as he is a child, is no better than a slave, though he is the owner of all the estate; 2 but he is under guardians and trustees until the date set by the father. (4.1-2)

The whole section (4.1-7) continues the argument started in 3.21, which contrasts the situation of those under the Law with those who are sons of God. With the former, it is subservience and lack of freedom; with the latter, it is freedom and joyous fellowship with God. TEV makes this continuity clear by not treating this as a new section.

Here, as in many other places throughout the Bible, the introduction of a new chapter does not indicate a major change in the discourse. The chapter divisions in the Bible were introduced by printers centuries after the original manuscripts were written, and these divisions often, although not always, betray a lack of insight into the divisions of the discourse.

4.1   But now to continue—the son who will receive his father's property is treated just like a slave while he is young, even though he really owns everything.

But now to continue is literally "but I say" (JB "Let me put this another way"), a type of expression which Paul frequently uses to introduce an expansion or explanation of a previous argument (cf. 3.17; 5.16; Rom 15.8; 1 Cor 1.12). One may also say "I would also like to say," or "But I will continue what I was just saying."

The son who will receive his father's property translates the one word "heir." The main problem in retaining this word in translation is the implication that the father is dead. While it can be proved from Roman law that property was transferred to a son only on the death of the father, this understanding cannot be applied here. It would create serious difficulties, particularly with the application of the illustration later in this section, for it would imply that God had died. It is more likely that Paul has in mind a situation where the father, for some reason, establishes a guardianship while he is still alive. In such a case, the word "heir" would simply refer to the son who would eventually receive his father's property. It is also possible to translate "heir" as "the son who has received what his father has promised to give him," or "...the property which his father has promised to give him."

The phrase while he is young involves a Greek word which literally means "infant" or "babe." It includes components of intellectual and moral immaturity.

Many commentators suggest that Paul is using the word here in much the same way as in 1 Cor 3.1. However, in view of the context, it is more likely that what Paul has in mind here is the child's characteristic as a "minor" (as in NEB), that is, the child is not old enough to assume legal responsibilities (cf. NAB "not of age," Mft "under age"). In a number of languages one may use "while he is still a small child." However, in other instances it is preferable to use a designation which indicates clearly his being literally "before maturity," expressed in some languages as "before he can act as a man," "before he sits with the men," or "before he takes his place among men."

The phrase is treated just like a slave refers primarily to legal status. The child, being a minor, cannot perform any act except through his legal representatives. However, he differs from a slave in that even though he has no freedom of action, he still owns everything. Potentially, he is the owner of his property, but in actual practice others make decisions for him.

A literal translation of is treated just like a slave, would imply in some languages that the son is ordered about, beaten, and forced to endure privations, even as slaves are generally treated. It may be necessary to say, therefore, "he has no legal rights; he is just like a slave," or, idiomatically, "he cannot speak in the council of elders; he is just like a slave."

4.2   While he is young, there are men who take care of him and manage his affairs until the time set by his father.

Men who take care of him and manage his affairs translates two Greek words, literally "guardians" and "trustees." The former is a general term, used to describe someone who is entrusted with the total care of the child, and the latter is a specific term, referring to one who has financial responsibilities (used also in Rom 16.23; Luke 12.42; 16.1). One should not, however, regard Paul as being precise in this statement; his main point is that there are persons who make decisions for the child and his property. The phrase take care of him may be rendered as "provide him with what he needs," but it is possible to understand this in a sense of "instruct him as to what to do." The expression manage his affairs may be rendered as "have responsibility for the property which will some day be his," or "make decisions about the property which will later belong to him."

The phrase until the time set by his father gives rise to a problem of legal interpretation. Under Roman law, a father had nothing to do with the setting of the time when his son became of age. This was set by law, which ordained that a minor whose father died remained under the care of a guardian until age fourteen, and then under a trustee until age twenty-five, at which time he attained maturity. However, this difficulty disappears when Paul is understood as referring to a special case, where a guardianship is established during the lifetime of the father, who then can appoint the guardians and set a limit to the duration of their authority. In some languages it may be necessary to make the clause until the time set by his father more specific, for example, "until the day which his father said would mark the time when he would no longer have other people manage his affairs." In other languages it may be better to render this clause as "for as long as the father said it would be necessary."

TEV	RSV
3 In the same way, we too were slaves of the ruling spirits of the universe before we reached spiritual maturity. 4 But when the right time finally came, God sent his own Son. He came as the son of a human mother and lived under the Jewish Law, 5 to redeem those who were under the Law, so that we might become God's sons. (4.3-5)	3 So with us; when we were children, we were slaves to the elemental spirits of the universe. 4 But when the time had fully come, God sent forth his Son, born of woman, born under the law, 5 to redeem those who were under the law, so that we might receive adoption as sons. (4.3-5)

Paul now applies his illustration to his readers in particular, although what he says has relevance for all Christians.

4.3   In the same way, we too were slaves of the ruling spirits of the universe before we reached spiritual maturity.

The pronoun we should be understood as referring to Christians generally, and not simply to Jewish or Gentile Christians. Paul first describes their pre-Christian condition.

Ruling spirits of the universe translates a phrase which can be literally rendered "the elements of the world." The various possible meanings of the phrase are reflected in the numerous ways in which it is translated (Phps "the authority of basic moral principles"; JB "the elemental principles of this world"; Knox "the school room tasks which the world gave us"; NEB RSV "the elemental spirits of the universe").

Paul uses the word "elements" three times (twice in this chapter and once in Col 2.8), and in these occurrences it may refer to one of three things: either (1) knowledge, with special reference to the Law; (2) the spirits or lesser deities which control human destiny; or (3) the physical universe, with special reference to the sun, moon, and other celestial bodies. The first of these would have reference to the pre-Christian religious experiences of those who had put their trust in impersonal moral principles, as defined by the Law. It is more likely, however, that a combination of the second and the third represents rather accurately what Paul is talking about. Not only was there widespread belief at that time in spiritual forces that rule the universe, but the celestial bodies were talked about as "spirits" endowed with power over man's destiny. It is clear from what Paul is saying that these powers (meanings 2 and 3) were contrary to God's will, since they put man in bondage and in a state of fear. The implication seems obvious: in Christ these powers are defeated, and mankind is no longer held in bondage.

In a number of languages the closest equivalent of ruling spirits of the universe is "spirits which control the world," or "spirits which command things in

the world." These would, of course, be references to so-called "demonic" spirits, but it may be difficult to say that people are "slaves of such spirits." It may
be more appropriate to restructure the sentence to read "the spirits that ruled
the world had made us their slaves," or "...had caused us to serve them like
slaves." If there is a term which would specify not only the "world" but the entire
"universe," this would be very appropriate, since the underlying Greek expression refers to the entire cosmos.

It may not, however, be possible to say that being slaves of the ruling spirits of the universe is precisely the same as the relationship of an heir to his
guardian (the one managing his affairs), even though the son in some respects
is treated like a slave before he inherits all that legally belongs to him. Therefore, in place of in the same way it may be necessary to say "in a very similar
way" or "similarly." The analogy is not exact, but it is parallel, and an appropriate equivalent term must be used in the receptor language.

The clause before we reached spiritual maturity translates "when we were
babes." The word for "babe" is the same word used in 4.1, where it refers to
legal status of a minor. Paul also uses this word to refer to spiritual immaturity
(as in 1 Cor 3.1), but here it describes primarily a person in his pre-Christian
state. An appropriate equivalent in some languages may be "before we could
fully understand," or "before we realized what the truth really was."

4.4   But when the right time finally came, God sent his own Son. He came
       as the son of a human mother and lived under the Jewish Law,

The right time translates the Greek phrase "the fullness of time," for
which a variety of meanings has been suggested by various commentators. The
most probable is that Paul has in mind the end of the reign of the Law (and therefore of man's hopelessness) and the beginning of a new era when the decisive
aspect is not what man does or attempts to do, but what God does on behalf of
man. Whatever meaning we can see in the expression, the main thing to remember is that the emphasis is on a time designated by God as appropriate for his
act in order to assure man's deliverance from helplessness and subservience to
the Law and to those forces that are opposed to God (cf. Phps "the proper time";
JB "the appointed time"; NAB "the designated time"). In a number of languages
one simply cannot speak of "time coming." One can often say, however, "when
it was the right time," "...the right occasion," "when the right day was happening," or "when it was the day that God had decided upon." In some languages it
may be necessary to indicate in what respect a particular time or occasion is
"right," and the quality of being right can only be stated in some languages with
reference to God's determining it as being right. For this reason one must specify the occasion as being appropriate in terms of God having designated it or
selected it.

It is possible to interpret the expression God sent his own Son to mean
God's sending of Jesus from Galilee to fulfill his ministry in other parts of Palestine. It is more likely, however, that Paul is referring to God's act of sending
his Son from his pre-existent state into the world. In some languages it is al-

most essential to indicate the place to which God's Son was sent, and therefore it may be necessary to say "God sent his own Son into the world." This particular interpretation seems to be by far the more acceptable of the two.

The son of a human mother is literally "born of a woman." In the Bible this is an idiomatic expression referring simply to what is human (see Job 14.1 and Matt 11.11). The emphasis, therefore, is not on the human mother, but on the fact that the Son took upon himself human nature; in other words, he became a human being. The closest equivalent of the son of a human mother may in some languages be simply "his mother was a human being," "a woman gave birth to him," or even "he had a mother just as other people do"; but often a more appropriate rendering would be "he became a person" or "he came as a man."

Lived under the Jewish Law is literally "born under law," although the Greek construction would suggest "subject to law" as a more accurate rendering. The absence of the article before "law" is interpreted by some to indicate the general nature of the phrase. It could then refer simply to Jesus' status as man, since all men are under law of some kind. There is, however, an undeniable reference to the Jewish Law. What Paul very likely means is that the Son of God took upon himself human form and was subject to all the requirements of the Jewish Law. There is a serious complication involved in a literal translation of the expression lived under the Jewish Law, since in a number of languages an expression such as "under the law" would suggest illegal activity, that is to say, he "lived like an outlaw." It may therefore be necessary to say "he lived in obedience to the Jewish Law," or better "he lived in a society which had the Jewish Law." It is true, of course, that Jesus did violate a number of the ceremonial laws in order to reach people, but it is equally true that his general pattern of life was in conformance with Old Testament regulations.

4.5   to redeem those who were under the Law, so that we might become God's sons.

The purpose of the Son of God becoming a human being and living under the Jewish Law is twofold: negatively, to redeem those who were under the Law, and positively, so that we might become God's sons.

For redeem, see the note on 3.13. The deliverance spoken of there is from the curse of the Law, but here it is deliverance from the Law itself. It may be difficult to render redeem in the sense of "paying back," for a commercial transaction would tend to be misinterpreted in this type of context. The focus here is upon deliverance, and it may be best in a number of languages to translate "to deliver those who lived under the control of the Law," or "...who had to obey the Law." If this means primarily the Law of Moses, it is obviously a direct reference to Jews. If, however, one understands "born under law" as applying to wider legal requirements, then it may be necessary to use the first person inclusive, for example, "to redeem all of us who are under law," or "...subject to law."

Under the Law is literally "under law." While Paul's primary reference is to the Jewish Law, it is possible that he includes Gentiles, for they too were subject to legal ordinances. The inclusive we would naturally and logically follow.

We might become God's sons is literally "we might receive adoption." Paul uses similar expressions in Rom 8.15 and 23. The term "adoption" should not be understood, however, as a legal term but as a religious term, in the sense that God gives us the status of sonship (see NEB) together with all its privileges. Paul would obviously wish to include the Galatian believers as those who had become God's sons, and therefore the inclusive "we" (for such languages as make a distinction between inclusive and exclusive first person plural) would be essential. Certainly Paul would not want to suggest that he and his colleagues had become God's sons, while excluding the Galatians. Here again it may be necessary, in order to indicate clearly what is involved, to employ an expression such as "we all."

TEV	RSV
6 To show that you are*f* his sons, God sent the Spirit of his Son into our hearts, the Spirit who cries out, "Father, my Father." 7 So then, you are no longer a slave but a son. And since you are his son, God will give you all that he has for his sons.	6 And because you are sons, God has sent the Spirit of his Son into our hearts, crying, "Abba! Father!" 7 So through God you are no longer a slave but a son, and if a son then an heir. (4.6-7)

*f*To show that you are; *or* Because
   you are.   (4.6-7)

<u>4.6</u>   To show that you are*f* his sons, God sent the Spirit of his Son into
our hearts, the Spirit who cries out, "Father, my Father."

   *f*To show that you are; *or* Because you are.

At the end of verse 5, Paul used the first person pronoun we, which would include all Christians. Now at the beginning of verse 6, he switches to the second person plural (to show that you are his sons), thus making a more direct appeal to his Galatian readers. In the second part of the verse, he reverts to the first person plural (God sent the Spirit of his Son into our hearts), thus completely identifying himself with his readers in the experience of sonship and the gift of the Holy Spirit. Because of the shift between second person plural and first person plural, it may be important to reinforce the first person plural by saying "into all of our hearts." However, in many languages one does not speak of the Spirit being "in one's heart" but rather "in one's life" or "in one's inner self." In fact, in some languages it would be more appropriate to translate the second clause of this verse as "God sent his Son's Spirit to control us," or "...to guide us." Such an expression would have much more significance than one which merely speaks of sending a Spirit into one's heart, particularly if the expression for "heart" has no relation to will or emotion.

TEV signals the presence of an exegetical problem in this verse by giving an alternative rendering to the expression to show that you are his sons. The alternative rendering, "because you are his sons," treats the expression as causal, giving the reason for God's act of sending the Spirit into the believers' hearts. Some translations follow this interpretation (e.g. Mft "it is because you are sons"), but most modern translations take the expression as a proposition to be established or to be proved (e.g. NEB "to prove that you are his sons"). In the former case, sonship is the reason for the gift of the Holy Spirit; but in the latter the gift of the Spirit confirms for the believer his status as a child of God. However, the concepts of reason and confirmation are thoroughly interrelated.

The expression the Spirit of his Son, referring to the Holy Spirit, is used only here in the New Testament. Elsewhere, Paul uses the expressions "the Spirit of Christ" and "the Spirit of Jesus Christ." It is essential that any term for "Spirit" be such that it may apply in the phrases "Holy Spirit" and "God's Spirit," for precisely the same term must be used of the Holy Spirit, the Spirit of God, and the Spirit of Christ.

The Spirit is sent into our hearts, that is, the center of intellectual, moral, and spiritual life. It is from the heart that the Spirit cries out Father, my Father. The Greek word for cries out is used to describe a loud or earnest cry or even a public announcement, but here primarily it describes prayer addressed to God and shows how intense is the Spirit's cry within the believer. The expression translated Father, my Father is a combination of both the Aramaic and the Greek terms for "father"; it was probably used by the early church as a liturgical formula. Jesus spoke Aramaic, and he may have started the Lord's prayer with the Aramaic "Abba." This liturgical formula suggests a passionate and intimate cry addressed to God in recognition of his fatherhood and in gratitude for the gift of sonship. It is true that the Spirit is the one that cries, but he cries from the believer's heart. A literal translation of the Spirit who cries out could be interpreted to mean that the Spirit engages in the activity of speaking of the Father as Father, my Father, but that the individual believer is himself in no way involved. It may, therefore, be necessary to say "the Spirit which causes us to cry 'Father, my Father.'"

In the translation of the verb cries out, it is important to avoid an expression which would suggest either shouting or weeping. What is in focus here is the earnestness with which one speaks.

In a number of languages it may be misleading and, in fact, inappropriate to translate literally "Father, my Father." A more satisfactory equivalent may be "my dear Father" or "my Father whom I love." It is, of course, important so to structure verse 6 that the expression Father, my Father will be translated as a reference to God as used in prayer.

This verse is interpreted by some as indicating that sonship precedes the experience of the Holy Spirit. Many commentators, however, see a difficulty in this position, for Paul makes it clear in other writings that the gift of the Spirit is the means through which believers become conscious of their sonship (cf. Rom 8.15). The difficulty is really not great, for there is indeed a close relation between sonship and the gift of the Spirit. However, in this verse, Paul should be allowed to say what he apparently intends to say, without being influenced by what he has written elsewhere.

4.7   So then, you are no longer a slave but a son. And since you are his son, God will give you all that he has for his sons.

In this verse Paul uses the second person singular pronoun, thus zeroing in, so to speak, on each individual reader.

So then connects this verse not only with verse 6, but with everything from verses 1 to 6. The gift of the Spirit, referred to in verse 6, confirms the gift of sonship. In some languages it may be useful to translate so then as "because of what God has done," or "as a result of what has happened." In other languages one may employ an adverbial connective such as "therefore."

The clause you are no longer a slave implies at least two things: (1) Sonship includes freedom from bondage; one who has been made a son of God is no longer under the bondage of the Jewish Law or of any other force in the world. (2) Paul's use of no longer makes it clear that his readers were formerly under bondage. You are no longer a slave must refer to the bondage of persons to the elemental spirits of the universe or to the Law. Since this is a direct reference to the Galatians, it may be useful to translate "you are no longer in bondage to the spirits that rule the universe," or "you no longer have to serve those spirits." Similarly the phrase but a son must often be expanded to indicate whose son, for example, "but you are a son of God."

And since you are his son, God will give you all that he has for his sons is literally "and if a son, also an heir through God." The use of the word "heir" reminds one of Roman law, where all the children, whether sons or daughters, natural or adopted, inherited alike. Paul reminds his readers that each one of them, as a son, enjoys the full privileges of sonship and will receive from God everything that he promised to Abraham. The addition of the expression "through God" reminds Paul's readers of two things: (1) their sonship is a gift from God alone and not through any effort or merit on their part; and (2) since it is all from God, then God will certainly see to it that whatever he has promised to his sons will be realized.

TEV	RSV
Paul's Concern for the Galatians	
8 In the past you did not know God, and so you were slaves of beings who are not gods. 9 But now that you know God--or, I should say, now that God knows you--how is it that you want to turn back to those weak and pitiful ruling spirits? Why do you want to become their slaves all over again? 10 You pay	8 Formerly, when you did not know God, you were in bondage to beings that by nature are no gods; 9 but now that you have come to know God, or rather to be known by God, how can you turn back again to the weak and beggarly elemental spirits, whose slaves you want to be once more? 10 You observe days,

4.8

special attention to certain days, months, seasons, and years. 11 I am worried about you! Can it be that all my work for you has been for nothing? (4.8-11)	and months, and seasons, and years! 11 I am afraid I have labored over you in vain. (4.8-11)

Paul has just finished a long theological discourse (3.1—4.7) in which he has shown quite clearly and forcefully that it is those who receive God's blessings as promised to Abraham, and not those who obey what the Law requires, who through Christ have now received the gift of sonship from God. Now Paul returns to his starting point, which is the occasion of the letter, namely, his concern for the Galatian Christians. In 3.1-5, he has addressed them directly, expressing bewilderment over their foolishness and apostasy. Now again he addresses them directly, appealing to them not to return to a slavery similar to or worse than that which held them in bondage before they heard and accepted the Christian message.

The section heading Paul's Concern for the Galatians may be expressed in a verbal form by rendering "Paul is worried for the Galatians," "Paul says that he is concerned about the Galatians," or "Paul is afraid of what will happen to the Galatians' faith."

4.8   In the past you did not know God, and so you were slaves of beings who are not gods.

In this verse Paul reminds the Galatians of their former state, to prepare them for the warning he is about to give regarding the folly of their proposed actions.

In the Greek the verse starts with "but then," and while most translations omit the connective, it is possible to interpret it to mean that Paul's description of the former state of the Galatians and of their apostasy is in direct contrast to their description as children of God in the previous section.

In the past may be expressed in some languages as "in former days," but past time may be characterized specifically in terms of having occurred prior to faith in Jesus Christ, and therefore one may translate "before you believed in Jesus."

The verb form of you did not know is a perfect (but used as a present) tense to refer to a period of time simultaneous with the main verb (you were slaves) and thus in the past (TEV in the past; NEB and others "formerly"). Most interpreters take the position that, since Paul says that in their former state the Galatians were ignorant of God, he had in mind primarily the non-Jews among them, for the Jews would have had a knowledge of God before they became Christians. It is possible, however, to understand the Jews' subservience to the Law as a form of ignorance of God. In fact, the phrase know God must be understood in this context (as well as in many other contexts in Paul's letters) as indicating intimate relationship with God. It is far more than merely "knowing about God." An equivalent expression in some languages may be "you really were not personally acquainted with God," or "you had never met with God."

And so implies the reason for Paul's mentioning the matter of their ignorance of God. Since they were ignorant of God, one could understand why they were in a state of slavery. It is interesting to note that the word translated you were slaves is related to the word Paul uses when he talks of being a "servant" of Jesus Christ. In Christ, of course, this relationship is characterized by freedom, not bondage.

The expression beings who are not gods is literally "the ones which by nature are not gods." The word for "nature" refers to one's essential character. While Paul does not deny that these beings are called "gods," he does deny that they are deities. In other words, they are "gods who are really no gods at all" (Mft).

The main difficulty here is to determine what Paul was referring to by this description. Was he referring to the idols which the Galatians formerly served, to the "elements of the world" referred to in verse 3, or to the pagan deities which in another letter he refers to as "demons"? (1 Cor 10.20). Or did he include in this description the Jewish Law which had taken the place of God in Jewish life? It is not easy to choose an answer, but in view of the nature of Paul's readers, an interpretation that would include both Jews and Greeks would be preferred. The only equivalent of beings who are not gods in some languages is "spirits who are not gods." This would be a reference to those spirits in the universe which indwell nature but which are not regarded as having supernatural power over certain domains of nature. If, however, one endeavors to include the Jewish Law in beings who are not gods, then it may be necessary to use some relatively impersonal expression such as "powers which are really not gods." Such a generic expression as "powers" is, however, relatively rare in receptor languages, and therefore one may be forced to settle for an expression such as "spirits."

4.9   But now that you know God—or, I should say, now that God knows you —how is it that you want to turn back to those weak and pitiful ruling spirits? Why do you want to become their slaves all over again?

But now relates verse 9 with the previous verse and emphasizes the strong contrast between their pre-Christian and Christian states. Whereas their pre-Christian state is characterized by ignorance of God, their Christian state is characterized by knowledge. The word for know is different from the word translated "know" in verse 8. The word used in verse 8 implies primarily knowledge of facts, whereas the word in verse 9 is often used in the deeper sense of recognition or acknowledgment, not simply of facts, but of persons, and can therefore be used to describe the relationship between God and man and between a husband and his wife (cf. JB NEB "acknowledge," Knox "recognize"). Clearly in this verse it is important to employ a term for know which involves personal knowledge or experience, for example, "you are personally acquainted with God," "you have yourselves met with God," or "you have acknowledged God as your God."

Paul describes the Galatians as knowing God. But immediately, in order to correct any wrong impressions they might deduce from his statement, he adds:

now that God knows you. The emphasis, of course, is that their reconciliation with God has not come through any effort or merit on their part; it came as a result of God's love and God's own initiative. In translating now that God knows you, it is essential to use the same type of expression used in the first part of verse 9. For example, one may say "but now that you have met with God—or, I should say, now that God has met with you." This type of expression may serve well to indicate God's initiative in the process of reconciliation.

After all that, it is hard to understand why the Galatians would want to go back into slavery. How is it (other translations "how can you") carries with it both unbelief and dismay. The whole question is rhetorical, making it clear that to Paul it is simply not possible for them to turn back to those weak and pitiful ruling spirits. The word translated spirits is literally "elements" and obviously refers back to verse 3. Paul, however, makes his description more intense by the addition of two adjectives: the first of these, weak, puts emphasis on ineffectiveness (NAB "powerless," JB "can do nothing," Phps "dead"), and the second describes the qualities of a beggar and refers to the poverty and total inadequacy of the religious system which the Galatians are in danger of embracing (cf. JB "can give nothing," NAB "worthless," NEB "beggarly"). Though the two rhetorical questions in this verse are very effective in some languages, it is impossible to employ such expressions in other languages, and therefore a strong negative statement must be employed, for example, "surely you do not want to turn back ...," and "you certainly do not want to become their slaves...."

In languages where such rhetorical questions may be used, how is it may be rendered simply as "why," but because of the special emphasis involved at this point, an expression such as "why in the world..." would be very appropriate.

It may not be sufficient simply to say turn back to those weak and pitiful ruling spirits. In some languages this would mean nothing more than "turning around to look at." What is really involved here is "turn around in order to serve," "return in order to do reverence to," or "turn back in order to obey."

There is a problem involved in rendering a phrase such as those weak and pitiful ruling spirits, since in many languages one cannot apply the attributives "weak," "pitiful," and "ruling" to a noun such as "spirits." There are various ways in which such a syntactic construction may be restructured; a typical one would be "those spirits that rule over the world; they are weak and have no value."

Why do you want to become their slaves all over again? is part of the single rhetorical question in the Greek, but it is made into another rhetorical question in TEV in order to make clear that the result of their turning back to these spirits is to become slaves all over again, thus losing the relationship of sons to a father which they were already enjoying. The reference to slaves must be made more specific in some languages, since one must indicate to whom the persons become slaves, for example, "Why do you want to become the slaves of those spirits all over again?" or "Why do you want to have to obey those spirits all over again?"

<u>4.10</u>   You pay special attention to certain days, months, seasons, and years.

Paul now gives an example of the way the Galatians are becoming slaves all over again, namely, their strict observance of all kinds of celebrations. The verb translated <u>pay special attention to</u> contains the elements of observing or keeping something religiously, or scrupulously observing something to the minutest detail. The other element that Paul obviously has in mind is that the Galatians are doing all these things because of their belief that it is through these observances they can be reconciled to God. <u>Pay special attention to</u> may be expressed in some languages as "you observe as being very important," "you have religious festivals on," or "you count as part of your worship to God."

The expression <u>days, months, seasons, and years</u> probably refers to the Jewish system of religious feasts, since it is the Judaizers who are the strong opponents of Paul in Galatia. If this is so, <u>days</u> could refer to the sabbaths, and other feasts celebrated only for a day; <u>months</u> to the monthly celebrations (e.g. new moons, as in Num 10.10); <u>seasons</u> to the annual festivals which were not limited to a single day, e.g. Passover, Tabernacles, etc. (see 2 Chron 8.13); and <u>years</u> to the New Year celebrations, the year of Jubilee, or perhaps the Sabbatical year. One cannot be very sure as to the contents of these terms, but, taken together, they simply refer to the total system of celebrations observed by the Jews at that time.

There is little or no difficulty involved in an expression such as <u>days</u>, since all languages have some means of expressing such a time unit. The term for <u>months</u> is often simply equivalent to "moons," and <u>seasons</u> may be rendered as "special times during the year." Words for <u>years</u> are often expressed in somewhat idiomatic forms, for example, "when the rains come back," "the seasons of the sun," or "tying up the sun" (an expression in the Quechua languages of South America in which special strings, called "khipus," were used as means of counting the years through tying particular types of knots).

Paul does not suggest that the observance of these feasts is bad in itself; the implication of what he says is that it is wrong to regard the observance of these feasts in a legalistic manner, that is, in order to win the approval of God.

It is observed by some that it is strange that Paul does not here refer to the practice of circumcision, and the suggestion is made that the Judaizers actually began their campaign among the Galatians with elements of Judaism which were less repulsive and which had affinity with the pagan practices the Galatians were used to. More probably, however, this is no reflection at all on the approach of the Judaizers; it is simply Paul's approach. He selects those elements in Jewish ritual which have obvious affinities with pagan worship to show that adoption of these and other practices related to the Jewish Law is practically a return to the paganism which they forsook when they accepted the Christian message.

4.11   I am worried about you! Can it be that all my work for you has been for nothing?

Paul ends this section with a statement expressing his fear that everything he has done among the Galatians might end up in nothing. This shows how seriously Paul regarded the effects of legalism; once the Galatians start to observe a legalistic system, they have for all intents and purposes repudiated the Good News of God's free gift of love and reconciliation.

In the Greek this verse is actually one declarative sentence, but TEV restructures it into two sentences. The first expresses Paul's concern and worry for the Galatians, and the second expresses, in the form of a rhetorical question, his doubt, unbelief, and dismay at what he fears may actually happen, if it has not already become a reality among them.

It is possible to translate the first part of this verse with the worry or fear being connected with the efforts of Paul rather than with the Galatians themselves (RSV "I am afraid I have labored over you in vain"; JB "you make me feel I have wasted my time with you"; NEB "you make me fear that all the pains I spent on you may prove to be labour lost"). It is more likely, however, that the meaning of the Greek is more as TEV renders this passage; that is, Paul is showing his concern for the Galatians themselves, and not simply expressing fear that his efforts have been in vain (cf. Knox "I am anxious over you").

I am worried about you is literally "I fear for you," but special care would have to be exercised in translating "I fear for you." It could be translated "I am afraid for you," but too often it has been rendered in such a way as to mean "I am afraid of you." In some languages one can best say "I'm afraid for what may happen to you." However, in some languages one cannot speak of "fear" in a context such as this one. What was in Paul's mind was not fright, but deep concern and worry, as TEV indicates, and therefore one may translate "I am very much worried because of you," or, as expressed idiomatically in one language, "My mind is killing me because of you."

In place of the rhetorical question Can it be that all my work for you has been for nothing?, one may have in some languages an emphatic statement, "I sincerely trust that all my work on your behalf has not been for nothing." In many languages, however, a double negative is quite inappropriate, and may even be grammatically improper. Thus it may be necessary to say "I do trust that my work for you has had results."

To avoid the implication that Paul's work has been merely physical effort, it may be important in some languages to translate all my work for you as "all that I have done on your behalf," or "all that I have done in order to help you."

TEV	RSV
12 I beg you, my brothers, be like me. After all, I am like you. You have not done me any wrong. 13 You remember why I preached the gospel to you the first time; it was because I was sick. 14 But	12 Brethren, I beseech you, become as I am, for I also have become as you are. You did me no wrong; 13 you know it was because of a bodily ailment that I preached the gospel to you at first; 14 and

even though my physical condition
was a great trial to you, you did
not despise or reject me. Instead,
you received me as you would an angel from heaven; you received me as
you would Christ Jesus. 15 You
were so happy! What has happened?
I myself can say that you would
have taken out your own eyes, if
you could, and given them to me.
16 Have I now become your enemy by
telling you the truth?

17 Those other people show a
deep interest in you, but their intentions are not good. All they
want is to separate you from me, so
that you will have the same interest in them as they have in you.
18 Now, it is good to have such a
deep interest if the purpose is
good--this is true always, and not
merely when I am with you. 19 My
dear children! Once again, just
like a mother in childbirth, I feel
the same kind of pain for you, until Christ's nature is formed in
you. 20 How I wish I were with you
now, so that I could take a different attitude toward you. I am so
worried about you!   (4.12-20)

though my condition was a trial to
you, you did not scorn or despise
me, but received me as an angel of
God, as Christ Jesus. 15 What has
become of the satisfaction you
felt? For I bear you witness that,
if possible, you would have plucked
out your eyes and given them to me.
16 Have I then become your enemy
by telling you the truth?ʰ 17 They
make much of you, but for no good
purpose; they want to shut you out,
that you may make much of them.
18 For a good purpose it is always
good to be made much of, and not
only when I am present with you.
19 My little children, with whom I
am again in travail until Christ be
formed in you! 20 I could wish to
be present with you now and to
change my tone, for I am perplexed
about you.

ʰOr *by dealing truly with you*
(4.12-20)

This passage concludes the section on Paul's concerns for the Galatians.
For a moment Paul stops presenting his theological arguments and makes a passionate appeal to his readers. It has been noted that in this letter Paul never
allows himself to be intimate in tone; the most intimate address he has used is
my brothers, and in this passage he uses it again. But he goes further than that.
He remembers his experiences with them, and how they loved and cared for him
in the past, despite the fact that when he was with them he was ill. This illness
did not prevent the Galatians from welcoming him openly and accepting the message which he preached.

4.12   I beg you, my brothers, be like me. After all, I am like you.
          You have not done me any wrong.

This personal section starts appropriately with I beg you, my brothers.
Two things should be noted: (1) in the Greek, this stands at the end of the sentence, thus giving it added emphasis; (2) the verb used occurs only five other
times in Paul's letters, and in four cases it connotes intense longing on Paul's
part. In a number of languages the rendering of I beg you in this type of context

may be translated as "I strongly ask you," "I urge you with pleading," or, expressed idiomatically in some languages, "I speak to you with my heart exposed."

The appeal be like me. After all, I am like you is capable of various interpretations (Phps "I do beg you to follow me here,...I am a man like yourselves"; Knox "stand by me: I have taken stand with you"; NEB "put yourselves in my place, my brothers, I beg you, for I have put myself in yours"). The whole appeal is connected with Paul's attitude toward the Law. Most likely he is exhorting the Galatians to imitate him in abandoning the Law as a means of being reconciled to God. In other words, although Paul was a Jew, he has become like the Galatians, that is, as a Gentile, free from the clutches of the Law. That he regarded himself as outside the Law is clear from 1 Cor 9.20-21.

It is extremely difficult in some languages to express an obscure meaning such as be like me. One must usually employ a more specific meaning, for example, "behave like I do," "look like I do," or "believe as I do." In other words, imitation is often restricted to specific kinds of activity. If, as seems quite clear, the emphasis here is upon Paul's specific relation to the Law, it may be necessary in some languages to say "make a break with the Law, even as I have," "do not be subservient to the Law, even as I am not," or, perhaps, "as far as the Law is concerned, be like me."

You have not done me any wrong is capable of various interpretations. Among them are (1) you have not done me any wrong in the past, but now you do; (2) you have not done me any wrong in the past, so don't start now; (3) it is true, as you have said, that you did me no wrong when I was with you; it is not true, however, that you are not doing me any wrong now; (4) you have not wronged me, it is Christ whom you have wronged; (5) you have not wronged me, it is yourselves whom you have wronged; (6) I have no ground for complaining about your conduct (cf. Phps "I have nothing against you personally"). Of these possible meanings the first and the third seem to fit the context best. Since we do not know the specific circumstances of which Paul speaks, it is impossible to tell precisely what he means by the statement You have not done me any wrong. Again, it is not possible to be obscure in some languages with regard to such a meaning, and it may be necessary to choose one of the possible interpretations. For example, one may say "In the past you did nothing bad to me," "...you did nothing to cause me harm," or "...to cause me trouble."

4.13   You remember why I preached the gospel to you the first time; it was because I was sick.

You remember is literally "you know" and implies that the general circumstances that led to Paul's visit to Galatia are common knowledge among the Galatian Christians. He reminds them that it was because he was sick that he was enabled to preach the Good News to them the first time. In rendering the verb remember, it is important not to select a term which will suggest that the Galatians had themselves forgotten what had happened. It may therefore be better simply to translate you remember as "you know" or "you have known all along."

It is possible to understand the sickness as simply something that afflicted

Paul while he was preaching to the Galatians. This position is followed by some translators (e.g. Phps "you know how handicapped I was by illness when I first preached the Gospel to you"). However, most interpreters understand the sickness as the cause of his preaching there.

The nature of the infirmity has elicited numerous suggestions from scholars. Some connect the sickness with verse 14 and suggest a sickness that seriously affected Paul's appearance and became a trial to the Galatian believers. But the illness may have been something which gave the impression that Paul was possessed by an evil spirit, pointing to epilepsy. Others connect the sickness with verse 15 and come to the conclusion that Paul had eye trouble. Others suggest that Paul contracted malaria while he was on the coast and had to travel up into Pisidian Antioch to recuperate. Still others connect it with the "thorn in the flesh" in 2 Cor 12.7. Finally, some claim that it was no physical sickness, but that Paul was referring to his sufferings when he brought the gospel to Galatia (cf. Acts 14.19 ff.). Interesting and ingenious as all these suggestions may be, we still have to admit that we do not know the exact nature of Paul's sickness. However, we can draw the conclusion that this sickness, whatever it was, was in some way offensive to the Galatians.

The expression translated the first time can be interpreted as implying a second visit (NEB margin "on the first of my two visits"). Some interpreters suggest that this second visit refers to the return journey of Paul on his way back to Syrian Antioch to conclude his first missionary journey, as recorded in Acts 14.21-28. It is possible, however, to understand the expression as referring to Paul's original mission to the Galatians, and not to a second occasion, for example, "at the beginning, when the illness gave the opportunity" (NEB "it was bodily illness that originally led me to my bringing you the Gospel").

Though it may be very convenient, as in TEV, to separate the fact of preaching the gospel in Galatia from the reason for it, namely, Paul's illness, and thus placing the two in separate clauses clearly marked by why and it was because, in some languages it may be much better to combine the two, for example, "You know that I preached the gospel to you the first time because I was sick." However, in some languages it may seem very strange to combine sickness with preaching the gospel as reason and result or cause and effect. It may therefore be important to indicate that the sickness produced circumstances which somehow permitted Paul to preach the gospel, that is, that his sickness was the occasion rather than the reason for it. In this case, sickness would not be an immediate but a secondary cause of his preaching the gospel, for example, "Because I was sick, it was possible for me to preach the gospel to you the first time," or "My sickness caused the circumstances which made it possible for me to preach the gospel to you at first."

4.14   But even though my physical condition was a great trial to you, you
        did not despise or reject me. Instead, you received me as you would
        an angel from heaven; you received me as you would Christ Jesus.

Paul expected a negative reaction from the Galatians because of his <u>physical condition</u>, which was a <u>great trial</u> to them. The rendering of <u>physical condition</u> would, of course, be determined by one's opinion regarding the nature of Paul's infirmity. <u>My physical condition was a great trial to you</u> may be expressed as cause and effect, for example, "my sickness caused great difficulty for you," or "because I was sick, you had great difficulty."

Paul does not spell out <u>how</u> his condition was a trial for the Galatians. Was it the nature of the sickness itself, or was it simply the problems that went along with having to take care of a sick man? Whatever it was, it is clear that Paul's condition was such that one might have expected the Galatians to reject him and his message. Fortunately, they did not succumb to the temptation of judging Paul or his message by his outward appearance.

Although Paul's sickness could have led the Galatians to <u>despise</u> or <u>reject</u> him and his message, they did not do so. The two verbs are strong terms. <u>Despise</u> has the meaning of "to regard as good for nothing." <u>Reject</u> can be literally rendered "to spit out," and some commentators regard this as a clue to Paul's sickness, since at that time it was a common practice for one to spit when a person thought to be possessed by an evil spirit passed by. This would imply that Paul had epilepsy or a similar sickness. However, it is better to interpret the term metaphorically as an expression of disgust. There are various ways in which languages may reflect the meaning of such terms as <u>despise</u> and <u>reject</u>. For example, <u>you did not despise...me</u> may be rendered as "you did not look down on me," "...say I was worthless," or "...frown upon me." Similarly, <u>you did not...reject me</u> may be rendered as "you did not throw me out," "...turn your backs on me," or "...throw my words back at me."

The verb for <u>received</u> suggests the idea of welcome more distinctly than other verbs more commonly used by Paul. In some languages <u>you received me</u> is best rendered as "you welcomed me in your homes," since this is often an expression for general acceptance. However, in other languages it may be more appropriate to say "you were happy with my words," "you spoke to me with kindness," or "you heard my words with open hearts."

The term "angel" can be taken in the sense of God's messenger. However, in view of Pauline usage, it is more likely that it refers here to a supernatural being. Since an <u>angel</u> is often called "a messenger from heaven," a phrase such as "an angel of God" (the literal translation) would then be expressed as "God's messenger which comes from heaven." In this way one can distinguish between earthly messengers sent by God (for example, the prophets) and those special messengers often spoken of as dwelling in heaven with God.

The idea of the whole clause is not that the Galatians received Paul as a superhuman being or as Jesus Christ himself, as some translations seem to suggest (e.g. JB "you welcomed me as an angel of God, as if I were Christ Jesus himself"; also NAB), but that they accorded him such respect and honor as they would have accorded an angel of God or even Jesus Christ. In other words, the Galatians could not have received an angel or Jesus Christ more courteously and more honorably. In order to make clear that what is being compared is the manner of reception, it may be useful to translate the final clause of this verse as "you received me in the same way as you would have received Christ Jesus himself," or "you received me so well; it was the same as if you were receiving Christ Jesus."

4.15   You were so happy! What has happened? I myself can say that you
        would have taken out your own eyes, if you could, and given them to
        me.

You were so happy! What has happened? is literally "Where is your happiness?" or "...your blessedness?"   The question is rhetorical and implies that when Paul was asking the question the Galatians no longer felt the same way they did when he was with them. This is made clear in TEV and other modern translations (RSV "what has become of the satisfaction you felt?"; JB "what has become of this enthusiasm you had?"; NAB "what has happened to your openhearted spirit?").

It is possible to interpret the happiness of the Galatians as related either to Paul's presence with them (NEB "have you forgotten how happy you thought yourselves in having me with you?") or to his teaching. However, it may be enough to take the question as a general statement describing the condition of the Galatians at that time.

A literal translation of You were so happy! might be interpreted as merely a description of the Galatians' normal personality, that is, that they were essentially happy people. Obviously, however, Paul is referring to the particular experience which made them happy, for example, "What happened to you made you so happy," "Because of your experience, you were so happy," or "As a result of what had happened, you were so happy." Thus it may be necessary to render What has happened? as "What has happened now?" or even "What has happened to change all this?"

I myself can say that is literally "I bear you witness that," and what follows is an illustration of the happiness and satisfaction of the readers (Phps "I guarantee," JB "I swear," NAB "I can testify on your behalf"). One may also translate this introductory statement as "I am absolutely sure that," "there is not the slightest doubt that," or "I would say to anyone that."

As already noted, the statement you would have taken out your own eyes, if you could, and given them to me has led some commentators to conclude that Paul's sickness was connected with poor eyesight. However, in view of the fact that the eye is a symbol of one's most precious possessions and is considered the most important part of the body (Deut 32.10; Matt 18.9), it is better to interpret this statement in a metaphorical sense and render it as "you would have given me even that which you valued most," or "you would have sacrificed everything for me, even your very eyes." One might even render this expression as "you would have done anything for me; why, you would even have taken out your eyes and given them to me if you could," or "there is nothing you wouldn't have done for me if you could; you would even have taken out your own eyes and given them to me."

<u>4.16</u>   Have I now become your enemy by telling you the truth?

The occasion of Paul's telling the Galatians the truth is quite disputed. Among the suggestions are (1) it was during a second visit or in an unrecorded letter, in which he warned them of the apostasy they are now confronted with; or (2) the reference is to the present letter, in which case Paul is simply expressing his fears that the strong language of his letter may lead the Galatians to treat him as an enemy. The first possibilities involve conjectures with no evidence at all. Against the second one must note that the verb form of "become" implies a result which already exists (though the verbal forms are not conclusive), and the Galatians have not yet read the letter. A third suggestion may be brought forth, and that is to interpret <u>truth</u> as the message which Paul preached among the Galatians during his first visit to them. The message of Paul's enemies is, of course, contrary to what he preached to the Galatians, and since the Galatians, or some of them, have already accepted the Judaizers' message, they are questioning the accuracy of Paul's gospel and his right to proclaim it. The word <u>enemy</u> then could be interpreted as hostility to Paul and his message. This fourth suggestion would fit the context best, though no modern commentary takes this line of interpretation.

It may be difficult to speak of Paul as having actually "become an enemy." Obviously he is not in reality an enemy; it is only that he is suggesting the possibility that the people in the congregations in Galatia might regard him as such. Therefore it may be better to render this verse as "Because I tell you the truth, do you now regard me as your enemy?", "Does my telling you the truth cause you to think of me as your enemy?", or "...cause you to say, He is now our enemy?"

<u>4.17</u>   Those other people show a deep interest in you, but their intentions are not good. All they want is to separate you from me, so that you will have the same interest in them as they have in you.

After speaking of his very satisfying experiences with the Galatians, Paul goes on to remark on their relationship with the false teachers (the Judaizers), who are obviously referred to in <u>those other people</u> (literally "they"). In some languages a literal translation of <u>those other people</u> may be satisfactory, but in some it is not enough, and it may be necessary to be more specific at this point, especially since the false teachers have not been specifically mentioned for a number of verses. Hence it may be better to render <u>those other people</u> as "those people who are trying to change the gospel," or "those people who are speaking lies about the Good News."

Paul has already implied what these false teachers were teaching; now he talks about their motives. They <u>show a deep interest in</u> the Galatians. The verb used here literally means "to be envious," and accordingly some translators take the literal meaning (NEB "are envious of you," Knox "they are jealous over you"). It could be, as some commentators suggest, that the false teachers are envious of the Galatians both for their new-found freedom in Christ and their good relationship with Paul. Most commentators and translators, however, understand the verb in the same way as TEV (NAB "courting your favour," Phps "how keen these

[104]

men are to win you over"). One of the difficulties with a literal rendering of
show a deep interest in you may be that it would seem to express a perfectly legitimate or even good attitude, and therefore the following clause would seem to
be contradictory. It may therefore be better to translate the first clause as
"Those others are trying very hard to win you over to their side," or ". . . are
very anxious for you to belong just to them."

Their showing of interest could be interpreted, of course, as a good thing,
but their intentions are not good. In other words, their motives are thoroughly
selfish (Phps "it is for their own ends," Knox "but for a dishonourable purpose").
In a number of languages their intentions may be rendered as "what they really
want to do," "what they have set out to do," or "what they are trying to do." It
may be very important to indicate clearly how good is to be interpreted; therefore one may say "but what they intend to do is not good for you," or ". . . not for
your benefit."

What is their aim? It is to separate you from me. Literally, the Greek
simply says "they want to shut you out" or ". . . exclude you." From what?, one
may ask. It could be from the church and from all other Christians who have
found freedom in Christ. Or it could be from Christ himself and his gift of a new
relationship with God. Or it could be, as TEV suggests, from Paul himself (cf.
Phps JB). Whatever it is, the intended effect of this act is "that you may make
much of them" (RSV), that is, so that the Galatians would turn to them for fellowship and guidance, since they would have no one else to turn to. Most modern
translations follow this interpretation (Phps "have your zeal all to themselves";
JB "they want to win you over to themselves"; NAB "so that you may court their
favour"). A literal rendering of all they want is to separate you from me may be
understood in entirely too literal a sense. What is involved here is not physical
separation but a shift of loyalty. Therefore it may be necessary to say "all they
want is to cause you no longer to be loyal to me," or ". . .to cause you to be opposed to me."

4.18   Now, it is good to have such a deep interest if the purpose is good—
         this is true always, and not merely when I am with you.

The first part of this verse seems to be a general principle which is in
direct contrast to the attitude of the false teachers. Accordingly, many translations, including TEV, interpret the verse in this manner (JB "it is always a good
thing to win people over, and I do not have to be there with you, but it must be
for a good purpose"; NEB "it is always a fine thing to deserve an honest envy—
always, and not only when I am present with you"). The phrase if the purpose is
good may be rendered "provided what one intends to accomplish is good," or "only
if what one is trying to do is good."

The last part of the verse, and not merely when I am with you, seems to be
out of place if the first part is indeed a general principle. Accordingly, various
interpretations are offered, all centering on the referents of the phrase to have
such a deep interest. If the object is the Galatians, then the subject could either
be Paul himself or men in general (Phps "don't think I'm jealous—it is a grand

thing that men should be keen to win you"; NAB "it would be well for you to be courted for the right reasons at all times, and not only when I happen to be with you"). If the object is Paul, then there is only one possible subject, namely, the Galatians themselves, as seems to be implied by Knox ("your jealousy should be for the honourable gifts you see in a man of honour; always, not only when I am at your side").

4.19   My dear children! Once again, just like a mother in childbirth, I feel the same kind of pain for you until Christ's nature is formed in you.

This verse is very closely connected with verse 18. Some translators retain the dependent construction, but most modern translators make verse 19 into a complete sentence in order to capture more effectively the emotional tone of what Paul is saying.

Previous to this verse, Paul has been rather formal. Here, however, he addresses his readers as my dear children!, an address of endearment and tender affection. The Greek form is diminutive (literally "my little children"), though some manuscripts have the nondiminutive form. It is a common form of address in 1 John, but it is used by Paul only here (although in some other cases he does use the nondiminutive form "my children"). The diminutive could be interpreted as a term of both affection and slight rebuke, expressing tenderness on the part of the apostle and feebleness on the part of his readers. Such an expression fits well the imagery of childbirth. In a number of languages, however, one cannot use an expression such as "my dear children" without its referring specifically to Paul's own offspring. A more satisfactory equivalent may be "my dear friends," "my dear people," or even "you whom I sincerely love."

What follows is metaphorical language. In another letter, Paul pictures himself as a nursing mother (1 Thes 2.7); here he speaks of himself as a mother in childbirth, suffering birth pangs for the Galatians, who, by implication, are thought of as again in the womb, needing spiritual rebirth. Birth pangs are the most painful and at the same time the most rewarding experience of an expectant mother, and therefore they are an appropriate figure for the pain and suffering that Paul was undergoing because of the problems in the Galatian church. Just like a mother in childbirth may be rendered in some languages as "I am just like a mother who is about to give birth to a child," or "I can compare myself to a woman who is about to have a child."

The second part of the metaphor presents some problems. One can (1) take it as a metaphor in reverse, that is, that the Galatians who were thought of as being formed in the womb are now spoken of as expectant mothers who must now wait for Christ to be developed in them; or (2) one can maintain the same metaphor in the first part and think of Christ being formed in the Galatians while they are still in the womb, so that at birth they would really be in Christ. Most translations, by keeping the form of the original, imply either of these interpretations; NEB, however, clearly takes the second of these. A third option is to drop the figure altogether and to understand until Christ's nature is formed in you as referring to the whole process by which the Galatians come to be in Christ and Christ in them.

I feel the same kind of pain for you may be rendered in some languages as "I feel pain for you, the same kind of pain that a mother feels at childbirth," or "...it is like the kind of pain a mother feels when she is going to have a baby." It may, however, be important to indicate clearly that the pain is to be interpreted figuratively; therefore one may translate "I feel, as it were, the same kind of pain." In general, the phrase for you may be rendered as benefactive, that is, "for your benefit" or "for your sake." However, in some languages this is more often rendered as a causative, "because of you."

It may be quite difficult to translate until Christ's nature is formed in you. One equivalent may be "until you become like Christ"; another, "until you have the characteristics of Christ himself." In some instances, however, the most satisfactory equivalent may simply be "until you become true followers of Christ."

4.20   How I wish I were with you now, so that I could take a different attitude toward you. I am so worried about you!

Paul ends this section with an expression of a desire to be with the Galatians at their moment of distress. How I wish I were with you now expresses Paul's strong desire, at the same time indicating that at the moment the impossibility of its fulfillment. He does not say, however, why he cannot be with them. Such a strong desire or wish may be expressed in some languages as "I want very much to be with you now," or "I desire with all my heart to be where you are now."

If he were present, Paul could take a different attitude toward them (literally, "to change my tone," RSV). Several things should be noted. First, it is not that Paul regrets what he has just said, but the way he had to say it. Secondly, the wished-for change of attitude should be understood as from a severe to a gentle attitude, and not vice versa. Finally, the change has reference to the manner of speech which dominates his letter or which he had when he told them the truth (v. 16), and not to that in the immediately preceding verses, in which he has spoken with affection and tenderness. It is often rather difficult to speak of "taking a different attitude toward someone." What is evidently uppermost in Paul's mind is the possibility of showing by his speech his true feelings about the Galatians. The purpose of Paul's desiring to be with them may in some cases be expressed as "so that I could show you by my speech how I really feel toward you," "...by a change in my language how I feel toward you," or "...by talking face to face with you...."

Finally, we can picture Paul, with a deep sigh, crying out I am so worried about you. The verb means "to be at a loss" or "to be disturbed," meanings reflected in some translations (Phps "I honestly don't know how to deal with you"; JB "I have no idea what to do for the best"; NAB "you have me at a complete loss!"; NEB "I am at my wits' end about you"; Knox "I am bewildered at you"). It is not the same verb which TEV translates "to be worried" in verse 11, where Paul's worry is characterized by fear. Here it is perhaps characterized by his feeling of doubt or helplessness.

The Example of Hagar and Sarah

21 Let me ask those of you who want to be subject to the Law: do you not hear what the Law says? 22 It says that Abraham had two sons, one by a slave woman, the other by a free woman. 23 His son by the slave woman was born in the usual way, but his son by the free woman was born as a result of God's promise. 24 These things can be understood as a figure: the two women represent two covenants. The one whose children are born in slavery is Hagar, and she represents the covenant made at Mount Sinai. 25 Hagar, who stands for Mount Sinai in Arabia, is*g* a figure of the present city of Jerusalem, in slavery with all its people. 26 But the heavenly Jerusalem is free, and she is our mother. 27 For the scripture says,

"Be happy, you childless woman!
Shout and cry with joy, you
who never felt the pains
of childbirth!
For the woman who was deserted
will have more children
than the woman whose husband
never left her."

28 Now, you, my brothers, are God's children as a result of his promise, just as Isaac was. 29 At that time the son who was born in the usual way persecuted the one who was born because of God's Spirit; and it is the same now. 30 But what does the scripture say? It says, "Send the slave woman and her son away; for the son of the slave woman will not have a part of the father's property along with the son of the free woman." 31 So then, my brothers, we are not the children of a slave woman but of a free woman.

*g*Hagar...is; *some manuscripts have* Sinai is a mountain in Arabia, and it is.   (4.21-31)

21 Tell me, you who desire to be under law, do you not hear the law? 22 For it is written that Abraham had two sons, one by a slave and one by a free woman. 23 But the son of the slave was born according to the flesh, the son of the free woman through promise. 24 Now this is an allegory: these women are two covenants. One is from Mount Sinai, bearing children for slavery; she is Hagar. 25 Now Hagar is Mount Sinai in Arabia;*i* she corresponds to the present Jerusalem, for she is in slavery with her children. 26 But the Jerusalem above is free, and she is our mother. 27 For it is written,

"Rejoice, O barren one that dost
not bear;
break forth and shout, thou who
art not in travail;
for the desolate hath more
children
than she who hath a husband."

28 Now we,*j* brethren, like Isaac, are children of promise. 29 But as at that time he who was born according to the flesh persecuted him who was born according to the Spirit, so it is now. 30 But what does the scripture say? "Cast out the slave and her son; for the son of the slave shall not inherit with the son of the free woman." 31 So, brethren, we are not children of the slave but of the free woman.

*i*Other ancient authorities read *For Sinai is a mountain in Arabia*

*j*Other ancient authorities read *you*   (4.21-31)

The section heading <u>The Example of Hagar and Sarah</u> may be rendered in some languages as simply "The story about Hagar and Sarah." In other languages it may be more appropriate to employ a section heading such as "Paul speaks about Hagar and Sarah," or "What happened to Hagar and Sarah is important."

In this section Paul resumes the argument which ended in verse 7 and which has been interrupted by his personal and intimate address to the Galatians (vv. 8-20). This renewing of the argument comes almost as an afterthought. It seems that Paul is making one last attempt to convince the Galatians of the fallacy of following the Law. The method he uses is that of allegory, a type of interpretation which he has already used in 3.15-18 and which is a very common exegetical device among the rabbis. Simply stated, allegory is interpreting scriptural events and personalities as foreshadowing religious truths. In this passage the two mothers represent two covenants and two communities, and the antagonism between the two sons represents in a sense the conflict between the false teachers and the Galatian believers. The point of the whole argument is that there are two groups claiming to be the sons of Abraham: those who are in bondage and those who are free.

One cannot help but wonder about Paul's motives in using allegory. Could it be that the Galatians are fascinated by rabbinical exegesis? Or is it Paul himself who is attracted to this kind of approach? Are the false teachers using rabbinical exegesis in their attempts to influence the Galatians? Whatever the reason, it is clear that Paul uses this form of interpretation effectively to achieve the aims of his letter.

<u>4.21</u>　　　　　Let me ask those of you who want to be subject to the Law: do you not hear what the Law says?

<u>Let me ask</u> (literally "tell me") signals the change in tone from the preceding section. It is still direct, but now it is less affectionate and more formal. The abruptness of the expression shows that the idea that Paul is about to present had just occurred to him. <u>Let me ask</u> should not be interpreted as requesting permission; rather it is equivalent to "I want to ask a question of those...," or "I want to pose a question to those of you...."

Paul is probably not addressing all his readers but only those <u>who want to be subject to the Law</u>. This statement suggests that not all the Galatians have succumbed to the false teachers, but that many have shown by their actions that they desire to be under the Law and are about to adopt the principles and practices which the Law provides. The phrase <u>subject to the Law</u> is literally "under law" and clearly means being obliged to do what the Law requires in order to win God's approval. In the Greek, "law" does not have an article, and accordingly it is suggested by some commentaries that it means law in general rather than the Jewish Law. It is clear, however, that Paul had in mind the Jewish Law, as this was what the false teachers were presenting to the Galatians. <u>Who want to be subject to the Law</u> may often be rendered simply as "who want to be under obligation to obey what the Law says," or "who want to be controlled by what the Law says." Note, however, that in this passage as well as in a great many others, it may be necessary to specify that this is "the Law of Moses," "the laws of Moses," or "the laws given by means of Moses."

In the question do you not hear what the Law says?, some commentaries see a touch of irony: "you want so much to be subject to the Law, so why don't you listen more carefully to what the Law says?" This is reflected in some translations (JB "you want to be subject to the Law? Then listen to what the Law says"; NEB "tell me ...will you not listen to what the Law says?"). Others, however, see no irony but an earnest and sincere desire on the part of Paul to reach his readers and even the false teachers who honestly believe that to obey the Law is to follow God's will. Do you not hear what the Law says? may be equivalent to "do you really understand what the Law says?" or "...what the laws really mean?" In this particular context hear should be understood in the sense of full comprehension or realization of what is involved. For a language which could not employ a rhetorical question at this point, a strong negative statement may be used, for example, "you do not really understand what the Law is saying."

Law here is specifically the Law, and would refer either to the whole Old Testament, or to the first five books, known as the Torah or the Pentateuch. The suggestion made by some scholars that this question has reference only to the public reading of scripture is too far-fetched to be taken seriously.

4.22   It says that Abraham had two sons, one by a slave woman, the other by a free woman.

Paul now starts his argument from the Law. It says is literally "it is written," a well-known authoritative formula used traditionally to introduce a quotation from scripture. What follows, however, is not a direct quotation but a summary statement. It says may be rendered in some languages as "in the Law one may read," or "in the Law are the words about."

Paul's illustration is again taken from Abraham, this time concentrating on his two sons, Isaac and Ishmael, a story familiar to every Jewish child and which Jewish preachers often used to prove the superiority of their nation to those outside the covenant. The mothers are not at first referred to by name but are described according to status. The slave woman is, of course, Hagar. The word for slave woman properly means a young woman, but by Paul's time it had come to mean a servant or a slave. The free woman is Sarah; free here is in antithesis to slave. The Old Testament account referred to is found in chapters 16, 17, and 21 of Genesis.

The statements one by a slave woman, the other by a free woman may be translated as "a woman who was a slave gave birth to one of his sons, and a free woman gave birth to the other." However, in a number of languages a literal rendering of free woman would be quite misleading, for it would tend to designate a woman who was not married, suggesting a prostitute or a paramour. It may therefore be necessary to say "his wife who was, of course, not a slave." It may also be important to indicate that the slave woman was a slave of his wife, and one may translate "a woman who was his wife's slave gave birth to one of his sons, and his wife gave birth to the other."

4.23 His son by the slave woman was born in the usual way, but his son by the free woman was born as a result of God's promise.

This verse is an expansion of the previous one. Whereas in the previous verse the focus is upon the status of the mothers, here the focus is upon the sons. Ishmael is described as born in the usual way, which is, literally, "born after the flesh." It is tempting to read ethical connotations into the expression, but what Paul has in mind is simply that Ishmael was born according to the natural process and not through divine intervention. When Hagar conceived a child by Abraham, she was obviously young and Abraham had not yet become too old a man to beget a child.

A literal translation of his son by the slave woman was born in the usual way may give rise to serious misunderstanding, particularly in contrast with the following clause. Born in the usual way may suggest that this was simply the normal kind of delivery, that is, with the head of the child coming out first, with the added inference that in some way or other the birth of Isaac was an unusual kind of birth, possibly a breech birth. What is involved here, of course, is not a reference to the manner of birth, but to the fact of coming into existence. One may therefore better translate the first part of this verse in some languages as "Abraham had a son by the slave woman in the same way that children are usually conceived and born."

On the other hand, Isaac was born as a result of God's promise (literally, "through promise"). Clearly this is a reference to the fact that when Isaac was conceived, Abraham and Sarah were already old and presumably incapable of having children and that therefore Isaac was conceived and born as a result of divine intervention. God promised Abraham and Sarah a son, and he fulfilled that promise in the birth of Isaac. Again the focus of attention is not on the manner of birth but on the conception. Therefore one may translate the second part of this verse as "Abraham had a son by his wife, who was not a slave, and this came about because God himself had promised such a son," or "the fact that Abraham had a son by his wife, who was not a slave, happened as a result of what God had promised to Abraham."

4.24 These things can be understood as a figure: the two women represent two covenants. The one whose children are born in slavery is Hagar, and she represents the covenant made at Mount Sinai.

Paul now starts to explain what he means by the Old Testament facts he has just cited. These things can be understood as a figure is literally "which things are being allegorized." To speak allegorically is to take a historical event or a statement and draw from it a meaning quite different from its original significance. In this case, the two women represent two covenants, that is they "stand for" (literally "are") two covenants. For "covenant" see the notes on 3.15 and 17.

It may be necessary to restructure rather radically the statement these things can be understood as a figure. In the first place, these things must refer to the conception and birth of the two sons, and figure must be understood as a comparison which is designed to teach a particular truth. In some languages the closest equivalent may be "What happened in the case of Abraham's two sons may be understood as referring to something important which is true," "...may be compared to something else," or "...may be understood as referring to something else." The statements which follow must then normally be treated as similes or comparisons, for example, "the two women may be compared to the two covenants," or "the two women are like, as it were, two covenants."

Here again Paul finds it unnecessary to add a word of explanation about the term "covenant," assuming common knowledge among his readers. The two covenants referred to are the covenant with Abraham (3.16-18), which has already been mentioned, and the covenant with Moses, enacted at Mount Sinai. Paul finds it more convenient and rewarding to mention the Sinai covenant first and to identify it specifically with Hagar, since no Jew would ever make the connection. Hagar was a slave, and her children would have the same status, unless the father was a free man and cared to adopt the children as his own. Paul concentrates on the status of the children as slaves and applies this to the covenant at Mount Sinai. Hagar represents this covenant, and those who are children of it (that is, share in it) are also born in slavery, since they are in bondage to the Law.

The arguments and the grammatical relations involved in verses 24 and 25 are unusually complex, and therefore it may be important to have some supplementary note indicating the basis for these allegorical comparisons. Such data can be given simply in terms of the historical facts in question. One of the difficulties involved in the second part of this verse is that the one may refer, as far as the Greek text is concerned, either to one of the women or to one of the covenants, because grammatically both terms are feminine in gender. One may therefore say "one of these covenants comes from Mount Sinai," or "one of these women, that is, Hagar, comes from Mount Sinai." In either case, of course, the covenant is made equivalent to Hagar, and Hagar is identified with it. The clause whose children are born in slavery may be made a separate sentence in a number of languages, for example, "Hagar's children became slaves when they were born," or "...were born as slaves."

4.25   Hagar, who stands for Mount Sinai in Arabia, is[g] a figure of the present city of Jerusalem, in slavery with all its people.

> [g]Hagar...is; *some manuscripts have* Sinai is a mountain in Arabia, and it is.

This verse presents difficulties, both in the text and in the interpretation. The textual problems center on two points: whether Hagar is in the text or not, and whether the verse starts with an additive connective, "but" or "and," or with "for" or "because." The omission of Hagar from the text is attested by many old and reliable manuscripts and is reflected in some translations (JB "since Sinai is in Arabia," NEB "Sinai is a mountain in Arabia"). It seems more likely, however, that Hagar was in the original text, and that the omission can be explained by the problems that arose out of trying to understand what Paul meant. In other words, it is much easier to explain the verse with the omission of Hagar (NEB

"Sinai is a mountain in Arabia and it represents the Jerusalem of today").

Assuming, then, that Hagar is part of the original text, we are confronted with the problem of interpreting it. What does Paul mean by the statement "Hagar is Mount Sinai in Arabia" (RSV)? The main explanations are as follows: (1) Hagar is sometimes used to refer to Mount Sinai. This could either be because Hagar in Arabic means Mount Sinai (Twentieth Century "the word Hagar meaning in Arabia [sic] Mount Sinai"), or that Mount Sinai is called Hagar by the Arabs (NAB "the mountain Sinai [Hagar] is in Arabia"). (2) This could be a play on words, based on the Arab word hajar which means "stone," and therefore corresponds to the Mosaic tablets. No translation takes this alternative. (3) It could be that Paul is simply continuing his argument in verse 24 and making the correspondence between Hagar and Mount Sinai more explicit, to make sure that the Jews will not miss the point. In this case, the relation would be understood as stands for (as in TEV) or "represents." This third point seems to be the most likely meaning.

In rendering Hagar, who stands for Mount Sinai, it is necessary in some languages to say "When one speaks of Hagar, one is speaking of Mount Sinai," or "In these comparisons, the name for Hagar is the name for Mount Sinai."

The addition of the phrase in Arabia also gives rise to many theories, among which are (1) Paul wants to emphasize that Mount Sinai is outside the Promised Land, accentuating the fact that the Law was given at a time when the Jews had not yet received the promise of God; (2) Paul wishes to specify Arabia as a land of slavery, thus suggesting that Hagar can only have children who are slaves; (3) Paul simply added the phrase as geographical information, to make sure that his Gentile readers will not miss the point; (4) Paul wants to emphasize that Mount Sinai is in Arabia, the land of the descendants of Ishmael. We cannot be sure as to Paul's motives, but the third of these options seems to be the least problematic and therefore to be preferred. One should resist the temptation of reading various kinds of interpretation into a simple statement of fact.

Hagar not only stands for Mount Sinai, but she is also a figure of (literally "corresponds to") the present city of Jerusalem. Jerusalem here should be understood as standing for the whole Jewish nation with Jerusalem as its center. The concluding phrase in slavery with all its people is literally "in bondage with her children," with "children" rightly understood as referring to the whole Jewish people and not simply to the inhabitants of Jerusalem. The connection with Hagar is clearly obvious: just as Hagar can only bear children who are slaves, so the whole Jewish system of seeking for God's approval by means of following the Law only results in the Jews becoming slaves to the Law and not children of God. Some commentators find a double sense in this reference to Jerusalem: a Jerusalem under Roman occupation and under bondage to the Law.

Is a figure of the present city of Jerusalem may be rendered as "may also be compared to the present city of Jerusalem," or "...to what is now the city of Jerusalem." The introduction of the comparison may also be stated as "we can also compare Hagar to the city of Jerusalem," with the first part of the verse rendered as an independent clause also.

4.26

The phrase in slavery with all its people may require some expansion in certain languages, for example, "Jerusalem is like a slave, and so are all of its people," "...all of the people related to Jerusalem," or "...all of the people who look to Jerusalem."

4.26   But the heavenly Jerusalem is free, and she is our mother.

Paul now presents the contrast between the present city of Jerusalem and the heavenly Jerusalem, the former in slavery while the latter is free. The image of the heavenly Jerusalem was evidently common among Jews even before the Christian era, and it occurs elsewhere in the New Testament, particularly in the book of Revelation (3.12; 21.2,9 ff.). Perhaps one should not understand the heavenly Jerusalem in an eschatological sense ("the Jerusalem up in heaven") or in a futuristic sense ("the Jerusalem which is to come") but simply in a figurative sense. Just as the present city of Jerusalem refers to the Jewish nation, so the Jerusalem above refers to the church as the community of those who have put their faith and trust in Jesus Christ. In this community there is freedom from bondage to law and freedom to become sons or children of God.

It may be quite difficult to find in some receptor languages a term such as heavenly which will suggest a qualitative distinction applicable to Jerusalem. The Greek text itself simply says "the above Jerusalem." The closest equivalent in some languages may be "the Jerusalem related to heaven" or "the Jerusalem which has to do with heaven." In some languages the most appropriate contrast seems to be between "the Jerusalem on earth" and "the Jerusalem of God."

As in various other contexts, it may be best to translate is free as "is not a slave."

Paul continues the figure of a mother: this heavenly Jerusalem is our mother. Sarah is not specifically named, but Paul assumes that his readers will make the appropriate connection. The term our refers to all Christian believers, and the idea of motherhood includes membership in the Christian community, together with nourishment and spiritual growth within its fellowship. It may be necessary to change the metaphor she is our mother into a simile, "this Jerusalem is just like our mother," or "...is like a mother to us."

4.27   For the scripture says,
              "Be happy, you childless woman!
                  Shout and cry with joy, you who never felt the pains of
                      childbirth!
              For the woman who was deserted will have more children
                  than the woman whose husband never left her."

Paul further supports his concept of two Jerusalems with a quotation from the Old Testament, specifically Isa 54.1 quoted from the Septuagint. The quotation has some slight variations from the Hebrew text, but the translator should translate the quotation as Paul has it and not the way it may appear in the Old Testament.

This Old Testament passage of scripture reflects the time that the Jews

[114]

were in exile in Babylon, away from their homeland. In this passage Jerusalem is viewed in two ways: (1) Jerusalem without its inhabitants, and therefore desolate, is represented as a childless woman (literally "barren one," that is, incapable of bearing children), while (2) Jerusalem before the exile is represented as a woman whose husband never left her. The "barren" or childless woman is exhorted to be happy and to shout and cry with joy (literally "break forth and shout," which calls for glad and loud exclamations). The first two lines of the prophecy are parallel to each other, and therefore the "barren" woman is the same as the one who never felt the pains of childbirth. The idea of having more children refers to the hoped for and expected return of the exiles from captivity.

In a number of languages it is necessary to identify who is being spoken to before a command can be given. Therefore, it may be necessary to alter the order in the first two lines of the scripture quotation so as to read "You woman, who has never had children, be happy! You who never had the pain of childbirth, shout and cry for joy!" In some languages, however, this kind of translation might suggest that two different women are being addressed. Since the two parallel lines obviously refer to the same person and the same experience, it may be more appropriate in some languages to translate "You woman who have never had children and have never felt the pain of giving birth to children, be happy, shout and exclaim with joy!"

In citing this passage from Isaiah, it is quite possible that Paul is referring to Sarah when he speaks of the barren woman and to Hagar when he speaks of the woman whose husband never left her. It is more likely, however, that the barren woman refers to the heavenly Jerusalem, and the woman with a husband to the present city of Jerusalem. The idea of having more children is perhaps best interpreted to refer not simply to the entrance of both Jews and Gentiles into the fellowship of the church, but primarily in terms of the more desired gifts of freedom and of becoming children of God. The woman who was deserted may be rendered as "the woman whose husband had abandoned her."

4.28   Now, you, my brothers, are God's children as a result of his
           promise, just as Isaac was.

Paul here starts to apply the allegory specifically to his readers, at the same time bringing to their attention the two sons of Abraham, whose mothers have so far been the focus of Paul's discourse. Now at the beginning of the verse is clearly continuative rather than temporal. The closest equivalent in some languages is "on the basis of this comparison," or simply "hence" or "therefore."

Some translations adopt the reading "we" instead of "you," but the latter seems to be the better reading, both from external and internal evidences. Paul once again addresses his readers with the more or less formal my brothers, which he has used twice before. As in many similar contexts, this may be rendered as "my fellow believers" or "you who trust Christ along with me."

They are God's children as a result of his promise (literally, "are children of promise"). The clue to the meaning of the expression is found in the last part of the verse: just as Isaac was. Just as Isaac was conceived, not through natural

[115]

means, but through the fulfillment of God's promise, so the Galatians also have become God's children, not through their own efforts, much less through natural and physical descent, but exclusively as a fulfillment of what God promised to Abraham.

As a result of his promise may be rendered as "because that was the way in which God had promised it would happen," or "because God had made a promise."

The final clause, just as Isaac was, may require certain expansion because of the rather severe ellipsis, for example, "in the same way Isaac became Abraham's son because of what God had promised," or "in the same way Abraham had a son, Isaac, because of what God had promised," or "...because God had promised Abraham that such would happen."

4.29   At that time the son who was born in the usual way persecuted the one who was born because of God's Spirit; and it is the same now.

In the relationship between the two sons of Abraham, Paul finds an allegorical reference to the relationship between the Jews, particularly the false teachers, and the Christians, particularly the Galatian believers.

The son who was born in the usual way (literally, "the one born according to the flesh," as in verse 23) refers to Ishmael, and the one who was born because of God's Spirit refers to Isaac. For God's Spirit, the Greek simply has "spirit," and while some translations take this in the sense of "spiritual" (NEB Phps Knox NAB), it is in accordance with Pauline usage to take this as referring to the Holy Spirit (TEV JB). The switch from "promise" (vv. 23, 28) to "spirit" reminds us of the language of chapter 3.

As in the case of verse 23, it is important to render the son who was born in the usual way in a manner which will not suggest some physical aspect of birth. In this context it may be necessary in some languages simply to say "At that time Abraham's son by means of Hagar persecuted the son who was born because of what God's Spirit had said," or "...because of what God's Spirit had done." The Greek text simply says "according to spirit," but since the focus has been upon the birth of Isaac resulting from the promise of God, it is quite legitimate to fill out the semantic ellipsis by indicating that the birth took place as "the result of what God's Spirit had promised," or "...caused to happen."

The final clause and it is the same now refers either to the persecution or to the type of personalities involved. One may therefore say "and the same kind of persecution takes place now," or "there are the corresponding kinds of persons even now."

4.30   But what does the scripture say? It says, "Send the slave woman and her son away; for the son of the slave woman will not have a part of the father's property along with the son of the free woman."

The connective but at the beginning of this verse marks Paul's alternative to the persecution mentioned in the previous verse (cf. Phps "yet").

For languages in which one cannot speak of the scripture or "the Hebrew

Scriptures (equivalent to the Old Testament) saying something, it may be possible, as in many other contexts, to read "But what does one read in the Scriptures?" or "...the Holy Writings?"

The quotation itself is from Gen 21.10 and consists of the words of Sarah to Abraham, asking him to do something either because of Ishmael's hostility towards Isaac or because of his inheriting along with Isaac. Paul quotes from the Septuagint, as is his usual practice, but he makes certain innovations. While the Septuagint ends with "will not inherit with my son Isaac," Paul changes this to "will not inherit with the son of the free woman." This should not bother us, for biblical writers frequently made adaptations in their quotations to suit their particular purposes. One should also remember that at that time very few copies of Scripture were available, and most quotations were made from memory, thus allowing a certain degree of freedom in rendering the meaning of a quotation rather than a strictly literal repetition of its words.

In place of Send the slave woman and her son away, it may be more appropriate in a number of languages to translate as "Banish the slave woman and her son," or "Make the slave woman and her son go away."

The phrase will not have a part of the father's property is literally "will not inherit." As employed by Paul in this context, "inherit" is used in the sense of receiving what God has promised. For translating this word, see the comments on Gal 3.18, 29; 4.1, 7. One must translate in some languages "the son of the slave woman must not have any of the father's property; it is to go to the son of the free woman," or "...the son of the father's wife who is not a slave."

4.31   So then, my brothers, we are not the children of a slave woman but of a free woman.

Paul now concludes his discussion with a statement of what he has been trying to say to the Galatians through this rather complicated and involved allegorical argument. Appropriately, he starts with so then, marking what follows as a conclusion of what has been said (Knox "you see, then"; NAB "therefore").

Once more there is a shift in pronouns from the second person plural you of verse 28 to a first person plural we. This we should be understood as inclusive, referring to all members of the Christian community, including Paul himself.

Paul maintains the figure of sonship. He denies that we are...the children of a slave woman and affirms that we are children of a free woman. One should note that there is no definite article before slave woman, thus emphasizing that slavery is not a monopoly of the Jewish system. What Paul is saying is that we are not children of any slave woman, whether it be Judaistic legalism or any form of heathen ritual and practice. The statement we are not the children of a slave woman must be marked as a simile in some languages, for example, "we are not, so to speak, the children of a woman who was a slave." In this context it may be necessary in certain languages to translate a free woman as "a wife who is free" or "a wife who is not a slave." This is required since in this type of context a free woman could be misconstrued as a woman of "free morals."

CHAPTER 5

TEV	RSV
Preserve Your Freedom	
1 Freedom is what we have--Christ has set us free! Stand, then, as free people, and do not allow yourselves to become slaves again.	1 For freedom Christ has set us free; stand fast therefore, and do not submit again to a yoke of slavery.
2 Listen! I, Paul, tell you that if you allow yourselves to be circumcised, it means that Christ is of no use to you at all. 3 Once more I warn any man who allows himself to be circumcised that he is obliged to obey the whole Law. 4 Those of you who try to be put right with God by obeying the Law have cut yourselves off from Christ. You are outside God's grace. 5 As for us, our hope is that God will put us right with him; and this is what we wait for by the power of God's Spirit working through our faith. 6 For when we are in union with Christ Jesus, neither circumcision nor the lack of it makes any difference at all; what matters is faith that works through love.	2 Now I, Paul, say to you that if you receive circumcision, Christ will be of no advantage to you. 3 I testify again to every man who receives circumcision that he is bound to keep the whole law. 4 You are severed from Christ, you who would be justified by the law; you have fallen away from grace. 5 For through the Spirit, by faith, we wait for the hope of righteousness. 6 For in Christ Jesus neither circumcision nor uncircumcision is of any avail, but faith working through love. (5.1-6)
(5.1-6)	

Paul spoke of freedom in the closing verse of chapter 4. Now he proceeds to discuss the subject further, starting with a general statement about freedom as a gift from Christ and a warning to his readers not to lose this freedom. In the next two verses he specifies the kind of slavery that he has in mind, namely, slavery to the Law, of which circumcision is the starting point. He ends this section with a profound statement regarding the Christian alternative to slavery.

The section heading <u>Preserve Your Freedom</u> may be rendered as "Remain free" or, negatively, "Do not become slaves again." It is equally possible to use the expression "Christ has set us free," since this so well characterizes the dominant theme in this portion of chapter 5.

<u>5.1</u>   Freedom is what we have—Christ has set us free! Stand, then, as free people, and do not allow yourselves to become slaves again.

There is an obvious connection between this verse and the preceding one (4.31); both are concerned with freedom. Accordingly, it is sometimes preferred to include 5.1 with the preceding section rather than with what follows, as is the case in the UBS Greek New Testament.

[118]

This close relation, coupled with the unusual construction of the first part of this verse, has given rise to serious textual problems, various solutions of which are reflected in modern translations. The decision we have to take regarding the textual variants centers primarily on whether one should take 5.1 with what immediately precedes or with what follows. If the former, the following rendering is possible: "We are children... of the free woman with the freedom for which Christ set us free" (Mft; cf. Knox "we are sons of the free woman, not of the slave; such is the freedom Christ has won for us"). The evidence, however, strongly favors the latter alternative, and this is reflected in TEV.

After deciding what text to follow, one has to determine what Paul means by the statements in this verse. The grammatical form of "freedom" is dative, and this can be either a dative of instrument or a dative of purpose or designation. If the dative of instrument is understood, the following rendering is possible: "by means of this freedom Christ set us free." Most translators, however, understand here a dative of purpose, so that Paul is understood to be saying "Christ has set us free in order that we can live as free people" (JB "when Christ freed us, he meant us to remain free"; NEB "Christ set us free, to be free men").

Freedom here should be understood as freedom from the Law, and the pronoun us is inclusive, referring to both Paul and his readers.

Though the TEV rendering Freedom is what we have—Christ has set us free! is rhetorically effective and indicates a close relation to the preceding verse, it may be difficult to reproduce this type of structure in another language, especially if the freedom which the Christian possesses is to be interpreted as the purpose for which Christ set believers free. Therefore one may translate "Christ has set us free so that we could truly be free." In a number of languages, however, there is no appropriate term for "free" which would suggest freedom from arbitrary obligations or control, and therefore it may be necessary to speak of being free in terms of "not being slaves," for example, "Christ has rescued us so that we need not be slaves at all," or "... so that we need not live like slaves."

The last part of the verse presents both exhortation and warning. Stand, then, as free people is intensive and is better translated "stand firm" or, in a figurative sense, "dig your heels in firmly." While the Greek does not have as free people, yet it is clear that what Paul wants the Galatians to be firm about is their freedom in Christ. Stand, then, as free people may be rendered as "Determine to remain free," or "Be sure that you remain as people who have been released."

Do not allow yourselves to become slaves again is literally "do not be caught again by a yoke of slavery." The verb Paul uses means "to be ensnared" and is in the passive form; the false teachers are the implied agents.

Paul refers to "a" yoke of slavery, not "the" yoke, thus addressing both Jews and Gentiles. Any legalistic system, whether Jewish or Gentile, is bound to make slaves of people. The yoke is an appropriate metaphor for bondage, since an animal under a yoke has to obey its master. The Jew spoke of "taking the yoke of the law" upon himself, and it could be that the false teachers have been using this kind of language with the Galatians.

It is interesting to note that Jesus also used the figure of the yoke, but to describe obedience and apostleship (Matt 11.29).

In translating this type of expression, there are three alternatives: (1) the figure can be retained, as long as the readers understand what it means ; (2) another metaphor can be substituted (as in Phps "shackles of slavery"); (3) the metaphor can be replaced by a nonmetaphor, as in TEV.

The addition of <u>again</u> makes it clear that Paul is referring to their former state of subservience either to the Jewish or to the pagan system before they accepted the Christian message.

In rendering <u>do not allow yourselves to become slaves again,</u> it may be important to indicate some type of agent, for example, "do not let people cause you to become slaves again," or "...to enslave you again." It may be, however, that a reference to "becoming slaves" or "enslaving" would be understood only in a literal sense. One may therefore change the metaphor into a simile, for example, "to become like slaves again," or "to live as though you were slaves again."

<u>5.2</u>   Listen! I, Paul, tell you that if you allow yourselves to be circumcised, it means that Christ is of no use to you at all.

Paul accents the importance of what he is going to say by the very way he starts. <u>Listen!</u> is emphatic and invites the readers to pay special attention to what follows (NAB "pay close attention to me"; NEB "mark my words"). The formula <u>I, Paul</u> is present in some other letters of Paul. It does not at this point indicate that Paul is personally doing the writing; one has to wait until 6.11 to learn that. The meaning here is that he is accenting the fact that this information is coming from him, and is therefore authoritative in two ways: (1) he is an apostle and (2) he knows what he is talking about, since he has gone through the pain and agony of seeking the approval of God through the path of circumcision. His audience is clearly the Galatian Gentile Christians, as indicated by Paul's use of the plural <u>you</u> and the way he talks about circumcision.

It may be important in some languages to combine <u>Listen!</u> with what immediately follows, for example, "Listen to what I, Paul, am telling you," or "... what I am going to say to you." In order to emphasize the force of the command, it may be important in some languages to use an idiomatic expression such as "Listen with both of your ears," "Listen to nothing else but what I am going to tell you," or, as in one language, "Take the wax out of your ears."

The way the conditional sentence is constructed in Greek may suggest that the Galatians have not yet taken the step of being circumcised, but that they are considering it and are at the verge of submitting to it. TEV makes this information explicit: <u>if you allow yourselves to be circumcised</u> (Phps "if you consent to be circumcised").

Circumcision, as already noted, was the rite of initiation among the Jews whereby a person was accepted into the Jewish fellowship.

The introduction of the subject of circumcision here seems rather abrupt, as Paul has not discussed it at all in the preceding chapters. He does, however, intimate that it is a problem when he mentions the case of Titus (2.1-5). The passive expression <u>allow yourselves to be circumcised</u> may be changed into an active one by saying "allow others to circumcise you," or "permit men to circumcise you."

Apparently, the false teachers have put forth the claim that for the Galatians to be really Christians, they must first accept the rite of circumcision; in other words, they must become Jews before they can become believers in Christ. That would explain the meaning of Paul's statement: <u>Christ is of no use to you at all</u>. Submission to circumcision would be to adopt the notion that one can win God's approval through some legalistic ritual or through doing what the Law requires, and this would constitute a complete denial of the fact that freedom and sonship are God's gifts through Jesus Christ. Paul's statement, therefore, could mean that the Galatians make meaningless what Christ has done for them in order that they might receive the gift of sonship from God. Since the term <u>Christ</u> as used here refers essentially to what Christ did rather than to Christ as a person, it may be important to say in some languages "This means that what Christ has done for you is of no value at all." The same thought may be stated in a rather different fashion in some languages, for example, "This means that you cannot benefit in any way from what Christ did." In some languages the closest equivalent would be "This means that Christ cannot help you at all."

<u>5.3</u>   Once more I warn any man who allows himself to be circumcised that he is obliged to obey the whole Law.

Paul now gives a further reason why a man should not submit to circumcision. In verse 2 he has stated what would be lost: they would lose Christ. Here he states what would be gained: they would gain the whole Law; but this would be at the price of loss of freedom.

<u>Once more</u> (literally "again") can be interpreted to refer either to an earlier statement of Paul (perhaps made on the occasion referred to in 4.16 and 1.9) or to the verse immediately preceding. The close relation between the two verses tends to give more weight to the latter of these (Phps "I will say it again").

<u>I warn</u> is literally "I testify." The verb can be used to mean "to declare" or "to protest," but here it has the primary meaning of "to warn" (JB "I repeat my warning"; Knox cf. NEB "you can take it from me"). After a verb such as <u>warn</u>, it may be necessary in a number of languages to use direct discourse, for example, "Once more I warn any man who lets others circumcise him, You must now obey the whole Law," or "...every regulation in the Law."

As in verse 2 Paul is addressing someone who has apparently not yet been circumcised but is about to submit to that rite. Paul's warning is clear: anyone who receives circumcision <u>is obliged to obey the whole Law</u>. Paul has already discussed certain aspects of this problem in relation to Christ (see the comments on 3.7-14, especially v. 10). Circumcision is only one part of the Law, but to accept it is to obligate oneself to obey everything in the Law. As in several other contexts, the reference to <u>Law</u> may need to be translated as "the laws given by means of Moses." However, the <u>Law</u> here may possibly be understood as referring to the whole body of laws found in the Old Testament, together, perhaps, with other laws that developed out of the Old Testament tradition. In that case the whole Law may be translated as "every one of the regulations of the laws," or "every one of the specific laws."

5.4   Those of you who try to be put right with God by obeying the Law have cut yourselves off from Christ. You are outside God's grace.

Paul further narrows down his audience and now addresses those among the Galatians who have already accepted the principle of winning God's approval by following the Law. This is made clear by those of you who try (NAB "any of you"). Other modern translations give the impression that Paul is still talking to all the Galatians, but the context does not support this interpretation.

To be put right with God by obeying the Law is literally "to be justified by the law" (compare the expressions used in Gal 2.16 and 3.11). In this context those of you who try to be put right with God may be rendered as "those of you who try to get right with God," "... put yourselves right with God," or "... become right with God." On the other hand, some languages would require some such expression as "try to make yourself acceptable to God," or "try to cause God to accept you."

The expression of means in the phrase by obeying the Law may be rendered as cause in some languages, "because you do what the Law says."

Those who put their trust in the Law as a means of winning God's approval have cut themselves off from Christ. The verb here is used by Paul elsewhere in this letter (3.17) to mean "nullify" or "make ineffective" (compare also Paul's use of this verb in Rom 7.2, where it relates to "being freed from a marriage bond"), and so here it would mean to be separated from Christ (NEB "your relation with Christ is completely severed"). That means that they are no longer in Christ, that is, in union and fellowship with him.

Have cut yourselves off from Christ may thus be rendered as "have completely separated yourselves from Christ." This meaning may be expressed idiomatically in some languages as "have destroyed your bond with Christ," or "have destroyed what ties you to Christ."

Furthermore, they are outside God's grace (literally, "you have fallen away from grace"). Grace here may refer either to God's or Christ's grace, but most translators prefer the former interpretation. For a discussion of grace, see under 1.6. So here also as in 1.6, grace includes the components of undeserved love and free gift. To obey the Law in order to win God's approval is to turn one's back on God's gift of sonship. The expression "you have fallen away" should be understood, not in the sense that grace has been taken away from them, but in the sense that they have turned their backs on it (NEB "you have fallen out of the domain of God's grace"; Phps "you put yourself outside the range of his grace"). One may also say "you have put yourself in a place where God's goodness cannot find you," "... where God cannot be good to you," or "... show you his goodness."

5.5 As for us, our hope is that God will put us right with him; and this is what we wait for by the power of God's Spirit working through our faith.

As for us is literally "for we." "For" indicates that Paul here presents an argument which in a sense explains the previous verse by pointing up the contrasts involved. "We" is emphatic and refers to Paul and others who do not depend on the Law but on Christ, in contrast to those who depend on the Law. An exclusive form of "we" would suit the context better: "we" in contrast to "you" in the previous verse.

The statement of verse 5 seems to summarize everything that Paul has been talking about. RSV translates it as "For through the Spirit, by faith, we wait for the hope of righteousness." "Righteousness" means here, as it does in 2.16 and 2.21, God's activity of putting men right with himself. This is what we hope for, and "hope" includes the elements of assurance and expectation. That is also what we wait for. The verb used is intensive and can be translated "to wait eagerly" or "to wait patiently." In a number of languages hope can only be expressed as involving a combination of confidence and expectation with regard to the future. One may translate our hope as "we look forward to what will happen and we are sure of it."

This "righteousness" is therefore in the future, and the TEV rendering is correct: God will put us right with him. One should not, however, deduce from this that Paul did not believe in the experience of a right relationship with God as a present reality. It may be that here he is talking eschatologically, that is, of the final day, when man will experience perfect and full reconciliation with God.

"Spirit" here does not have the article, and while some understand that this means "spirit" in contrast to "flesh," most translators take it to refer to the Holy Spirit, in accordance with general Pauline usage (cf. 3.3). "By faith" could have as its object either "God" or "Christ." As elsewhere, "faith" here has the element not only of belief, but also of trust and confidence in someone.

Some take "through the Spirit" to be connected with the waiting (NAB "it is in the spirit that we eagerly await"), while others take it to be connected with the hoping (Knox "all our hope of justification lies in the spirit"). "By faith," on the other hand, is sometimes connected with the hoping (Knox "it [hope] rests on our faith"), while others connect it with the waiting (Phps "it is by faith that we await in His Spirit the righteousness we hope to see"). TEV connects "through the Spirit" with the waiting; whereas NEB connects "the Spirit" with the hoping. Both TEV and NEB relate "faith" to the work of the Spirit. But the other renderings can also be regarded as legitimate.

And this is what we wait for is essentially equivalent to "this is what we are looking forward to"; expectation is one of the components of hope.

If the phrase by the power of God's Spirit is to be understood with hope, one may need to translate "we hope because of what God's Spirit has done." Similarly, if through our faith is likewise to be combined with hope, one may also say "we hope by means of our faith in Christ," "...because of our confidence in Christ," or "...because we trust in Christ." If, however, by the power of God's

Spirit and through our faith are regarded as qualifying the way in which we wait for God to put us right with him, one may translate "this is what we are waiting for; God's Spirit helps us and we are sustained by our trust in Christ."

5.6   For when we are in union with Christ Jesus, neither circumcision nor the lack of it makes any difference at all; what matters is faith that works through love.

Paul now expands the statement of verse 5. To be "in Christ Jesus" is to be united with him in faith and in fellowship. As has been noted in several other contexts, the expression "in Christ Jesus" may be rendered in various ways, for example, "one together with Christ Jesus," "tied closely with Christ Jesus," or "closely related to Christ Jesus."

In this state, Paul does not find room for either circumcision nor the lack of it. The phrase translated makes any difference at all expresses the idea of irrelevance or insignificance (JB "makes no difference," Knox "means nothing," NAB "neither...counts for anything").

It is interesting that Paul here includes the lack of circumcision. He has been very harsh against those who have been advocating circumcision. Now he wants to make it clear that, on the other hand, he would not allow the Gentiles to use their state of uncircumcision as an occasion for claiming that they are in the right with God. If a man is in Christ Jesus, physical conditions of any kind are not essential to that relationship.

The phrase neither circumcision nor the lack of it must be rendered in some languages as conditional expressions, for example, "if a man is circumcised or if he is not circumcised," or "if men have been circumcised or if they have never been circumcised." The following expression makes any difference at all may then be rendered as "this does not make any difference," or "it is all the same." In some languages the same meaning may be communicated by a rendering such as "whether a man is circumcised or not makes no difference," "... is all the same," or "...is not important."

If that is the case, then what is important? Paul says it is faith that works through love. "Faith" here once again is trust in, submission to, and commitment of oneself to Christ. This kind of faith works through love. (Paul's mention of love here seems to anticipate what he is going to say later in verses 13 ff.) The verb phrase should probably be understood as "expresses itself through love" (NAB). Love should probably be understood primarily as care and concern for people, and not as a reference to God's love for man or man's love for God.

The expression what matters may be rendered as "but what is important" or "but what does make a difference." The particular form of expression to introduce the final part of this verse will depend, of course, upon the corresponding form used in the immediately preceding clause.

In some languages it is quite impossible to use nouns such as faith and love as they occur in this verse, for faith and love do not do anything apart from the persons who have faith and who show love. Therefore one may translate this clause as "but what does make a difference is the fact that we (or, people) trust

Christ, and this becomes evident through our (or, their) loving other people," or "... showing love to other people."

It is possible, however, to interpret the verb <u>works</u> as passive and to understand <u>love</u> in the sense of God's love rather than human love. <u>Faith that works through love</u> would then mean "faith which is made effective by God's love." No translation, however, has this interpretation.

TEV	RSV
7 You were doing so well! Who made you stop obeying the truth? How did he persuade you? 8 It was not done by God, who calls you. 9 "It takes only a little yeast to make the whole batch of dough rise," as they say. 10 But I still feel confident about you. Our life in union with the Lord makes me confident that you will not take a different view and that the man who is upsetting you, whoever he is, will be punished by God. (5.7-10)	7 You were running well; who hindered you from obeying the truth? 8 This persuasion is not from him who called you. 9 A little leaven leavens the whole lump. 10 I have confidence in the Lord that you will take no other view than mine; and he who is troubling you will bear his judgment, whoever he is. (5.7-10)

Once again (as in 4.12) Paul introduces a type of parenthetical theme. He temporarily postpones the topic of faith and love, and deals once more with reminiscences of the Galatians' behavior before they succumbed to the false teachers.

5.7   You were doing so well! Who made you stop obeying the truth? How did he persuade you?

You were doing so well! is literally "you were running well." The figure of running a race is one of Paul's favorites when talking of moral efforts. Most translations keep the metaphor, but TEV drops it in favor of a simple statement of its meaning (also Phps "you were making splendid progress"). It may be useful in this particular context to indicate that the progress the believers were making was in their relationship to Christ, for example, "You were progressing so well in your relationship to Christ," or "... in the way in which you trusted Christ."

The verb translated <u>made you stop</u> has the primary meaning of "to hinder" (RSV). It is tempting to continue the metaphor of the race track and to interpret the verb as "put you off the course" (Phps) or "diverted you from the path of truth" (NAB). But perhaps it is better to assume that Paul is mixing metaphors, since the verb here is used in military operations and signifies breaking up a road to render it impassable.

The tense of the verb (aorist) indicates that the work of the false teachers has already been done and that in some way the Galatians have stopped <u>obeying the truth</u>. <u>Truth</u> here is the message which Paul had proclaimed to the Galatians. <u>Who made you stop obeying the truth?</u> may be rendered as "who caused you to

stop obeying the true words?", or even "...the true words about God?" In some
languages it is simply impossible to speak of "truth" without indicating what is
true. One may therefore have "true words," "true words about God," or "the true
Good News." This could be an indirect reference to the initial presentation of the
gospel in chapter 1.6-9.

The question How did he persuade you? really belongs to verse 8; it is an
expansion of a nominal form of the verb "to persuade."

5.8   It was not done by God, who calls you.

Some suggest a play on words between "persuade" and "obey," since their
roots are related. However, this is hard to reproduce in English, and few translators attempt it.

The action of the Galatians is hard to explain, and whoever caused it must
have had some special method. Paul is only sure of one thing: this kind of per-
suasion did not come from God. Literally, the text has "him who calls you," but
from Pauline usage this clearly means God (see 1.6, 15).

It was not done by God, who calls you may be understood as a negative response to the question Who made you stop obeying the truth? This verse may
therefore be rendered as "It was certainly not God, since he is the one who calls
you," or "...has called you." As in other contexts, it is important in employing
a verb meaning call to avoid an expression which would simply mean "to shout
at." The meaning here is essentially "invite you to become his own," or, as in
some languages, "urges you to come to him."

5.9   "It takes only a little yeast to make the whole batch of dough rise," as
          they say.

Paul here quotes a proverbial saying which he uses elsewhere (see 1 Cor
5.6). The amount of yeast is very small in proportion to the total lump of dough,
but it is used to make...rise (that is, to ferment or leaven) the whole lump. In
the New Testament yeast is used as a symbol of the pervasive influence either of
evil or of good (as in Matt 13.33). Paul's emphasis is on the former. The meaning of the proverb is fairly obvious: evil, no matter how small it seems, will
always in the end result in great harm. Paul may be applying the proverb either
to the teachers, who obviously were only a handful, or to their teaching, especially to their possible insistence on circumcision as only a small thing.

The action of yeast on a batch of dough is expressed quite differently in
various languages, for example, "only a little yeast can make a large batch of
dough grow big," "...can soon sour a great deal of dough," or "...is needed for
a big loaf of bread."

The expression as they say is not in the Greek text but is legitimately
added here to mark the previous statement as a proverb or popular saying. It
may be rendered in some languages as "there is a saying that," "one often hears
it said," or even "people often say."

5.10   But I still feel confident about you. Our life in union with the Lord
        makes me confident that you will not take a different view and that the
        man who is upsetting you, whoever he is, will be punished by God.

Paul switches from an attitude of despair (4.19-20) to an expression of
confidence in his readers.

The first part of the verse is literally "I have confidence in the Lord." Several things should be noted.

I is emphatic and has the sense either of "I know you well, and therefore I
am confident," or "I, regardless of what others might think."

The phrase "in the Lord" occurs some forty times in Paul's writings. In
accordance with his usage, it should refer to Christ. The meaning of the expression in this particular context depends on one's conclusion regarding its relation
to Paul's confidence. It could denote the object of Paul's confidence, that is, "I
am confident about your being in the Lord," or "...united with the Lord." Most
modern translators, however, understand "in the Lord" as the basis for Paul's
confidence (JB "I feel sure that, united in the Lord"; NEB "united with you in the
Lord, I am confident"). The causal relation between our life in union with the
Lord and Paul's confidence may be expressed in some languages by a clause of
cause, for example, "because we are all joined together with the Lord, I am
sure that...."

You will not take a different view may have as its reference Paul's general
position as reflected in the letter (RSV "you will take no other view than mine";
Knox "you will be of the same mind with me") or Paul's statement in verses 7-9
(as it seems to be in JB "you will agree with me"). Many translations, including
TEV, leave the statement ambiguous (NEB "you will not take the wrong view";
NAB "you will not adopt a different view").

It is possible to interpret the man who is upsetting you as referring to all
the false teachers, with a singular standing for the whole (Knox "leaving the disturbers of your peace, be they who they may"), or as a general statement referring to no one in particular but to anyone who disturbs (JB "anybody who troubles
you," NAB "whoever it is that is unsettling you"). Many scholars, however, take
the position that Paul has a specific person in mind, perhaps the leader of the
false teachers. In that case, the expression whoever he is might indicate that
he has quite a high position within the group. It could, however, only emphasize
the indefiniteness of the reference.

The expression will be punished by God is literally "will bear the judgment,"
but it is clear from the context that this has reference to God's act in regard to
the disturber, and that this act carries with it both judgment and punishment.

Paul's confidence expresses itself with respect to two situations: (1) that
the believers in Galatia will ultimately not have a different view from what Paul
has, and (2) that the man who has been causing the trouble will be punished by
God. It is necessary in a number of languages to divide the content of these two
expressions of confidence into two completely different sentences, for example,
"Because we are joined together with the Lord, I am sure that you will not see
things differently from the way in which I see them. I am also sure that the man

who is disturbing you, whoever that man happens to be, will suffer punishment by God," or "...God will punish the one who is upsetting you, it makes no difference who he is."

TEV	RSV
11 But as for me, my brothers, if I continue to preach that circumcision is necessary, why am I still being persecuted? If that were true, then my preaching about the cross of Christ would cause no trouble. 12 I wish that the people who are upsetting you would go all the way; let them go on and castrate themselves! (5.11-12)	11 But if I, brethren, still preach circumcision, why am I still persecuted? In that case the stumbling block of the cross has been removed. 12 I wish those who unsettle you would mutilate themselves! (5.11-12)

Again, Paul shifts rapidly to another closely related topic, namely, the relation of circumcision to his preaching and to other people's attitudes towards him.

5.11   But as for me, my brothers, if I continue to preach that circumcision is necessary, why am I still being persecuted? If that were true, then my preaching about the cross of Christ would cause no trouble.

The first part of this verse consists of a conditional clause, "if I still preach circumcision," and a rhetorical question, "why am I still persecuted?" The conditional clause could reflect either a charge against Paul by his enemies or a hypothetical case: "if I were preaching...." Most translators favor the former position, in which case it is implied that there was a time ("still") when Paul actually advocated circumcision. To "preach circumcision" is of course to advocate that circumcision is necessary in order for one to be accepted by God (Knox "I preach the need of circumcision"). In order to make it quite clear that Paul no longer was preaching that circumcision was necessary, it may be essential to indicate that this was an accusation brought by some of the Judaizers. The condition may then be translated as "if, as they say, I continue to preach that men must be circumcised."

The passive expression why am I still being persecuted? may be made active by translating "why do people still persecute me?" or "...cause me harm?"

As in other contexts, my brothers may be understood as "you, my fellow believers," or "you who also believe in Christ."

It may be necessary in some languages to relate the phrase as for me somewhat more closely to what follows, for example, "now consider my situation. Why am I still persecuted...?"

The rhetorical question denies the charge contained in the conditional clause. What the whole sentence means is that if it were really true that Paul was still preaching the necessity of circumcision, he would not be persecuted; or, to state it another way, since Paul is still being persecuted, then it is not true that he continues to preach that circumcision is necessary. If one adopts the interpretation that the condition is purely hypothetical and so contrary to fact, it may be necessary to translate it as "if I were continuing to preach that men must be circumcised—but, of course, I am not preaching that—then...."

The condition if that were true must refer not to circumcision being true, but to the preaching concerning the necessity of circumcision. Therefore, if that were true may be rendered as "if I were really doing that," or "if I really were preaching that."

A further consequence of Paul's alleged continuing advocacy of circumcision would be that his preaching about the cross of Christ would cause no trouble. The expression would cause no trouble translates two words, a noun which is traditionally rendered "stumblingblock" and a verb which means "to cease" or "to pass away" (the same verb as in 5.4). The stumblingblock of the cross is that element in the death of Christ that would lead the Jews to oppose the whole event and hinder them from accepting Jesus as the Messiah. This is expressed in various ways (e.g. Phps "the hostility which the preaching of the cross provokes"; JB "scandal"). Paul does not say explicitly what this stumblingblock is, but it is clearly implied that it is his interpretation of Christ's death as making it possible for anyone to be accepted by God on simple trust, and not by doing what the Law requires.

What Paul is saying here is that if it were true that he is still advocating circumcision, then his preaching about the death of Christ on the cross would no longer cause any trouble for the Jew. But, since his preaching is still causing trouble, it is not true that he continues to advocate circumcision.

Preaching about the cross of Christ may require some minor amplification in order to indicate that Paul was not merely talking about the cross as an object but about the cross as an instrument of Christ's death or a symbol of his death, for example, "preaching about Christ's dying upon the cross," or "preaching about the meaning of Christ's death on the cross."

5.12   I wish that the people who are upsetting you would go all the way; let them go on and castrate themselves!

Once again Paul refers to the false teachers in the plural, describing them as the people who are upsetting you, that is "unsettle, disturb, agitate" (used only here by Paul). He even expresses a strong wish that they would go all the way (that is, go beyond circumcision) and castrate themselves. Most scholars understand Paul here to be referring to actual self-emasculation, similar to the practices of the priests of certain mystery cults with which the Galatians would be familiar. This sense is found in most translations (e.g. NEB "had better... make eunuchs of themselves"; RSV "would mutilate themselves"; Knox "should lose their own manhood"). One may also translate "cut off their male organs."

A possible alternative interpretation is that Paul may have had in mind the Old Testament understanding of castration which involved exclusion from God's people (Deut 23.1). This would mean, therefore, that Paul here is using the figure of self-mutilation to speak of an intended result, which is exclusion from the church. This interpretation is followed by Phps: "would cut themselves off from you altogether."

TEV	RSV
13 As for you, my brothers, you were called to be free. But do not let this freedom become an excuse for letting your physical desires control you. Instead, let love make you serve one another. 14 For the whole Law is summed up in one commandment: "Love your neighbor as you love yourself." 15 But if you act like wild animals, hurting and harming each other, then watch out, or you will completely destroy one another. (5.13-15)	13 For you were called to freedom, brethren; only do not use your freedom as an opportunity for the flesh, but through love be servants of one another. 14 For the whole law is fulfilled in one word, "You shall love your neighbor as yourself." 15 But if you bite and devour one another take heed that you are not consumed by one another. (5.13-15)

The topic of these verses is that which Paul began in verse 1, namely, the freedom of the believer. In the light of their freedom, believers are exhorted to love one another, for love is the fulfillment of the whole Law (v. 14). In verse 15 he accents the importance of what he has just said by a warning to his readers on what happens if the opposite of love is operative among them.

5.13   As for you, my brothers, you were called to be free. But do not let this freedom become an excuse for letting your physical desires control you. Instead, let love make you serve one another.

Again Paul turns his attention to his readers, addressing them as my brothers (see the remarks on 1.11). You is emphatic, accenting the difference between the Galatians and those referred to in verse 12.

Paul asserts that the Galatians were called to be free. The implicit agent is either God or Christ, but in accordance with Pauline usage, God would seem to be a better choice. Called to be free may be rendered in some languages as "called to no longer be slaves." As in verse 8, the verb call may be equivalent in some languages to "urge" or "strongly invite."

It seems that Paul pauses abruptly and adds a warning against the abuse of freedom in order to avoid any misunderstanding on the part of his readers: Do not let this freedom become an excuse for letting your physical desires control you. Actually, Paul does not use a verb with the noun freedom (literally, "not this freedom" etc.), but the objective form of the noun indicates that a verb is understood, and TEV supplies become (cf. Phps "be careful that freedom does not become"). Other verbs are supplied in other translations (RSV "do not use your freedom," NEB "do not turn your freedom," JB "be careful, or this liberty will provide an opening"). In some languages one cannot speak of freedom as doing or becoming anything. However, the circumstance of being free may be related to what follows in this verse, and so one may translate "But because you are free in this way, do not think that you can now let yourselves be controlled by what your bodies desire," or "...what you desire in your bodies."

The word translated excuse is used only by Paul among New Testament writers. It was originally a military term meaning "a base of operations." In this verse it means primarily "occasion" or "opportunity to do something." In some languages become an excuse may be rendered as "become your reason for," or "become the way in which you justify."

The word translated physical desires is "flesh." This is a difficult word to translate, simply because it is used to refer to many things. A literal translation (as in RSV and NAB) should be ruled out, since it would not depict what Paul is talking about. In the light of verses 14 and 15, the TEV rendering seems to be justified. However, many commentators take the position that "flesh" here has the same meaning as in verse 16 (where TEV renders it human nature). It refers to that aspect of the human self which refuses to acknowledge God and which leads to the doing of evil instead of good. This is reflected in some translations (e.g. Phps NEB "your lower nature").

Letting your physical desires control you may be rendered as "permitting yourselves to be ruled by what your bodies desire," "letting yourselves obey whatever your bodies tell you to do," or "...urge you to do."

The last part of the verse is an alternative to the abuse of freedom. Here the Galatians are exhorted to engage in mutual service.

As in verse 6, love is either God's love for man as shown in Jesus Christ or the believers' love for one another. If the former, a proper translation would be "let God's love make you serve one another," or "because God loves you, you should serve one another"; but note verse 14, which focuses on love for others. Such love defines the quality or the motivation of the service rendered (Knox "serving one another in a spirit of charity"; NAB "out of love, place yourselves at one another's service"). One may also translate "because you love one another, help one another," or "show your love for one another by helping one another." (For a discussion of "love," see under 2.20.)

5.14   For the whole Law is summed up in one commandment: "Love your neighbor as you love yourself."

The whole Law here is, of course, the Jewish Law, not understood as a legalistic system but as an expression of God's will. The verb translated summed up is literally "fulfilled" and can mean either "to summarize" (TEV Knox JB NEB), "to complete," or "to make perfect," as some commentators suggest. If the meaning is "to summarize," the content of the whole Law can be summed up in one statement. If the meaning is "to complete" or "to make perfect," the intent of the Law can be carried out in the activity of love.

The whole Law may be rendered as "all the laws" or "all the laws given through Moses," and an equivalent for summed up in one commandment may be "are equal to just one commandment" or "to one law." Accordingly, the introductory statement in this verse may be translated as "for all the different laws together are really equal to only one law."

The quotation is from Lev 19.18, and once more it is taken from the Septuagint. In its Old Testament setting, it is simply a command for Israelites to love their fellow Israelites; here, it is understood as a command for Christians to love one another, regardless of their race or nationality. Jesus also applies this quotation in a similar sense (Luke 10.25-37, where the one who does the loving is a Samaritan and the neighbor is a Jew).

As you love yourself is literally just "as yourself." What the quotation is saying is that you must love your neighbor as you love your own self. TEV makes this clear by supplying you love. In order to make this commandment applicable to all persons rather than simply a specific command to a particular individual to love a particular neighbor, it may be necessary in some languages to employ a plural form, for example, "you all must love your fellowmen as you love your own selves."

5.15   But if you act like wild animals, hurting and harming each other, then watch out, or you will completely destroy one another.

The warning in this verse indicates that Paul pictures the Galatians as furiously fighting each other. The verb translated hurting is literally "to bite" and refers primarily to snakes and beasts. The verb translated harming is literally "devour" or "gulp down," again used of wild beasts. It is clear, therefore, that Paul is comparing the Galatians to wild animals, and TEV makes this explicit. Other translations do not mention animals at all (the phrase like wild animals does not occur in the Greek text) but try to recapture the image by the way they render the verbs (JB "if you go snapping at each other and tearing each other to pieces"; NEB "if you go on fighting one another, tooth and nail"). In referring to animals, it is important to identify the kinds of animals which would normally be wild or vicious, for example, "if you behave like wild animals," or "... savage animals." Hurting and harming each other may be rendered in some languages as "causing pain and suffering to one another."

The expression watch out may be rendered simply as "beware," or "I warn you."

The result of all this, Paul asserts, is mutual destruction: you will completely destroy one another. The verb translated "completely destroy" is literally "to consume." It is often used to describe the destruction caused by fire. The basic idea is that everything is destroyed—nothing remains.

What will be destroyed is either the Galatians themselves (NAB "you will end up in mutual destruction!"; also TEV NEB) or the Christian fellowship (Phps "you destroy your fellowship altogether"; JB "you will destroy the whole community").

In light of Paul's use of the present tense in the verbs, he is evidently thinking of an actual case. This means that the false teachers' efforts have resulted in chaos and confusion among the Galatian believers, and one should translate this as an actual fact.

	TEV	RSV

The Spirit and Human Nature

16 What I say is this: let the Spirit direct your lives, and you will not satisfy the desires of the human nature. 17 For what our human nature wants is opposed to what the Spirit wants, and what the Spirit wants is opposed to what our human nature wants. These two are enemies, and this means that you cannot do what you want to do. 18 If the Spirit leads you, then you are not subject to the Law.

(5.16-18)

16 But I say, walk by the Spirit, and do not gratify the desires of the flesh. 17 For the desires of the flesh are against the Spirit, and the desires of the Spirit are against the flesh; for these are opposed to each other, to prevent you from doing what you would. 18 But if you are led by the Spirit you are not under the law.

(5.16-18)

Having warned his readers of the danger of abusing freedom and not living in love, Paul now assures them that they will not succumb to such abuse as long as their lives are controlled by the Spirit of God.

In place of the section heading The Spirit and Human Nature, one may employ "The Spirit of God and human nature," or, as in some languages, "The difference between God's Spirit and human nature," or, perhaps better, "The difference between being controlled by God's Spirit and being controlled by our own natures."

5.16   What I say is this: let the Spirit direct your lives, and you will not satisfy the desires of the human nature.

What I say is this is literally "but I say," a common way by which Paul starts a section. In 3.17 and 4.1 such an expression is used to introduce a further explanation of a subject already under discussion. Here, as in verse 2, Paul uses it to get his readers' attention to a personal appeal. In some languages an expression such as what I say is this would seem to be so self-evident as to be either meaningless or misleading. An equivalent expression may be "what I mean is this," or "what I am trying to say is the following."

Let the Spirit direct your lives is literally "walk by the Spirit." Some take the Spirit here to mean spiritual life as opposed to "flesh." Most translators, however, understand it as referring to the Holy Spirit. The verb "to walk" is frequently used in the New Testament in a moral sense, that is, as equivalent to "to live" or "to conduct one's self." The present tense of the Greek verb denotes action that is already in progress. Hence it can be rendered as "continue to walk." The whole expression means that the Galatians should allow their whole life to be controlled, or regulated, by the Holy Spirit (JB "guided by the Spirit"; also NEB). Let the Spirit direct your lives should not be understood merely as a kind of "permission." The imperative form of the Greek text may be translated as "live in accordance with the way in which the Spirit tells you to," or "...the way God's Spirit directs you."

The next clause in this verse has been interpreted as equivalent to an imperative (as in RSV), but most translations employ a future indicative (as in TEV). In the former case, it is an emphatic command; in the latter, it is a strong assertion that once they allow the Spirit to guide them, "then you will never satisfy the passions of the flesh" (Mft).

There are three words in this clause that need to be commented on: satisfy, desires, and human nature (literally "flesh"). Satisfy is literally "to fulfill," but it is used here in the sense of "to gratify" (RSV). Desires or "passions" refers to any kind of desires, both good or bad, but the New Testament usage points more to the bad. Human nature ("flesh") is the same word used in verse 13, and refers once again to that part of human nature which does not submit to God. This is not easy to translate; there is danger even in the TEV way of rendering it, since it makes human nature all bad, and all its desires evil.

In a number of languages there is no closely corresponding way to speak of human nature. The closest equivalent may simply be "you yourselves," for example, "do not do just what you yourselves want to do." In other languages one may say "do not do what you as a human being want to do," or "...just as a person wants to do." In still other languages human nature is best spoken of as "the heart," for example, "do not do just whatever your heart wants you to do," or "...just whatever you want to do in your heart."

5.17   For what our human nature wants is opposed to what the Spirit wants, and what the Spirit wants is opposed to what our human nature wants. These two are enemies, and this means that you cannot do what you want to do.

Paul starts this verse with for, which connects it with verse 16. We will not satisfy the desires of the human nature, if we live by the Spirit, because of the fact that human nature and the Holy Spirit are at enmity with each other.

The word translated human nature is "flesh," and is to be taken in the same sense as in the previous verse. Here flesh and the Spirit are pictured as opposing each other. The contrast between the desires of the human nature and of the Spirit of God may be expressed in some languages as "For what we as human beings want is against what God's Spirit wants, and what God's Spirit wants is against what we as human beings want." There may, however, be difficulties involved in some languages since a verb such as "want" may require a goal. Therefore, one may need to translate "For what we as human beings want to do is against what the Spirit of God wants us to do, and what the Spirit of God wants us to do is against what we as human beings want to do."

After expressing the conflict, Paul comes up with another statement: These two are enemies, and this means that you cannot do what you want to do.

There are different ways of interpreting these two are enemies. One is to regard this statement as simply a summary of the first part of the verse. On the other hand, the first part of the verse can be taken as a general statement of the conflict, and the second part as a statement of the conflict in the experience of the individual believer. In both cases, the last clause you cannot do what you want to do is interpreted as expressing result. Further, it is neutral, referring to both good and evil desires. What Paul would mean, then, is that since the Spirit and the flesh are in conflict within the believer, this results in the believer's loss of his freedom.

These two are enemies may be translated as either "What we want to do and what God's Spirit wants us to do are opposed," or "We as human beings and God's Spirit are enemies of one another," or "...opposed to one another."

However, a third interpretation of these two are enemies is possible. That is to take you cannot do what you want to do to refer to doing what the flesh wants, which would take Paul's meaning to be that since the Spirit opposes the flesh, then the believer is not free to do what he wants to do, insofar as following the flesh is concerned. The last part of this verse would then read: "These two are enemies, and this means that if the Spirit directs your lives, you cannot do what you want to do, which is to satisfy the desires of the human nature."

The merit of this last interpretation is that it connects this verse more closely with both what precedes and what follows.

5.18   If the Spirit leads you, then you are not subject to the Law.

This verse is almost universally regarded as a summary of Paul's argument in the whole chapter. It reinforces verse 16, where Paul has asserted that those who are led by the Spirit do not satisfy the desires of the human nature. Here Paul is asserting that if they are led by the Spirit, they are not subject to the Law.

The expression the Spirit leads you (literally,"you are being led by the Spirit") is to be taken as more or less equivalent to "walk by the Spirit" in verse 16. Actually, the two expressions come out almost the same in TEV and other translations (Phps "live your whole life in the spirit...follow the leading of the Spirit"; NAB "live in accord with the spirit...guided by the spirit"; NEB "guided by the Spirit...led by the Spirit"). The tense of the verb suggests continuing action, which makes it possible to come out with a translation such as "if you continue to be led by the Spirit." One may also translate "if you do what the Spirit tells you to do," or "if you obey what the Spirit of God says you should do."

You are not subject to the Law is literally "you are not under law." "Law" here is taken by the majority of scholars to refer to the Jewish Law. However, since the noun does not have an article, some scholars understand it as referring to any law, whether Jewish or Gentile. This latter position is reflected in NEB ("you are not under law") and JB ("no law can touch you").

Not subject to the Law is "not being a slave to the law," that is, not following the law's precepts in order to win God's approval.

One may also render you are not subject to the Law as "you are not compelled to do all that the laws say," or "it is not necessary for you to be obedient to all the laws." The relation between the person and the Law may, however, be reversed in some instances, and one may translate "then the laws do not command you," or "...do not have authority over you."

[135]

TEV	RSV
19 What human nature does is quite plain. It shows itself in immoral, filthy, and indecent actions; 20 in worship of idols and witchcraft. People become enemies and they fight; they become jealous, angry, and ambitious. They separate into parties and groups; 21 they are envious, get drunk, have orgies, and do other things like these. I warn you now as I have before: those who do these things will not possess the Kingdom of God.	19 Now the works of the flesh are plain: immorality, impurity, licentiousness, 20 idolatry, sorcery, enmity, strife, jealousy, anger, selfishness, dissension, party spirit, 21 envy,^{k} drunkenness, carousing, and the like. I warn you, as I warned you before, that those who do such things shall not inherit the kingdom of God.
22 But the Spirit produces love, joy, peace, patience, kindness, goodness, faithfulness, 23 humility, and self-control. There is no law against such things as these. 24 And those who belong to Christ Jesus have put to death their human nature with all its passions and desires. 25 The Spirit has given us life; he must also control our lives. 26 We must not be proud or irritate one another or be jealous of one another. (5.19-26)	22 But the fruit of the Spirit is love, joy, peace, patience, kindness, goodness, faithfulness, 23 gentleness, self-control; against such there is no law. 24 And those who belong to Christ Jesus have crucified the flesh with its passions and desires. 25 If we live by the Spirit, let us also walk by the Spirit. 26 Let us have no self-conceit, no provoking of one another, no envy of one another.

^{k}Other ancient authorities add *murder*   (5.19-26)

This section is an expansion of the previous one. Having mentioned that the Spirit and human nature are enemies, Paul becomes more concrete and proceeds to enumerate the manifestations of these two. He first deals with the manifestations of human nature (vv. 19-21), to which he later contrasts the "fruits of the Spirit" (vv. 22-23). He ends this section with an appeal parallel to that of verse 16, that is, that the Spirit should be allowed to control the lives of the Galatian Christians.

5.19   What human nature does is quite plain. It shows itself in immoral, filthy, and indecent actions;

In describing what human nature does as quite plain, Paul is simply saying that it is well-known to everyone; in other words, that anyone can recognize it as "works of the flesh" (NEB "anyone can see the kind of behaviour that belongs to the lower nature"; NAB "it is obvious what proceeds from the flesh").

Human nature translates "flesh" as in verses 16 and 17.

In a number of languages one cannot speak of human nature doing certain things. Rather, one must speak of people doing certain things because of their human nature. One may therefore render the first sentence in this verse as "Because of what people really are, it is clear to everyone how they act; they are immoral...."

Scholars have suggested that what Paul enumerates falls logically into four groups. The first group includes "immorality," "impurity," and "licentiousness," which seem to be acts connected with sex or sensuality. "Immorality" translates a word which originally meant "prostitution" but came to mean sexual unfaithfulness and was used as a general term for any kind of sexual sin or immoral acts.

"Impurity" translates a Greek word which originally was used to describe the contents of graves and came to mean ceremonial or moral uncleanness with no special emphasis on sexual vice. In Paul's thinking, however, it is associated with "immorality" seven times (out of nine), and therefore in this passage also it may be interpreted as sexual uncleanness.

The third word in this series "licentiousness" (RSV), probably refers here to sexual excesses, resulting in indecent conduct.

It is always possible to find some general term for immoral, but it may not be so easy to find two other corresponding terms which would indicate other aspects or increasingly evil degrees of sexual immorality. In some languages terms such as filthy and indecent actions may be expressed as idioms, for example, "acting like dogs," or "copulating in evil ways."

5.20-21   in worship of idols and witchcraft. People become enemies and they fight; they become jealous, angry, and ambitious. They separate into parties and groups; (21) they are envious, get drunk, have orgies, and do other things like these. I warn you now as I have before: those who do these things will not possess the Kingdom of God.

The second group consists of two which are associated with heathen worship: "idolatry" and "sorcery." "Idolatry" is worship of idols in a specific sense, and in a general sense worship of anything other than the one God. "Sorcery" translates a word which originally meant simply "use of medicine or drugs," but which had the derived meaning of the use of drugs for magical purposes. Therefore it came to mean, in the biblical writings, magic, sorcery, or witchcraft.

Worship of idols may be rendered simply as "people worshiping idols," "people bowing down before idols," or "... statues of their gods."

Witchcraft may be rendered as "they practice black magic against one another," "they do sorcery," "they cause curses to come upon people," or "they cause curses by magic." In some instances witchcraft is identified by very specific idiomatic expressions, for example, "they burn hair," "they mutter curses," or "they mix saliva." One should not, however, employ an idiomatic expression for witchcraft unless it has a broader meaning than merely the designation of some technique appropriate only to some usage in an individual culture.

The third group includes eight which can be generally designated as describing social evils. Except for two, "strife" and "jealousy" (see below), all these are plural in the Greek, stressing numerous and repeated occurrences. TEV indicates this plural form by starting a new sentence and focusing on the people who perform them rather than on the acts themselves. Thus, for "enmity"

TEV has people become enemies, and so on. In most languages the remaining types of evil behavior are expressed either by verbs or by a general term of action qualified by a word such as "angrily" or "with envy."

Paul starts this third list with "enmity," a general term referring to hostility or unneighborly acts of any kind or form.

"Strife" refers to "dissensions, wranglings" (JB), "bickering" (NAB), "quarrels" (Knox). Though TEV translates they fight, the fighting should be regarded primarily as an aspect of dissension and arguing. One may therefore translate "they quarrel with one another," or "they fight one another with words."

"Jealousy" should not be understood as a term which refers simply to a lover's attitude toward his rivals, but the eager desire to have or attain what belongs to another, hence "envy" (NEB). Quite frequently "jealousy" here is rendered as "they want what other people have," or "they look with envious eyes at one another."

"Anger" is the same word often rendered "passion," but here it is used in the sense of "wrath," "rage," "outbursts of anger" (Knox); "outbursts of rage" (NAB). Paul is not simply describing a characteristic, as some translations might suggest (JB "bad temper"), but an act in which anger is expressed.

"Selfishness" is a word which suggests the act of pushing oneself ahead regardless of what happens to others, or of working zealously for one's own interests, together with the resulting intrigues and rivalries (TEV ambitious, NEB "selfish ambitions," NAB "selfish rivalries"). Since ambitious can be understood in a perfectly proper sense, it may be essential to have some qualifying phrase or word, for example, "selfishly ambitious," "ambitious only for themselves," or "wanting to get ahead of others."

"Dissension" refers to divisions and schisms, while "party spirit" translates a word which means "sect" or "faction," usually a heretical one. Since the two concepts are related, both referring to the act of separating from one another or creating divisions and so destroying the unity of any group, TEV joins them together: They separate into parties and groups. It is possible to understand parties as temporary divisions, and groups as permanent divisions, and some translations reflect this kind of understanding (JB "disagreements, factions"; NAB "dissensions, factions"). One may also translate "they divide themselves into cliques and oppose one another."

"Envy" is similar to "jealousy." Perhaps, as some scholars have suggested, the use of the plural denotes different acts or specific forms of envious desire.

A number of Greek manuscripts and so some translations include a ninth "work of the flesh," namely, "murder." The manuscript evidence in favor of its inclusion is considerable.

The fourth group includes two sins of intemperance. "Drunkenness" is self-explanatory, and it results in "carousing," which is a word to describe "excessive feasting" or "orgies." In heathen worship, these acts were usually part of the festal processions in honor of the gods. The distinctions here in terms of two levels of intemperance may be expressed in some languages as "they get drunk, and they are drunk in religious festivals," or "they get very drunk during fiestas."

Paul concludes his enumeration with the clause and do other things like these. This indicates that his list is by no means exhaustive, but that the Galatians will be able to recognize other "works of the flesh," in addition to what Paul has mentioned.

Paul now spells out the consequences of all these "works of the flesh" in the form of a warning. As I have before probably refers to the same occasion which he has referred to previously (see 1.9; 4.16; 5.3).

The people who practice these "works of the flesh" will not possess the Kingdom of God (literally,"shall not inherit the Kingdom of God"). The expression the Kingdom of God does not refer to a place where God is king, or to a realm where God exercises his kingship, but to his rule, to his activity as King. To "inherit the Kingdom of God," therefore, is to reach the point of acknowledging God as King or to be under God's rule and authority. Will not possess the Kingdom of God may be rendered in some languages as "will not enjoy having God rule over them," or "will never have the joy of God ruling them."

5.22-23   But the Spirit produces love, joy, peace, patience, kindness, goodness, faithfulness, (23) humility, and self-control. There is no law against such things as these.

In contrast to "the works of the flesh," Paul now presents a listing of "the fruit of the Spirit."

Before going through the list, three things should be noted. First, in talking of human nature, Paul uses the word "works" (TEV what human nature does), whereas in talking of the Spirit, Paul uses "fruit" (TEV the Spirit produces). This is significant, for Paul wants to emphasize that the manifestations of human nature stem from human endeavor. The whole expression "works of the flesh" is therefore roughly equivalent to "works of the law." On the other hand, the "fruit" of the Spirit is the natural product of the Christian's relationship with the Spirit, and so it issues forth spontaneously in the Christian's behavior.

Secondly, one should note that "fruit" is singular, indicating that to Paul spiritual life is a unity, and that all of these qualities which he is about to mention are found whenever one is led by the Spirit.

Finally, Paul talks elsewhere of "the gifts of the Spirit" (1 Cor 12.1-11). These should not be confused with the "fruit" of the Spirit. The "gifts" are functions and capacities which are given to various people to enable them to serve the Christian community. Obviously, then, all Christians would not share the same gifts. However, the "fruit" which Paul talks about here is found in its entirety in every believer whose life is led by the Spirit of God.

The list itself consists of nine qualities. In view of their being contrasted with the previous list, they should be understood as referring primarily to the believer's relationships with his fellowmen, that is, in the same areas where the works of the flesh are manifested.

There have been attempts to come out with some kind of classification of the list. One such attempt is to divide the list into three: the first dealing with Christian mental habits in their more general aspects ("love, joy, peace"), the second including special qualities relating to a man's relationship with his fellowmen ("patience, kindness, goodness"), the final trio including principles which guide a Christian's conduct ("faithfulness, gentleness, self-control"). But one should not put too much emphasis on trying to fit these into a neat logical sequence. Most translations, including TEV, simply enumerate them in the order in which they are found in the Greek text and separate them with commas.

In most languages it is impossible to speak of what the Spirit produces as being a kind of "fruit," since the metaphorical extension of a receptor language term for "fruit" seems to be quite inappropriate when talking about such human qualities and experiences as love, joy, peace, patience, etc. In general, the fruit of the Spirit must be spoken of in terms of verbal or predicate expressions, for example, "people love," "people are joyful," etc. The relation of the Spirit to these experiences of the believer must often be expressed as causative, for example, "the Spirit of God causes people to love...."

Love is the opposite of "enmity," and should be taken not as referring to a person's love for God, but primarily to a person's love for other persons.

Joy is something independent of outward circumstances, since it is grounded in God. In some languages joy is essentially equivalent to "causes people to be very happy." In order to indicate that this joy is not merely some passing experience, one may say "to be truly happy within their hearts." In some languages joy is expressed idiomatically as "to be warm within one's heart," or "to dance within one's heart."

Peace may refer either to tranquility of mind as a result of a right relationship with God, or to restoration of right relationships between people. The latter should be preferred in view of the fact that Paul's emphasis here is on human relationships. If one adopts the first interpretation of peace, it may be translated as "God calls his people to experience peace in their hearts," or, idiomatically as in some languages, "to sit down in their hearts." On the other hand, if the preferred interpretation is followed, then one may often translate as "causes people to be reconciled to one another," "causes people to live in peace with one another," or, stated negatively, "to live together without quarreling."

Patience connotes endurance and forbearance in the midst of provocation and injury from others (NAB "patient endurance"). In a number of languages patience may be rendered as "enduring troubles" or "remaining quiet when persecuted." Patience may be expressed idiomatically in some languages as "not answering the threats of others," or "sitting quiet while others rage."

Kindness and goodness both refer to one's favorable disposition toward his neighbor, with goodness probably being general and kindness specific. Kindness is often expressed as "causes people to be kind to one another," or "causes people to help one another." Goodness is often expressed in very similar ways, for example, "the Spirit causes people to be good to one another," or "...to cause good for others."

Faithfulness translates the same word which is elsewhere translated "faith."

It is tempting to understand this in terms of man's relation to God, but here it probably includes the elements of faithfulness, trustworthiness, honesty, trustfulness, and reliability in one's dealings with others. Faithfulness is often expressed by a verbal phrase, for example, "causes people to be trustworthy," or "causes people to be such that others can trust them."

Humility can be understood as humble submission to God, but here primarily in the sense of gentleness and patience in dealing with others. Humility is often expressed negatively as "not being harsh with others," or "not pushing others around."

Finally, self-control refers to mastery over the desires and passions of the self. Since the verb form of the noun is used in 1 Cor 7.9 in the sense of controlling sexual desires, it is possible to read that meaning here also. However, since it seems to be antithetical to drunkenness and orgies, it may mean restraint in a wider context. Perhaps Paul here means self-restraint in a general way rather than in a specific area. Self-control is often rendered as "being able to say no to one's own desires," "commanding one's own desires," or "being able to refuse what one's body wants to do."

What does Paul mean by concluding this enumeration with the statement There is no law against such things as these? What he probably means is that the law just has no part to play in the realm of the Spirit. The law exists for restraint, but there is nothing to restrain in these qualities. This meaning is reflected in NEB: "There is no law dealing with such things as these." One may also translate as "The laws do not even speak about such matters as these," or "These actions are not even contained in any of the laws."

It is possible to understand the statement in another sense, and that is to read the Greek word for such things as these as masculine, in which case Paul would be saying "There is no law against such men." This is reflected in Knox: "No law can touch lives such as these." The law was never meant for people who demonstrate these qualities, since no law can check or condemn their conduct. One may also translate "There are no laws which speak against people who live in this way," or "...who do these things."

5.24   And those who belong to Christ Jesus have put to death their human nature with all its passions and desires.

This verse is closely connected with the previous verses, the point being that those who are in Christ can no longer indulge in the "works of the flesh" which were previously mentioned.

Those who belong to Christ Jesus translates a possessive genitive (literally "those of Christ Jesus"), the meaning of which is synonymous with "in Christ" or "those who are led by the Spirit" in verse 16. One may also render those who belong to Christ Jesus as "those who are the people of Christ Jesus," or "those who are Christ Jesus' followers."

Have put to death is literally "crucified." It is, of course, a figurative expression, suggesting a connection between this action of the believer and the death of Jesus Christ on the cross. The verb is in the aorist tense, suggesting

either that the action took place in the past (at conversion or baptism), or that
the action resulted in a complete and decisive change. Since this action is presently reflected in the experience of every believer, it is better to translate it in
the perfect tense, as in TEV and most other translations. In many languages it
is quite misleading to say have put to death their human nature, since this would
be equivalent to "they killed themselves." It is sometimes possible to employ a
simile, for example, "they have, as it were, put to death their human nature,"
but even this can be misleading and it is often quite meaningless. An equivalent
in some languages is "have caused their own selves not to control them," "have
not given themselves over to be ruled by their own human nature," or "have
caused their human nature no longer to command them."

What is put to death is human nature with all its passions and desires.
"Passion" is used to mean "suffering," in a good sense, or "disposition," in a
bad sense. Here it is almost synonymous with "desires." It is even possible to
translate passions and desires as "passionate desires." The two taken together
should be understood to refer to "the works of the flesh" which Paul has just previously enumerated. The final phrase in this verse, with all its passions and
desires, must often be rendered as a complete sentence, for example, "This includes all that their human nature wants so much to do," or "Their human nature
has all of these strong and evil desires."

5.25   The Spirit has given us life; he must also control our lives.

The Spirit has given us life is a conditional clause in the Greek (literally
"if we live by the Spirit"). As in verse 18, the "if" clause refers to something
that is presently existing, but it is usually better to translate "if" as "since."
In a number of languages one cannot speak of "giving life." One can, however,
say "the Spirit has caused us to live," or possibly "...to really live" (as a means
of indicating a significant new quality in life).

"To live by the Spirit" is related to two other expressions which Paul has
used in this chapter, namely, "to walk by the Spirit" (v. 16) and "to be led by
the Spirit" (v. 18). These expressions are essentially equivalent. If one wishes
to make a distinction, perhaps "to live" would refer to the believer's relationship with the Spirit, "to walk" would refer to the believer's conduct, and "to be
led" to the believer's willingness to follow the Spirit's guidance. But some translators understand "to live by the Spirit" as the Spirit being "the source of our
life" (NEB), rather than the basis of the believer's relationship with the Spirit
(JB "since the Spirit is our life").

Since it is true that the Spirit has given us life, it follows that he should
also control our lives. The Greek literally says "let us also walk by the Spirit,"
and this is an exhortation to live in accordance with the implications of the believer's relation to the Spirit. It is not the inevitable or automatic consequence
of such a fact. This should not be understood as synonymous with the expression
in verse 16, since Paul here uses a different word for "walk." The word used
here can be literally translated "to walk in a straight line" and probably means
in this context "to behave properly according to accepted standards." In this

sense, then, the expression here is synonymous with the expression in verse 18. Some other ways of translating "walk" are "guided" (Phps) and "directed" (JB NEB). He must also control our lives may simply be rendered as "he must be the one to tell us how to live," "he should command how we live," "we should let him command our lives," or "we must let him tell us what we should do."

5.26   We must not be proud or irritate one another or be jealous of one another.

This verse is closely connected with the previous one, as indicated by the absence of any connectives. One may understand this verse as expressing negatively in three points what Paul means by being controlled by the Spirit, but it is also possible to understand the Greek as one initial point, that is, being proud, manifested by being "irritated" and "jealous."

It is very possible that Paul has in mind the Galatian situation, and is applying this concept of the Christian life to the actual state of affairs in the Galatian churches. A general application of this concept, however, without necessarily excluding the Galatian situation, is perhaps the best way to understand this verse.

The word translated proud is used only here in the whole New Testament; it can be literally rendered "vain-gloried." In its use in secular literature, it is often associated with boastfulness and has the sense of "glorying in vain things" or "seeing value in things not really valuable." Here it probably means either "conceited" (NEB RSV JB) or "boastful" (NAB). The rendering "ambitious" (Phps Knox) is taken from a cognate word usually translated "vanity" or "excessive ambition." Proud may often be rendered as "always saying how great we are," or, as expressed idiomatically, "always saying, Look at me."

The phrase translated irritate one another is also used only once in the New Testament. In accordance with its secular usage, it means either "to provoke" (JB RSV) or "to challenge" (NEB NAB). The meaning of the underlying Greek term may be expressed idiomatically in some instances as "always putting one's self ahead of others."

The phrase translated jealous of one another is also used only once in the New Testament, although its nominal form is used in many other places. It means "to be jealous" (NAB NEB Phps) or "to be envious of one another" (RSV JB Knox).

CHAPTER 6

TEV

RSV

Bear One Another's Burdens

1 My brothers, if someone is caught in any kind of wrongdoing, those of you who are spiritual should set him right; but you must do it in a gentle way. And keep an eye on yourselves, so that you will not be tempted, too. 2 Help carry one another's burdens, and in this way you will obey[h] the law of Christ. 3 If someone thinks he is something when he really is nothing, he is only deceiving himself. 4 Each one should judge his own conduct. If it is good, then he can be proud of what he himself has done, without having to compare it with what someone else has done. 5 For everyone has to carry his own load.

6 The man who is being taught the Christian message should share all the good things he has with his teacher.

[h]you will obey; *some manuscripts have* obey. (6.1-6)

1 Brethren, if a man is overtaken in any trespass, you who are spiritual should restore him in a spirit of gentleness. Look to yourself, lest you too be tempted. 2 Bear one another's burdens, and so fulfil the law of Christ. 3 For if any one thinks he is something, when he is nothing, he deceives himself. 4 But let each one test his own work, and then his reason to boast will be in himself alone and not in his neighbor. 5 For each man will have to bear his own load.

6 Let him who is taught the word share all good things with him who teaches. (6.1-6)

The last two verses of the previous section not only give a summary of Paul's appeal, but they also represent a general statement of what it means to be guided by the Spirit, both positively and negatively. In this new section, Paul now applies the statement to specific cases in the life of the Galatian churches.

The close relation between this section and the last two verses of chapter 5 has led some scholars to start a new section with 5.24. Most translations, however, including TEV (following the UBS Greek New Testament), begin a new section with 6.1.

The section heading <u>Bear One Another's Burdens</u> may be made more specific as, for example, "Help carry one another's burdens." On the other hand, one may employ a more general expression, such as "Help one another," or "Believers should help each other."

6.1   My brothers, if someone is caught in any kind of wrongdoing, those of you who are spiritual should set him right; but you must do it in a gentle way. And keep an eye on yourselves, so that you will not be tempted, too.

[144]

As in many similar contexts, My brothers may be rendered as "My fellow believers," or "You who along with me trust Christ."

Paul's first application of his general appeal is that of dealing with someone who falls into sin.

Paul's words here should be interpreted as stating a hypothetical case. This is indicated first of all by the nature of the conditional clause, particularly in the word he uses for "if" (for a similar construction, see 1.8); and secondly, by his use of the generic someone or "anyone." Yet he probably has in mind a specific situation, in which case, someone would refer to a member of the Christian community. This is the interpretation in some translations (e.g. JB "if one of you").

The Greek expression translated is caught in any kind of wrongdoing is capable of two interpretations. First, it could mean that someone is doing something wrong and is found out by others (TEV, also NAB "is detected in sin," Knox "found guilty of some fault"). Secondly, it could mean that someone, on a sudden impulse, does something wrong (NEB "should do something wrong," JB "misbehaves"). Both are possible because the verb which Paul uses here can mean either "detect" or "overtake," with the element of surprise. If one follows the first interpretation and at the same time must change the passive expression into an active one, it is possible to render the condition as "if some of you discover that someone has done something wrong." On the basis of the second type of interpretation, the condition may simply be rendered as "if someone does something bad," or "if someone sins."

Wrongdoing (literally "trespass" or "transgression") is best understood here to refer to wrongdoing of any kind.

Those ... who are spiritual are those whose lives are guided by the Spirit. This is made clear in some translations (e.g. NEB "endowed with the Spirit"). As in 5.4, Paul is not referring to all the Galatians, but only to some of them, hence the phrase of you is added in TEV to make this explicit. Those of you who are spiritual may be rendered as "those of you whom the Spirit guides," or "those of you who do what the Spirit of God says you should do."

Interpretations of the whole statement vary. Some see in it Paul's act of contrasting those who are guided by the Spirit with those who are still doing the "works of the flesh." Others see a tone of irony in the statement, as if Paul is saying, "if you are really spiritual, as you claim to be ...." Still others speculate that one party in Galatia called themselves by the name "the spirituals." The first of these seems to fit the context best, for Paul seems to be challenging his readers, not with any tones of irony, but in a sincere and honest manner.

Those who are in the Spirit should set the wrongdoer right, that is, "help him to stop doing wrong." But this should be done in a gentle way, literally "in a spirit of gentleness." (For "gentleness," see 5.23, where TEV has humility.) In a gentle way may be expressed in some languages negatively as "you must not treat him rough," but stated positively, one may say "you must be kind to him," or "you must speak to him with a tender heart."

Keep an eye on yourselves involves a Greek verb which means "to look at" or "to observe," but here it probably means "to take care" or "to look out." One should note that Paul switches from the plural to the singular pronoun at this point. He does this often in his letters (see 4.6-7). But since this admonition is applicable to all the individuals involved, it is normally necessary to continue the use of a plural form, for example, "you (plural) must watch out for yourselves," or "you (plural) must be careful about your own conduct" (that is, as individuals).

In you will not be tempted, the verb carries with it not only the idea of being attracted to doing wrong, but also the implication of yielding to this attraction. So that you will not be tempted, too may be rendered as "so that you also will not want to do the same kind of thing," or even "so that you also will not be guilty of doing something bad."

A more vital question is how to state the relation between the first and second parts of this statement. Some take the connection to be purposive, that is, the purpose for taking care is so that one will not fall into temptation. Others interpret this as a warning, that is, one should take care, or else he will fall into temptation. The first of these interpretations is found in TEV, while the second is found in RSV and most other modern translations. The relation of result may be expressed as "for if you are not careful, you will also be tempted to do the same."

6.2 Help carry one another's burdens, and in this way you will obey[h] the law of Christ.

 [h]you will obey; *some manuscripts have* obey.

When Paul exhorts his readers to help carry one another's burdens, he may have in mind what he has referred to in the previous verse, namely, the act of setting right a wrongdoer in the fellowship. The root of the word translated burdens, however, refers metaphorically to anything borne, either good (2 Cor 4.17) or bad (Acts 15.28; Rev 2.24; Gal 5.10). It is possible, therefore, to interpret burdens as a general term, referring to any problems that might befall a Christian.

The position of one another in the Greek is emphatic, meaning that Paul wants to stress it, but what he intends is not completely clear. Two interpretations are possible: (1) he may be harking back to 5.10 and therefore exhorting his readers to put emphasis, not on the burdens of following the Law, but on the burdens of helping each other; or (2) he may be emphasizing the nature of the Christian fellowship, where concern for one another is the basic rule, as he has already expounded it (5.13-14).

Though the figurative language involved in help carry one another's burdens is very meaningful in many languages, it can be relatively meaningless in others. In some instances it may be possible to change the metaphor into a simile, for example, "help carry one another's burdens, as it were," but in other instances it may be better to shift the metaphor into a nonfigurative expression, for example, "help one another in difficulty," or "if anyone is in difficulty, you should help him."

In this way is literally "thus," which has the connotation of "in doing this" (Knox "then"). In other words, it is in helping each other that they obey the law of Christ. The word translated obey is literally "to fulfill," a verb which denotes the idea of completeness (Phps "live out").

The expression the law of Christ means either the law of God as shown by Christ in his life or the law which Christ taught. In either case, Paul is asserting, that if the whole law is fulfilled in the concept of love (as he has already expressed in 5.14), then to share in each other's burdens is to be obedient to that law. In this context you will obey the law of Christ may be rendered as "you will obey the commandment that Christ gave," "...the law that Christ taught," or "...what Christ commanded."

As the footnote in TEV indicates, there is an alternative to the reading translated you will obey. This reading has another imperative, rather than a future indicative. The meanings of both readings, however, are essentially the same, especially in light of the word "thus," for this word makes it clear that it is by bearing the burdens of others that a person obeys the law of Christ—it is not as if there were two separate commands, one about bearing and one about obeying. This is really just what the future tense is also saying.

6.3   If someone thinks he is something when he really is nothing, he is
        only deceiving himself.

There seems to be a close connection between verses 2 and 3, since the Greek has a transitional "for" (see RSV) at the beginning of the latter verse, but the connection is not altogether clear. It may even be that Paul wants to remind his readers that often the sight of an erring brother (v. 1) creates in some a sense of spiritual superiority rather than a genuine desire to help. Or perhaps he is asserting the obvious fact that the proud man finds it difficult, if not impossible, either to lend a helping hand or to receive help of any kind. A third possibility is to connect verse 3 with verse 1, particularly the last part of that verse. There Paul was saying that a man should take care of himself in order not to be tempted. Here he continues to warn those who feel sure of themselves.

The word translated think is the same word used by Paul when talking of the three leaders of the Jerusalem church in 2.2,6,9. There the meaning is "to be regarded by others as important"; here the word is reflexive: "to regard oneself as important."

When he really is nothing could be understood as a statement that describes believers in general, for since they owe their very lives to Christ, they have no right to claim importance or status of any kind. It is possible, however, that Paul has in mind those who think of themselves as important, and he is trying to show them how insignificant they really are.

The relation between the conditional clause if someone thinks he is something and the temporal clause when he really is nothing must be expressed in some languages as a conditional clause with an embedded relative clause, for example, "if someone, who really is nothing, thinks he is something." However, to say merely that "he thinks he is something" may not carry any significance, for everyone is in a sense "something." Therefore it may be necessary to say "if someone—and he really amounts to nothing at all—thinks he is something big," or "...thinks he is very important."

The verb translated deceiving is one which seems to have been coined by Paul himself; it cannot be found in earlier writings, and later it is used only by ecclesiastical writers. It is used only here in the New Testament, and a cognate noun ("deceiver") occurs in Titus 1.10. RSV NAB Phps agree with TEV in translating this verb as "deceive"; NEB Knox have "delude." He is only deceiving himself may be expressed in some languages as "he is only lying to himself," or "it is just the same as though he were calling himself a fool."

The relation between the three parts of this verse will depend on the exegetical viewpoint one takes. One way of rendering it would be "if a man thinks he is something, he is only fooling himself, for the truth is he is nothing." Another way, representing another exegetical viewpoint, is "if a man thinks he is 'somebody', he is deceiving himself, for that very thought proves that he is nobody" (Phps), or "it is the people who are not important who often make the mistake of thinking that they are" (JB).

6.4 Each one should judge his own conduct. If it is good, then he can be proud of what he himself has done, without having to compare it with what someone else has done.

This verse seems to connect logically with verses 2 and 3 taken together. A man's pride must be based on his own achievement and condition, not in comparison with others, especially the weaker ones.

The word translated judge is seemingly one of Paul's favorite words; it means to "test" or "discriminate," hence "examine" (JB NEB Knox; cf. Phps "learn to assess properly").

Conduct is literally "work," but primarily in this context it means "deed" or "action," related to or as proof of character.

Each one should judge his own conduct may be rendered as "Each one must look at what he has done and decide whether it has been good," or "Each person must think about his own behavior (or "...about how he has acted") and decide whether he has done good or bad."

If it is good may then be rendered as "if what he has done is good," or "if his deeds are good."

He can be proud is literally "he will have reason for boasting." The word "boast" may not be the right one in this instance, for it implies excessive or unjustified claims about oneself. Perhaps "he can have some reason for self-satisfaction" or a similar expression would approximate what Paul is saying (Phps "he can then be glad when he has done something worth doing"). He can be proud in the sense of having "self-satisfaction" may be expressed in some instances as "he can thank himself."

Someone else translates "the other one," and should be understood as a generic statement, referring to "anyone else" (NEB) rather than to a specific individual.

The final part of this verse, <u>without having to compare it with what some-one else has done</u>, must often be rendered as a completely separate sentence, for example, "He should not compare what he has done with what someone else has done," or "He should not judge what he has done by judging what others have done."

<u>6.5</u>   For everyone has to carry his own load.

The main problem posed by this verse is its relation to verse 2. Are these verses contradictory? If not, how can one explain the relation? The context in which verse 5 appears seems to point to a different interpretation from that of verse 2. In the light of verse 4, <u>load</u> here seems to refer to one's own conduct, in which case Paul may be saying "Everyone is responsible to God for his own conduct."

Another angle that can be considered is the fact that Paul uses two different words to describe what is being carried. The <u>burden</u> in verse 2 seems to refer to a load which is heavy and somewhat oppressive, and therefore it would be for the person's own good if he could get rid of it. In verse 5, however, Paul uses a word (<u>load</u>) which is used of a ship's cargo or a man's pack or a soldier's knapsack. Accordingly, some see in this verse the figure of a soldier going to battle and bearing his own kit. The emphasis then would be on everyone doing his own share of normal duty (Mft "Everyone will have to bear his own load of responsibility").

One must not, however, press the linguistic difference between the two words, for no really sharp distinctions can be drawn between them. Another possibility is to understand <u>load</u> in verse 5 as referring to weakness and sin, and to interpret all of verse 5 as related to verse 2a, but in the form of a paradox. What Paul would be suggesting, then, is that it is only the man who knows he has to carry his own load who is able and willing to help carry the loads of others. Thus it is possible to understand "burden" in both verses as referring to the same thing, i.e., weakness, sin, etc., and to interpret the two verses as forming two parts of a paradox.

<u>6.6</u>   The man who is being taught the Christian message should share all the good things he has with his teacher.

The relation of this verse to what precedes cannot easily be seen. Some have assumed a connection because of the Greek connective ("and" or "but") which begins the sentence. This particular connective, however, is sometimes used to start a new section, and its presence here is not necessarily significant. Furthermore, the subject matter of the verse is entirely new and does not seem to be connected either with what immediately precedes or with the theme of the entire epistle. In view of this, some take this verse as the beginning of a new section (vv. 6-10), consisting of unrelated general exhortations.

At any rate, this verse speaks of the relationship between "the one who is being taught the word" and "the one who is teaching." The "word" in this context clearly refers to the whole <u>Christian message</u>, and the man being taught is one who is "under Christian instruction" (Phps, cf. NEB "under instruction in the faith"), that is, a catechumen.

Paul describes the relationship between catechumen and teacher as a partnership (the word he uses means "share" or "be a partner in"). But what does it mean to be partners "in all good things"? Does "good things" refer to spiritual matters? In other words, is Paul saying that the disciple must be receptive to everything that the teacher is imparting? Or does "good things" refer to material goods? That is, is Paul admonishing the disciple to make a financial contribution toward the support of the teacher? The latter interpretation seems to be more probable, and so it is made clear in some translations (JB "People under instruction should always contribute something to the support of the man who is instructing them"; cf. Phps).

Some suggest that Paul is being intentionally ambiguous here, for he wants both material and spiritual aspects included in the partnership between disciple and teacher. Retention of the Greek form (as in TEV NEB RSV NAB Mft etc.) would, of course, preserve this ambiguity.

TEV	RSV
7 Do not deceive yourselves; no one makes a fool of God. A person will reap exactly what he plants. 8 If he plants in the field of his natural desires, from it he will gather the harvest of death; if he plants in the field of the Spirit, from the Spirit he will gather the harvest of eternal life. 9 So let us not become tired of doing good; for if we do not give up, the time will come when we will reap the harvest. 10 So then, as often as we have the chance, we should do good to everyone, and especially to those who belong to our family in the faith. (6.7-10)	7 Do not be deceived; God is not mocked, for whatever a man sows, that he will also reap. 8 For he who sows to his own flesh will from the flesh reap corruption; but he who sows to the Spirit will from the Spirit reap eternal life. 9 And let us not grow weary in well-doing, for in due season we shall reap, if we do not lose heart. 10 So then, as we have opportunity, let us do good to all men, and especially to those who are of the household of faith. (6.7-10)

These four verses form a unity. Verse 7b is a proverbial saying taken from the world of agriculture; similar expressions are common both in secular and biblical literature (Job 4.8; 2 Cor 9.6). Here the proverb is applied to the relation between "flesh" and "Spirit." The section ends with two appeals (vv. 9-10) which result logically from the previous discussion.

The relation of this section to what immediately precedes is, as already mentioned, hard to determine. A possible solution is that Paul is continuing the theme of liberality which he has introduced in verse 6 and is applying the proverb in the same way as in 2 Cor 9.6. Thus Paul proceeds from a discussion of liberality into a discussion of life in general. Another possibility is simply to take this section as related not specifically to the previous verse, but to the general themes of "flesh and Spirit" and of "helping one another." A third possibility is to relate all this to the theme of verses 4-5.

6.7   Do not deceive yourselves; no one makes a fool of God. A person will reap exactly what he plants.

Paul uses the expression do not deceive yourselves to introduce a general principle. The form of the Greek is passive (RSV "do not be deceived"), and it is possible that Paul is thinking of the false teachers as those who would do the deceiving. It is better, however, to interpret this passive as being reflexive, as TEV does. The general import of what Paul wants to convey is captured by such expressions as "make no mistake about it" (NAB NEB Knox), or "you can be doubly sure of this."

In no one makes a fool of God, the word God is emphatic, emphasizing that God is not a man and therefore cannot be "mocked." The Greek word for "mock" is related to the word "nose," and can be translated literally as "to turn up the nose at." Possible meanings are "to treat with contempt," "to outwit," "to cheat" (JB Knox). The sense of the whole statement is captured by TEV (cf. Phps "you cannot make a fool of God!"; JB "don't delude yourself into thinking God can be cheated"). One may also simply translate "you cannot cheat God."

If the proverbial saying is dropped in favor of nonfigurative language, what he plants could refer to anything that a man does while he is alive, and will reap could refer to God's response to these actions or to his verdict in the day of judgment. An equivalent of this proverbial saying may be rendered in some languages as "Whatever a man plants in his field, that is exactly what he is going to harvest," or "The kind of grain a man plants is the kind of grain he will harvest."

6.8   If he plants in the field of his natural desires, from it he will gather the harvest of death; if he plants in the field of the Spirit, from the Spirit he will gather the harvest of eternal life.

The metaphor of verse 7 is continued here, but with a slight change, for attention is now drawn not to the seed, but to the ground on which the seed is sown. "Flesh" and "spirit" are presented as two kinds of fields yielding different harvests: "corruption" from the former, and "eternal life" from the latter.

There is a divergence of opinion as to whether "flesh" and "spirit" here mean the same thing as in 5.16-17. Some difference can be detected in the way these terms are used. In the previous case "flesh" and "spirit" are sources of action; here they seem to be recipients or beneficiaries. Accordingly, some take these terms to refer to two aspects of the human personality: the physical and the nonphysical (spiritual, intellectual, etc.). To "sow to his own flesh" then would mean to concentrate on satisfying bodily appetites, like food, drink, and other physical needs. Conversely, to "sow to the spirit" is to channel one's energies in the enrichment of the nonphysical aspects of life. Most translators, however, take Paul's usage here to be the same as in chapter 5.

It is frequently necessary to change the figurative expressions in this verse from metaphors to similes, for example, "If a person, so to speak, plants his natural desires in the field ...." Or it may be necessary to make the figurative comparison even more obvious, for example, "If a man encourages his natural desires, like a person who plants grain in a field, then the result is going to be his death," or "...he will have a harvest just as the farmer does, but the harvest will be his death."

The word which TEV translates as <u>death</u> is literally "corruption," which some take to refer primarily to moral and spiritual decay. It is likely, however, that it also refers to physical decay and therefore should be understood as a term for <u>death</u> in a general sense.

If "spirit" here has the same reference as in 5.16, then it means the Holy Spirit. To <u>plant in the field of the Spirit</u> is to concentrate on the fruit of the Spirit as previously mentioned, the result of which is <u>eternal life</u>. This term is quite common in the Johannine writings, but Paul uses it less frequently. The emphasis is not on something which does not end but on the positive qualities that go with a life which is lived in the Spirit.

The second condition in this verse, referring to the <u>field of the Spirit</u>, is even more complicated than the first figurative condition and in some instances may require considerable amplification for the relations to be made clear, for example, "If like a farmer who plants grain in a field, a person does his deeds by the help of the Spirit, then the Spirit will cause him to have a harvest, and this will be the true life that never ends." While specifying the various relations in this manner may be necessary to convey the meaning, a considerable amount of the impact of the figurative language is lost in the explicit details.

The future tenses in this verse lead some scholars to interpret it eschatologically, as referring primarily to the ultimate harvest, perhaps at the Day of the Lord, an interpretation which seems to be reinforced by the next verse.

<u>6.9</u>   So let us not become tired of doing good; for if we do not give up, the time will come when we will reap the harvest.

The introductory <u>so</u> connects this verse with the one immediately preceding. In the light of what Paul has just said, he now defines for his readers and for himself a corresponding course of action.

The verbs translated <u>become tired</u> and <u>give up</u> are similar in meaning, both containing the elements of fatigue and exhaustion. The first verb puts emphasis on losing interest (i.e., "spiritless") and the second on becoming discouraged or relaxing one's efforts. These are reflected in some translations (RSV "grow weary...lose heart"; NAB "grow weary...relax our efforts").

The word translated <u>good</u> is literally "well-being"; a different word for <u>good</u> is used in verse 10. Perhaps we should not press the distinction between these two words, but if one is to be made, <u>doing good</u> in this verse would refer generally to any action done for others or for oneself that results in well-being. In verse 10 it would refer primarily to things done for the benefit of others.

The last part of verse 9 suggests that Paul is thinking eschatologically. It could be that <u>the time will come</u> refers to the expected return of the Lord or to the end of the world. In place of this expression one may say, in some languages, "there will be a day," or "the day will happen."

An expression for reaping the harvest must refer to something beneficial or good. This may be expressed in some languages as "we will have the benefit of a harvest," or "we will have a good harvest."

6.10   So then, as often as we have the chance, we should do good to every-one, and especially to those who belong to our family in the faith.

For so then, see the remark on the previous verse.

The expression as often as we have the chance is literally "as we have op-portunity." It can be understood either in the sense of taking every opportunity as it presents itself (NEB "as opportunity offers") or in the sense of taking ad-vantage of the opportunity which is now available (JB "while we have the chance"). Both of these interpretations are possible, but the second seems to be more ap-propriate if the time will come of verse 9 is understood in an eschatological sense, that is, as referring to the return of the Lord or the end of the world. In view of the two possible interpretations, one may translate as often as we have the chance as either "as often as we can" or "now that we can."

Paul exhorts his readers to do good to everyone, whether he belongs to the Christian community or not. But now he adds a specification and lifts it up as a very important obligation of the Christian, as indicated by the word especially, namely, to do good to those who belong to our family in the faith. The family in the faith is, literally, "the household of faith." The imagery suggests that Chris-tians are like members of one family, the distinguishing aspect of which is their faith in Jesus Christ. The church is thus the "household of God" (Eph 2.19). Our family in the faith may be rendered in some languages as "our fellow believers in Christ," or "those who along with us also trust Christ and are thus a kind of family."

TEV	RSV
Final Warning and Greeting	
11 See what big letters I make as I write to you now with my own hand! 12 The people who are trying to force you to be circumcised are the ones who want to show off and boast about external matters. They do it, however, only so that they may not be persecuted for the cross of Christ. 13 Even those who practice circumcision do not obey the Law; they want you to be circumcised so that they can boast that you sub-mitted to this physical ceremony. 14 As for me, however, I will boast	11 See with what large letters I am writing to you with my own hand. 12 It is those who want to make a good showing in the flesh that would compel you to be circumcised, and only in order that they may not be persecuted for the cross of Christ. 13 For even those who receive cir-cumcision do not themselves keep the law, but they desire to have you circumcised that they may glory in your flesh. 14 But far be it from me to glory except in the

only about the cross of our Lord
Jesus Christ; for by means of his
cross the world is dead to me, and
I am dead to the world.   15 It does
not matter at all whether or not
one is circumcised; what does matter is being a new creature.   16 As
for those who follow this rule in
their lives, may peace and mercy be
with them--with them and with all
of God's people!   (6.11-16)

cross of our Lord Jesus Christ, by
which^l the world has been crucified
to me, and I to the world.   15 For
neither circumcision counts for
anything, nor uncircumcision, but a
new creation.   16 Peace and mercy
be upon all who walk by this rule,
upon the Israel of God.

^{l}Or *through whom*   (6.11-16)

This section is part of the conclusion of the letter. Written at least in part
in Paul's own handwriting, it contains his reiteration of some points which he has
already made in the body of the letter, centering primarily on the issue of circumcision.

One may also employ, as a section heading, "Paul himself warns the people
and greets the believers," "...adds a warning," or "...writes a warning."

6.11   See what big letters I make as I write to you now with my own
          hand !

Paul begins this section by calling attention to (1) the fact that he is doing
the writing himself and (2) his large handwriting.

There is no unanimity of opinion as to what parts of the letter are written
by Paul and what parts by a scribe. Some scholars believe the whole letter was
written by Paul and that the big letters are a form of emphasis, similar to the
modern practice of italicizing or underscoring.

In view of the fact, however, that it was apparently Paul's practice to employ a scribe (e.g. Rom 16.22), it seems better to assume that it is only at this
point in the letter that Paul picks up the pen. This seems to be a regular part of
Paul's letters, as can be deduced from its presence in other letters (2 Thes 3.17;
1 Cor 16.21; Col 4.18). The purpose is apparently to authenticate the letter as
genuine. This position is made clear in some translations, including TEV (JB
"Take good note of what I am adding in my own handwriting"; NEB "You see these
big letters? I am now writing to you in my own hand").

As to the purpose of the big letters, there is a variety of opinion. As already noted, this may be a form of emphasis, calling attention to the important
points which are about to be made. Or it may be a deliberate attempt on Paul's
part to distinguish his own handwriting from that of his scribe. A third possibility is that Paul's handwriting is simply awkward in comparison with the experienced handwriting of the scribe, in which case the statement contains the element
of an apology. The last of these explanations is attractive, but the word for big
simply denotes size and not irregularity or ugliness. All things considered, the
first possibility is probably the closest to Paul's intention.

In view of the fact that those who were to receive the letter were not per-

[154]

sonally present when Paul was writing, it may be better to employ an expression such as "You can see what big letters I make" rather than the direct imperative See what big letters.

As I write to you now with my own hand may be best expressed in some languages as "as I myself am now writing to you," or "... am now using the pen."

6.12   The people who are trying to force you to be circumcised are the ones who want to show off and boast about external matters. They do it, however, only so that they may not be persecuted for the cross of Christ.

Paul now engages in a final blistering attack on the false teachers, those who have been trying to force the Galatians to accept circumcision. First he describes them as those who want to show off and boast about external matters. The expression to show off and boast translates a verb which is used only here in the New Testament. It means "to make a good showing before men," with the intent of becoming popular and acceptable. The word translated external matters is literally "flesh," but here it refers to outward things, with special reference to the external rite of circumcision. In some languages one may simply say "boast about their bodies," or "brag about how their bodies appear." On the other hand external matters may be rendered in some instances as "about things that are seen," "about those things which appear to men," or "about things people think are important."

Who are trying to force you to be circumcised may be expressed in some languages as direct discourse following a verb of command, for example, "are trying to command you, You must be circumcised."

Secondly, Paul mentions that their motive in all of this is so that they may not be persecuted for the cross of Christ. The cross here stands for the whole event of the death of Christ together with its significance, particularly that of effecting a relationship with God based, not on circumcision and other external rites, but on faith alone. Anyone preaching the whole meaning of the cross would, of course, be persecuted by Jews. Paul accuses the false teachers of modifying the message in a way that would guarantee their remaining in good standing within the Jewish community. This purpose may be expressed in some languages as "they do that because they do not want people to persecute them," or "they want to avoid having to suffer."

The relation between the possible persecution and the cross of Christ is rather tenuous because of the negative involved. It may therefore be necessary to say "so that they would not be persecuted, since they would be persecuted if they preached about the death of Christ on the cross," or "... preached about the importance of the death of Christ on the cross." If one merely translates literally "persecuted for the cross of Christ," it might appear that somehow the persecution would be for the sake of the literal cross, which, of course, would be meaningless.

6.13   Even those who practice circumcision do not obey the Law; they want
you to be circumcised so that they can boast that you submitted to this
physical ceremony.

Scholarly opinion is divided as to whether those who practice circumcision
(literally,"the ones who are being circumcised") are identical with the people
Paul is talking about in verse 12. Some hold that in verse 13 Paul is referring in
a general way to all who accept the validity of circumcision, both in Galatia and
elsewhere. Others interpret this to refer to those among the Galatian Gentile
Christians who have submitted to circumcision through the influence of the false
teachers. A third view is that the reference is to the false teachers themselves.
Most translators preserve some degree of ambiguity (Knox "they do not even observe the law, although they adopt circumcision"; cf. JB). The merit of this
position is that it makes it easier to explain the remaining parts of the verse, as
is seen below. In any case, those who practice circumcision should not be understood merely in the sense of "those who cause others to be circumcised," but
primarily in the sense of "those who cause themselves to be circumcised."

What is accented in Paul's statement that these people do not obey the Law
is not their inability to follow the law but their indifference toward obeying it.
There is a touch of sarcasm in Paul's tone; in a sense he is saying "They want
you to follow the Law, but they themselves don't obey it!" As in so many contexts, do not obey the Law may be rendered as "do not do what the Law commands," or "...the laws command." The passive form to be circumcised may
be expressed actively as "they want to circumcise you."

The motive of these people in wanting the Galatians circumcised is so that
they can boast that you submitted to this physical ceremony (literally, "so that
they may glory in your flesh"), which is very similar to the statement in the
first part of verse 12. As there, but even more so here, "flesh" has reference
to the rite of circumcision. These people were probably boasting, perhaps to
the Jews, that they had gotten Gentiles to be circumcised and therefore techni-
cally to become members of the Jewish community. You submitted to this physical ceremony may be simply rendered as "you allowed yourselves to be
circumcised," or "...for them to circumcise you."

6.14   As for me, however, I will boast only about the cross of our Lord
Jesus Christ; for by means of his cross the world is dead to me, and
I am dead to the world.

In contrast to the false teachers and others who brag about circumcision,
Paul now proceeds to declare that he boasts only in the cross of Christ.

He starts this verse with a formula which he often uses to deny something
vigorously, a formula he has already employed twice in this letter (in 2.17 and
3.21, where it is especially translated By no means! and No, not at all!). The
implication of this formula here is that Paul's ground for boasting is not any of
those things which his opponents are boasting of; his ground for boasting is the
cross of Christ.

Some translations retain the negative form (NEB "but God forbid that I should boast of anything but the cross of our Lord Jesus Christ"; NAB "may I never boast of anything but the cross of our Lord Jesus Christ!"), but TEV captures this vehement denial in an entirely positive construction: as for me, however, I will boast only.... The expression as for me, however may often be rendered as "but as far as I am concerned," or "but with respect to me."

It may be very difficult to use the same term for boast in verse 13 and verse 14, since in verse 13 the term is used in a decidedly pejorative or bad sense, while in verse 14 the boasting is a legitimate expression of utmost confidence. It may therefore be necessary in verse 14 to translate I will boast as "I will state my full confidence in," "I will express my full reliance on," or "I will speak unreservedly about." The contrast must be indicated by the force of the transitional conjunction.

For cross, see the comment on 6.12. By means of his cross, a phrase which clearly expresses means in its relation to the world becoming dead to Paul, must be rendered as cause in some languages, for example, "because Christ died on the cross." It may not be sufficient simply to say "because of his cross," since the reference is not to the cross as such, but to the event which took place on the cross.

Paul now mentions the double effect of the cross for him: the world is dead to me, and I am dead to the world. The word "world" is used in Scripture in so many ways that it is hard to ascertain what it really means here. Some take it to mean the whole natural order, insofar as it is independent of the control of the Holy Spirit. It is more likely, however, that world is used here to describe a way of life in which human worth is measured by external circumstances. In this meaning, it is similar to external matters ("flesh") in verse 12. To be dead to this kind of world, then, is to regard all those external factors as without value, insofar as one's being related properly to God is concerned. Christ's death on the cross made this possible, for in that event is clearly demonstrated God's way of accepting men, not on the basis of external circumstances such as law, circumcision, religious observances, etc., but purely on the basis of faith.

In place of saying the world is dead to me, it may be necessary in some languages to specify certain aspects of the world as "becoming dead," since this is essentially a reference to a process which took place as a result of the death of Christ on the cross. Furthermore, the figurative language in dead must sometimes be indicated as a simile, for example, "the things of this world have become, as it were, dead as far as I am concerned," or "the ways in which people of the world value things have become dead for me." Conversely, I am dead to the world may be translated as "I am the same as dead as far as these ways of the world are concerned."

6.15　　It does not matter at all whether or not one is circumcised; what does matter is being a new creature.

This verse is quite similar to 5.6. The idea is that the matter of being circumcised or not is entirely irrelevant insofar as relationship with God is concerned. What is most important is being a new creature. The expression new creature can also be translated as "new creation" (RSV NEB). In "new creation" the emphasis is on the act of God in effecting a new thing, while in new creature it is on the result of God's action.

It is possible to translate "circumcision" and "uncircumcision" in this verse as "Jews" and "Gentiles," although no modern translator opts for this rendering.

The condition involved in the clause whether or not one is circumcised must often be expressed as a simple condition with an alternative, for example, "If one is circumcised or if one is not circumcised, that is not important." A number of languages employ a substantive equivalent of such an alternative condition in a form more or less equivalent to "whether or not a person is circumcised does not matter," or "...is not important." Corresponding to the form of the first sentence, the second sentence in this verse may be translated as "but being a new creature is important," "but being a new kind of person is what matters," or "...does make a difference." In some instances a new creature may be rendered as "being created new by God," or "being made over again by God."

6.16   As for those who follow this rule in their lives, may peace and mercy be with them—with them and with all of God's people!

The closing verse of this section is a benediction addressed to those who follow this rule, that is, those who obey Paul's injunctions in the last two verses.

The word translated rule (from which we get the word "canon") is literally "cane," "reed," or "measuring rod," but the term is also used in reference to a carpenter's measuring tape. Paul probably uses it in the sense of "rule" or "principle." The technical meaning "rule of faith" or "canon" arose much later.

The Greek term translated follow may also be rendered as "walk" (see comments on 5.25). Other ways of rendering it are "live by" (Phps) and "take this principle for their guide" (NEB). Those who follow this rule may accordingly be translated as "those who live according to this principle," "...according to this way of seeing things," or even "...in accordance with what I have just said."

In this benediction, Paul uses two theological terms, peace and mercy. For peace, see the comments on 1.3. Here it probably refers to eschatological salvation. Mercy is perhaps to be interpreted as God's kindness or good will. May peace and mercy be with them is a type of wish or prayer, and it may be necessary in some languages to introduce it as a benediction based upon what God will do on behalf of the people. Therefore one may translate as "may God grant them peace and mercy," "may God cause them to have peace and be kind to them," or "I pray that God will...."

The expression translated all of God's people is literally "the Israel of God." Some take the position that this refers to the faithful remnant in Israel who are seeking an alternative to the Law. If this is the case, then one may see a chiastic construction in the verse, with peace referring to those who follow this rule, and mercy to "the Israel of God." Mercy would then be interpreted more as clemency than as kindness. But such an interpretation is very unlikely.

Most interpreters understand "the Israel of God" as TEV does, namely, that it is another term for the Christian church. To Paul the church is the new Israel, related to God, not through physical descent, but by faith. This is made clear in many translations (Phps "to all who live by this principle, to the true Israel of God, may there be peace and mercy"; JB "all who follow this rule, who form the Israel of God").

With them and with all of God's people may be expressed in some languages as "I pray not only for them but also for all of God's people," "I ask this for them as well as for all God's people," or "...all the people who belong to God."

TEV	RSV
17 To conclude: let no one give me any more trouble, because the scars I have on my body show that I am the slave of Jesus.	17 Henceforth let no man trouble me; for I bear on my body the marks of Jesus.
18 May the grace of our Lord Jesus Christ be with you all, my brothers. Amen. (6.17-18)	18 The grace of our Lord Jesus Christ be with your spirit, brethren. Amen. (6.17-18)

In these two short verses, Paul combines a statement reasserting his authority with a closing benediction.

6.17   To conclude: let no one give me any more trouble, because the scars I have on my body show that I am the slave of Jesus.

To conclude may be expressed in some languages as "These are my final words," or "The last I have to say is this."

In this verse Paul exhorts the Galatians not to give him any more trouble (literally, "henceforth, let no man trouble me"), giving as his reason "I bear on my body the marks of Jesus" (RSV). The metaphor probably refers to the practice of branding slaves with the mark or name of their master. To Paul, the "marks of Jesus" are distinguishing marks which show undeniably that he is a slave of Jesus Christ. While it is possible to understand this in a spiritual sense, the better and more probable interpretation is that Paul has in mind the scars, the marks of suffering and affliction, which he carries on his body as a result of his obedience to his Lord.

Let no one give me any more trouble must not be understood as suggesting permission; rather, it is a command that no one should cause Paul any more difficulty. This may be expressed in some languages as "no one must give me any more trouble." In some languages this must be introduced by a command, for example, "I command that no one give me any more trouble," or "...cause me to suffer further."

In some languages the scars I have on my body must be rendered as "the scars on my skin," "the results of the wounds I have had," or "my healed wounds."

<u>6.18</u>   May the grace of our Lord Jesus Christ be with you all, my brothers. Amen.

The blessing is as terse as the salutation. Only Jesus Christ is mentioned, a departure from Paul's usual practice of mentioning also the Father and the Holy Spirit. For <u>grace</u>, see the comments on 1.3. One should remember that this term is used here also as part of a benediction formula. One should not read too much theological meaning into it here.

Instead of addressing the Galatians directly, Paul refers to their spirit (RSV "grace...be with your spirit"). It is a fitting ending, since the letter, particularly the last two chapters, has been dealing with the subject of the Spirit.

This final benediction is essentially a type of prayer, and in some languages it must be introduced as such, for example, "I pray that the grace of our Lord Jesus Christ will be with you all." In a number of languages, however, <u>grace</u> is translated as "showing mercy" or "being good to" in the sense of kindness which is unmerited. Therefore, one may translate "I pray that our Lord Jesus Christ may be good to you all."

Finally, Paul again addresses the Galatians as <u>my brothers</u>. Despite all his misgivings, he has kept faith with them to the end, and in this way he voices the confidence that they will overcome.

Many translators simply transliterate the word <u>Amen</u> since it is widely used in Christian circles for the conclusion of a prayer. In this particular context a transliteration would be quite fitting. However, <u>Amen</u> may be translated as "Indeed, let it be so," or "That is just what should be." A number of languages have their own equivalents to <u>Amen</u>, more or less literally translatable as "Yes, indeed," or "And so it should be."

BIBLIOGRAPHY

BIBLE TEXTS AND VERSIONS CITED

Bible, The: A New Translation. 1922. James Moffatt. New York: Harper and Row. Cited as Mft.

Good News for Modern Man: The New Testament in Today's English Version. Fourth edition, 1976. New York: United Bible Societies. Cited as TEV.

Greek New Testament, The. Second edition, 1968. Kurt Aland, Matthew Black, Carlo M. Martini, Bruce M. Metzger, and Allen Wikgren, eds. Stuttgart: United Bible Societies.

Gute Nachricht, Die: Das Neue Testament in heutigem Deutsch. 1971. Stuttgart: Württembergische Bibelanstalt. Cited as GeCL.

Holy Bible, The: a translation from the Latin Vulgate in the light of the Hebrew and Greek originals, by Ronald A. Knox. 1950. New York: Sheed & Ward. Cited as Knox.

Holy Bible, The. King James Version. 1611. Cited as KJV.

Jerusalem Bible, The. 1966. London: Darton, Longman & Todd. Cited as JB.

New American Bible, The. 1970. Washington: Confraternity of Christian Doctrine. Cited as NAB.

New English Bible, The. 1970. London: Oxford University Press, and Cambridge: Cambridge University Press. Cited as NEB.

New Testament in Modern English, The. 1962. J. B. Phillips. New York: Macmillan. Cited as Phps.

New Testament, The: a new translation. 1968. William Barclay. London: Collins. Cited as Brc.

Revised Standard Version. 1952. New York: Nelson. Cited as RSV.

COMMENTARIES

Burton, E. de Witt. A Critical and Exegetical Commentary on the Epistle to the Galatians. 1921. International Critical Commentary. Edinburgh: T. and T. Clark.

Cole, R. A. The Epistle of Paul to the Galatians. 1965. Tyndale New Testament Commentaries. Grand Rapids: Eerdmans.

Duncan, G. S. The Epistle of Paul to the Galatians. 1934. The Moffatt New Testament Commentary. London: Hodder and Stoughton.

Guthrie, Donald. Galatians. 1969. The Century Bible (New Series). London: Nelson.

Lightfoot, J. B. Saint Paul's Epistle to the Galatians. 1865. Grand Rapids: Zondervan.

Ridderbos, Herman N. The Epistle of Paul to the Churches of Galatia. 1968. The New International Commentary on the New Testament. Grand Rapids: Eerdmans.

Stamm, R. T. Galatians. 1953. The Interpreter's Bible, Volume X. Nashville: Abingdon.

Williams, A. L. The Epistle to the Galatians. 1910. Cambridge Greek New Testament.

GLOSSARY

active voice is the grammatical form of a verb which indicates that the subject
of the verb performs the action. "John hit the man" is an active expression,
while "the man was hit" is called a passive expression. The Greek language
has a middle form, in which the subject may be regarded as doing something
to or for himself.

adjective is a word which limits, describes, or qualifies a noun. In English,
"red," "tall," "beautiful," "important," etc. are adjectives.

adverb is a word which limits, describes, or modifies a verb, an adjective, or
another adverb. In English, "quickly," "soon," "primarily," "very," etc. are
adverbs.

adverbial refers to adverbs. An adverbial phrase is a phrase which functions as
an adverb. See phrase.

adversative expresses something opposed to or in contrast to something already
stated. "But" and "however" are adversative conjunctions.

agency, agent. In a sentence or clause, the agent is that which accomplishes
the action, regardless of whether the grammatical construction is active or
passive. In "John struck Bill" (active) and "Bill was struck by John" (passive),
the agent in either case is "John." See secondary agency.

allegory is a story in which persons (or other figures) and actions are used to
symbolize spiritual forces, truths, human conduct, experience, etc. Allegorical interpretation of scripture sees similar symbolic meaning in the historical
parts of the Bible.

ambiguity is the quality of being ambiguous in meaning. See ambiguous.

ambiguous describes a word or phrase which in a specific context may have two
or more different meanings. For example, "Bill did not leave because John
came" could mean either (1) "The coming of John prevented Bill from leaving"
or (2) "The coming of John was not the cause of Bill's leaving." It is often the
case that what is ambiguous in written form is not ambiguous when actually
spoken, since features of intonation and slight pauses usually specify which of
two or more meanings is intended. Furthermore, even in written discourse,
the entire context normally serves to indicate which meaning is intended by
the author.

antithesis is a point of view, idea, argument, etc. which is directly opposite to
another point of view, etc. For example, the idea that salvation is a reward

[163]

for service is said to be <u>antithetical</u> to the idea that salvation is a freely bestowed gift.

<u>aorist</u> refers to a set of forms in Greek verbs which denote an action completed without the implication of continuance or duration. Usually, but not always, the action is considered as completed in past time.

<u>apposition</u> (<u>appositional construction</u>) is the placing of two expressions together so that they both identify the same object or event, for example, "my friend, Mr. Smith." The one expression is said to be the <u>appositive</u> of the other.

<u>Aramaic</u> is a language whose use became widespread in Southwest Asia before the time of Christ. It became the common language of the Jewish people in place of Hebrew, to which it is related.

<u>aspect</u> is a grammatical category which specifies the nature of an action; for example, whether the action is completed, uncompleted, repeated (repetitive), begun, continuing (continuative), increasing in intensity, decreasing in intensity, etc.

<u>benefactive</u> refers to goals for whom or which something is done. The pronoun "him" is the benefactive goal in each of the following constructions: "they showed him kindness," "they did the work for him," and "they found him an apartment."

<u>causative</u> (also <u>causal relation</u>, etc.) relates to events and indicates that someone caused something to happen, rather than that he did it himself. In "John ran the horse," the verb "ran" is a causative, since it was not John who ran, but rather it was John who caused the horse to run.

<u>chiastic construction</u> (<u>chiasmus</u>) is a reversal of the order of words or phrases in an otherwise parallel construction. Example: "I (1) / was shapen (2) / in iniquity (3) // in sin (3) / did my mother conceive (2) / me (1)."

<u>clause</u> is a grammatical construction normally consisting of a subject and a predicate. An <u>independent</u> clause may stand alone as a sentence, but a <u>dependent</u> clause (functioning as a noun, adjective, or adverb) does not form a complete sentence.

<u>collective</u> refers to a number of things (or persons) considered as a whole. In English, a collective noun is considered to be singular or plural, more or less on the basis of traditional usage; for example, "The crowd is (the people are) becoming angry."

<u>complement</u> is a word or phrase which grammatically completes another word

or phrase. The term is used particularly of expressions which specify time, place, manner, means, etc.

components are the parts or elements which go together to form the whole of an object. For example, the components of bread are flour, salt, shortening, yeast, and water. The components of the meaning (semantic components) of a term are the elements of meaning which it contains. For example, some of the components of "boy" are "human," "male," and "immature."

concessive means expressing a concession, that is, the allowance or admission of something which is at variance with the principal thing stated. Concession is usually expressed in English by "though" ("even though," "although"). Example: "Though the current was swift, James was able to cross the stream."

conditional refers to a clause or phrase which expresses or implies a condition, in English usually introduced by "if."

conjunctions are words which serve as connectors between words, phrases, clauses, and sentences. "And," "but," "if," "because," etc. are typical conjunctions in English.

connective is a word or phrase which connects other words, phrases, clauses, etc. See conjunction.

connotation involves the emotional attitude of a speaker (or writer) to an expression he uses and the emotional response of the hearers (or readers). Connotations may be good or bad, strong or weak, and they are often described in such terms as "colloquial," "taboo," "vulgar," "old-fashioned," and "intimate."

connotative refers to connotation.

construction. See structure.

context is that which proceeds and/or follows any part of a discourse. For example, the context of a word or phrase in Scripture would be the other words and phrases associated with it in the sentence, paragraph, section, and even the entire book in which it occurs. The context of a term often affects its meaning, so that it does not mean exactly the same thing in one context that it does in another.

continuative means continuing. The term is used of certain adverbs ("now," "then," "still," etc.).

converse means reversed in order, relation, or action.

dependent. See clause.

deprecatory means expressing strong disapproval.

deuterocanonical books is another term for the apocryphal books (Apocrypha), writings included in the Septuagint and Vulgate but excluded from the Jewish and Protestant books of the Old Testament.

diminutive is a word form indicating primarily smallness of size, but also familiarity, endearment, or (in some cases) contempt.

direct discourse. See discourse.

discourse is the connected and continuous communication of thought by means of language, whether spoken or written. The way in which the elements of a discourse are arranged is called discourse structure. Direct discourse is the reproduction of the actual words of one person embedded in the discourse of another person. For example, "He declared, 'I will have nothing to do with this man.'" Indirect discourse is the reporting of the words of one person embedded in the discourse of another person in an altered grammatical form. For example, "He said he would have nothing to do with that man."

Eastern refers to "the East," those parts of Asia collectively lying east of Europe; more specifically (in some instances), the Bible lands.

editorial "we" is the plural pronoun "we" ("us," "our") when used by a writer in place of "I" ("me," "my").

ellipsis (plural ellipses) or elliptical expression refers to words or phrases normally omitted in a discourse when the sense is perfectly clear without them. In the following sentence, the words within brackets are elliptical: "If [it is] necessary [for me to do so], I will wait up all night." What is elliptical in one language may need to be expressed in another.

embedded clause is a dependent clause inserted within the structure of another clause. See parenthetical statement.

emotive refers to one or more of the emotions (anger, joy, fear, gratitude, etc.). The emotive impact of a discourse is its effect on the emotions of the person(s) to whom it is addressed.

eschatological refers to the end of the world and the events connected with it. In this connection, the term "world" is understood in various ways by various persons.

exclusive first person plural excludes the person(s) addressed. That is, a speaker may use "we" to refer to himself and his companions, while specifically excluding the person(s) to whom he is speaking. See <u>inclusive first person plural</u>.

<u>exegesis</u>, <u>exegete</u>, <u>exegetical</u>. The process of determining the meaning of a text (or the result of this process), normally in terms of "who said what to whom under what circumstances and with what intent," is called <u>exegesis</u>. A correct exegesis is indispensable before a passage can be translated correctly. <u>Exegetes</u> are men who devote their labors to exegesis. <u>Exegetical</u> refers to exegesis.

<u>expletive</u> is a word or phrase which appears in the place of the subject or object in the normal word order, anticipating a subsequent word or phrase which will complete the meaning. For example, in the statement "It is difficult to sing the high notes," the word "it" is an expletive which anticipates the real subject, "to sing the high notes."

<u>explicit</u> refers to information which is expressed in the words of a discourse. This is in contrast to <u>implicit</u> information. See <u>implicit</u>.

<u>figurative extension of meaning</u>, <u>figurative language</u>, or <u>figure of speech</u> is the use of words in other than their literal or ordinary sense, in order to suggest a picture or image or for some other special effect. <u>Metaphors</u> and <u>similes</u> are figures of speech.

<u>first person</u>. See <u>person</u>.

<u>first person plural</u> includes the speaker and at least one other person: "we," "us," "our," "ours." See <u>exclusive first person plural</u> and <u>inclusive first person plural</u>.

<u>first person singular</u> is the speaker: "I," "me," "my," "mine."

<u>generic</u> has reference to all the members of a particular class or kind of objects. It is the contrary of <u>specific</u>. For example, the term "animal" is generic, while "dog" is specific. However, "dog" is generic in relation to "poodle."

<u>genitive</u> case is a grammatical set of forms occurring in many languages, used primarily to indicate that a noun is the modifier of another noun. The genitive often indicates possession, but it may also indicate measure, origin, characteristic, etc.

<u>goal</u> is the object which receives or undergoes the action of a verb. Grammatically, the goal may be the subject of a passive construction ("John was hit," in which "John" is the goal of "hit"), or of certain intransitives ("the door shut"), or it may be the direct object of a transitive verb ("[something] hit John").

hypothetical refers to something which is not recognized as a fact but which is assumed to be true in order to develop an argument or line of reasoning.

idiom or idiomatic expression is a combination of terms whose meanings cannot be derived by adding up the meanings of the parts. "To hang one's head," "to have a green thumb," and "behind the eight ball" are English idioms. Idioms almost always lose their meaning completely when translated from one language to another.

imperative refers to forms of a verb which indicate commands or requests. In "go and do likewise," the verbs "go" and "do" are imperatives. In most languages imperatives are confined to the grammatical second person; but some languages have corresponding forms for the first and third persons. These are usually expressed in English by the use of "may" or "let." For example, "May we not have to beg!" "Let them eat cake!"

imperfect tense is a set of verb forms designating an uncompleted or continuing kind of action, especially in the past.

implicit refers to information that is not formally represented in a discourse, since it is assumed that it is already known to the receptor. This is in contrast to explicit information, which is expressed in the words of a discourse. See explicit.

inclusive first person plural includes both the speaker and the one(s) to whom he is speaking. See exclusive first person plural.

independent clause. See clause.

indicative refers to a group of modal forms of verbs that indicate action or state as an objective fact. See modal.

indirect discourse. See discourse.

irony is a sarcastic or humorous manner of discourse in which what is said is intended to express its opposite; for example, "That was a wise thing to do!" is intended to convey the meaning "That was a stupid thing to do."

Judaism. The religion of the Jews, particularly as opposed to the teachings of Jesus and his apostles.

Judaize means to attempt to impose some of the distinctives of Judaism on the teachings of the apostles. See Judaism.

Maccabees was a name given to a family of Jewish military leaders who flourished in the period between the Old and New Testaments. There are four Books of

Maccabees, two of which are included in the Apocrypha. See <u>deuterocanonical</u> <u>books</u>.

<u>marginal helps</u> in Bible Society usage are notes, normally occurring on the same page as the text and providing purely objective, factual information of the following types: alternative readings (different forms of the source-language text), alternative renderings (different ways of rendering the source-language text), historical data, and cultural details, all of which may be necessary for a satisfactory understanding of the text. Notes which are doctrinal or homiletical interpretations of the text are excluded from Scriptures published by the Bible Societies.

<u>metaphor</u> (<u>metaphorical term</u>) is likening one object to another by speaking of it as if it were the other, as "flowers dancing in the breeze." Metaphors are the most commonly used figures of speech and are often so subtle that a speaker or writer is not conscious of the fact that he is using figurative language. See <u>simile</u>.

<u>modal</u> refers to forms of verbs in certain languages which indicate the attitude of a speaker to what he is saying; for example, wish, hesitancy, command, etc. The various categories of verb forms are called "moods" (or "modes"). In English they are expressed by such auxiliary verbs as "can," "do," "may," "shall," etc. See <u>imperative</u> and <u>indicative</u>.

<u>nominal</u> refers to nouns or noun-like words. See <u>noun</u>.

<u>nonrestrictive attributives</u>. See <u>restrictive attributives</u>.

<u>noun</u> is a word that is the name of a subject of discourse, as a person, place, thing, idea, etc. See <u>proper name</u>.

<u>paratactic expression</u> (<u>parataxis</u>) refers to two or more clauses of equal rank which stand together without being joined by a connective. Example: "I came, I saw, I conquered." See <u>connective</u>.

<u>parenthetical statement</u> is a digression from the main theme of a discourse which interrupts that discourse. It is usually set off by marks of parenthesis ( ).

<u>participial phrase</u> is a phrase governed by a participle. See <u>participle</u>.

<u>participle</u> is a verbal adjective, that is, a word which retains some of the characteristics of a verb while functioning as an adjective. In "singing waters" and "painted desert," "singing" and "painted" are participles.

<u>particle</u> is a small word whose grammatical form does not change. In English the most common particles are prepositions and conjunctions.

[169]

passive voice. See voice.

pejorative means having a disparaging effect or force. For example, the suffix "-ish" in "childish" is pejorative.

perfect tense is a set of verb forms which indicate an action already completed when another action occurs. The perfect tense in Greek also indicates that the action continues into the present.

perfective participle is a participle in the perfect tense. See participle and perfect tense.

person, as a grammatical term, refers to the speaker, the person spoken to, or the person(s) or thing(s) spoken about. First person is the person(s) or thing(s) speaking ("I," "me," "my," "mine"; "we," "us," "our," "ours"). Second person is the person(s) or thing(s) spoken to ("thou," "thee," "thy," "thine"; "ye," "you," "your," "yours"). Third person is the person(s) or thing(s) spoken about ("he," "she," "it," "his," "her," "them," "their," etc.). The examples here given are all pronouns, but in many languages the verb forms distinguish between the persons and also indicate whether they are singular or plural.

Pharisees (Pharisaic sect). A Jewish religious party. They were strict in obeying the Law of Moses and other regulations which had been added through the centuries.

phrase is a grammatical construction of two or more words, but less than a complete clause or a sentence. A phrase may have the same function as the head word of the phrase. For example, "the old man" has essentially the same functions as "man" would have, or it may have a function which is different from the function of either set of constituents, for example, "to town," "for John."

plural refers to the form of a word which indicates more than one. See singular.

possessive pronouns are pronouns such as "my," "our," "your," "his," etc. which indicate possession. See genitive.

predicate is the division of a clause which contrasts with or supplements the subject. The subject is the topic of the clause and the predicate is what is said about the subject.

preposition is a word (usually a particle) whose function is to indicate the relation of a noun or pronoun to another noun, pronoun, verb, or adjective. Some English prepositions are "for," "from," "in," "to," "with."

prepositional refers to prepositions. A prepositional phrase or expression is one governed by a preposition.

proper name or proper noun is the name of a unique object, as "Jerusalem," "Joshua," "Jordan." However, the same may be applied to more than one object, for example, "John" (the Baptist or the Apostle) and "Antioch" (of Syria or of Pisidia).

pseudo passive is the same as substitute passive.

qualitative and quantitative are terms which are frequently used in contrast to each other. Qualitative has to do with quality, and quantitative with quantity. Certain words ("great," for example) are sometimes used qualitatively ("a great man") and at other times quantitatively ("a great pile").

rabbinical refers to the rabbis, religious teachers among the Jews. They had many peculiar interpretations of the meanings of the Old Testament writings. See exegesis.

reading. See textual.

receptor is the person(s) receiving a message. The receptor language is the language into which a translation is made. The receptor culture is the culture of the people for whom a translation is made, especially when it differs radically from the culture of the people for whom the original message was written. See source language.

redundancy is the expression of the same information more than once. Anything which is completely redundant is entirely predictable from the context.

referent is the thing(s) or person(s) referred to by a pronoun, phrase, or clause.

reflexive has to do with verbs where the agent and goal are the same person. Sometimes the goal is explicit (as "he dresses himself"); at other times it is implicit (as "he dresses").

relative clause is a dependent clause which qualifies the object to which it refers. In "the man whom you saw," the clause "whom you saw" is relative because it relates to and qualifies "man."

repetitive. See aspect.

restrictive attributives are so called because they restrict the meaning of the objects which they qualify, while nonrestrictive attributives do not. In the expression "the soldiers who were retreating were commanded to halt and regroup" (no commas), the clause "who were retreating" indicates that the

[171]

command was restricted to a particular class of soldiers, namely, those who were retreating. But in the expression "the soldiers, who were retreating, were commanded to halt and regroup," the same clause (this time set off by commas) qualifies all the soldiers referred to in the discourse and simply provides supplementary information about them.

restructure is to reconstruct or rearrange. See structure.

rhetorical refers to special forms of speech which are used for emphasis or to create an effect on the receptor. A rhetorical question, for example, is not designed to elicit an answer but to make an emphatic statement.

second person. See person.

secondary agency (agent) involves the immediate agent of a causative construction. In the sentence "John made Bill hit the man," the primary agent is "John," and the secondary agent is "Bill." "John" may also be regarded as the responsible agent and "Bill" as the immediate agent. Similarly, in the sentence "God spoke through the prophets," the primary agent is "God," and the secondary agent is "the prophets." These do the actual speaking, but the responsible agent is "God." See agency.

semantic domain is a definable area of experience which is referred to by a set of words whose meanings are in some way related. For example, kinship terms constitute a semantic domain. Similarly, the color terms of a language may be said to form a semantic domain.

Septuagint is a translation of the Old Testament into Greek, made some two hundred years before Christ. It is often abbreviated as LXX.

simile (pronounced SIM-i-lee) is a figure of speech which describes one event or object by comparing it to another, as "she runs like a deer," "he is as straight as an arrow." Similes are less subtle than metaphors in that they use "like," "as," or some other word to mark or signal the comparison.

singular refers to the form of a word which indicates one thing or person, in contrast to plural, which indicates more than one.

source language is the language in which the original message was produced. For the New Testament it is the Greek spoken at that particular period.

specific implies the precise or individual designation of an object. The term is used in contrast to generic.

structure is the systematic arrangement of the form of language, including the ways in which words combine into phrases, phrases into clauses, and clauses into sentences. Because this process may be compared to the building of a house or a bridge, such words as structure and construction are used in reference to it. To separate and rearrange the various components of a sentence or other unit of discourse in the translation process is to restructure it.

subject. See predicate.

substantive is a noun or anything (pronoun, phrase, clause, adjective, etc.) that functions as a noun.

substitute passive is a form which is passive in meaning, though active in form. For example, in the expression "they received punishment," the subject "they" is really the goal of the activity of the "punishment." The same is true of such expressions as "he got kicked" and "they obtained mercy."

supplementary notes. See marginal helps.

synonyms are words which are different in form but similar in meaning, as "boy" and "lad." Expressions which have essentially the same meaning are said to be synonymous.

Synoptic Gospels are Matthew, Mark, and Luke, which share many characteristics that are not found in John.

syntactic refers to syntax, which is the arrangement and interrelations of words in phrases, clauses, and sentences.

temporal refers to time. Temporal relations are the relations of time between events. A temporal clause is a dependent clause which indicates the time of the action in the main clause.

tense is usually a form of a verb which indicates time relative to a discourse or some event in a discourse. The most common forms of tense are past, present, and future.

textual refers to the various Greek manuscripts of the New Testament. A textual reading is the reading of a particular manuscript (or group of manuscripts), especially where it differs from others. Textual evidence is the cumulative evidence for a particular reading. Textual problems arise when it is difficult to reconcile or to account for conflicting readings.

third person. See person.

transitionals are words or phrases which mark the connections between related events. Some typical transitionals are "next," "then," "later," "after that," "the day following," "when this was done."

[173]

translation is the reproduction in a receptor language of the closest natural
equivalent of a message in the source language, first, in terms of meaning,
and second, in terms of style.

translational refers to translation. A translator may seem to be following an in-
ferior reading (see textual) when he is simply adjusting the rendering to the
requirements of the receptor language, that is, for a "translational reason."

transliteration is to represent a word from the source language in the letters of
the receptor language rather than to translate its meaning.

verbal has two meanings. (1) It may refer to expressions consisting of words,
sometimes in distinction to forms of communication which do not employ words
("sign language," for example). (2) It may refer to word forms which are derived from verbs. For example, "coming" and "engaged" may be called ver-
bals.

vocative refers to the person addressed (spoken to). Some languages have dis-
tinctive vocative forms for nouns.

voice in grammar is the relation of the action expressed by a verb to the participants in the action. In English and many other languages, the active voice indicates that the subject performs the action ("John hit the man"), while the
passive voice indicates that the subject is being acted upon ("the man was hit").
The Greek language has a middle voice, in which the subject may be regarded
as doing something to or for himself (or itself).

Vulgate is the Latin version of the Bible translated and/or edited originally by
Saint Jerome. It has been traditionally the official version of the Roman Cath-
olic Church.

Zealots were a Jewish political party in Palestine at the time of Christ. They
were intensely nationalistic.

INDEX

Abraham
  descendants 52,57,59,60,70,71,73,
    74,75,85,109,110,111,112,115
  faith 57,58,59,60
  God's promise to him 66,67,68,70,
    72,73,75,77,85,93,116
adoption 90
angels 14,75,102
Antioch 39,40,41,43,44,101
apostles 1,3,4,5,23,24,36
apostleship See Paul
Arabia 23,112,113
Aramaic 24

baptism 84
Barnabas 28,29,31,37,38,41,42
brothers 6,14,17,68,99,100,115,
    130,145,160

Canaan 72
Cephas 24
Christ
  cross of 49,50,54,65,66,129,141,
    155,156,157
  death of 49,50,51,54
  work of 8,9
church(es) See Antioch, Jerusalem,
    Judea, Galatian churches
Cilicia 25
circumcision 1,30,31,32,59,84,120,
    121,124,128,129,155,156,157,158
covenant 68,69,70,71,72,111,112
crucifixion See Christ
curse 61,62,63,64,65,73

Damascus 15,23,24
demons See spirits
disciples of Jesus See Twelve

Egypt 72
English style 4

faith 26,44,45,80,81,82,83
  See also Abraham

false gods 95
false teachers 1,32,33,110,121,125,
    127,155,156
flesh 131,134,135,136,137,138,141,
    142,151

Galatia 1,6,14,53,100,101
Galatian Christians 4,11,12,13,15,
    33,44,94,95,98,99,100,101,102,103,
    104,105,106,107,109,117,119,120,
    122,125,126,130,132,155
Galatian churches 1,4,5,6,11,14,15,
    52,83,104,106,143
Galatian letter 1,3,4,6,7,15
Galilee 89
Gentiles 1,22,28,30,34,36,38,39,
    40,41,43,44,45,47,59,60,67,69,83,
    84,85,88,94,100,119,158
Good News 4,11,12,13,22,26,29,30,
    33,42,54,57,60,104,126
gospel 11,13,17,18,30,33,36,42,43,
    100,126 See also Good News
grace 12,21,37,51,122

Hagar 109,112,113,116
heirs 93
hell 14
Holy Spirit 1,2,54,55,56,57,67,73,
    79,91,92,116,123,133,134,135,136,
    139,140,141,142,144,145,151,152,
    160

incarnation 89
Isaac 110,111,115,116,117
Ishmael 110,111
Israelites 132

James 24,25,37,40,41
Jerusalem 7,23,24,25,28,29,30,34,
    35,37,38,113,114,115,147
Jewish beliefs, concepts, etc. 7,18,
    19,20
Jewish Christians 44,45,46,47,69,88
Jewish customs, etc. 1,2,3,33

Jewish Law See Law of Moses
Jews   1, 19, 20, 21, 36, 37, 39, 43, 44, 45,
   46, 83, 84, 85, 94, 110, 114, 119, 120,
   121, 155, 158
John   37
Judea   25, 26
Judaism   18, 19, 97
Judaizers   13, 97   See also false teach-
   ers
justification   45, 47, 51, 63, 64, 122

law   19, 44, 46
Law of Moses   1, 12, 40, 43, 46, 47, 48,
   49, 50, 51, 54, 55, 57, 61, 62, 63, 64, 65,
   67, 72, 73, 74, 76, 77, 80, 81, 82, 86, 89,
   90, 93, 94, 95, 100, 109, 110, 118, 121,
   122, 123, 131, 135, 146, 156
letters   3, 6

Maccabees   18
mediator   75, 76
Messiah   8

non-Jews   See Gentiles

Palestine   38, 89
Paul
   apostleship   1, 3, 4, 5, 16, 17, 21, 22,
      36, 52

authority   3
companions   33
missionary journeys   7, 28
Pentateuch   110
Peter   24, 36, 37, 38, 39, 40, 42, 43, 44
persecution   19, 26, 128, 155
Pharisees   19, 20

rabbinical exegesis   76, 109
religious feasts   97
resurrection   5, 6
Roman law and practices   1, 86, 87, 93

Sarah   109, 111
Septuagint   46, 58, 59, 69, 72, 114, 117,
   132
Sinai   111, 112, 113
Spirit   See Holy Spirit
spirits   88, 89, 96
Synoptic Gospels   8
Syria   18, 25, 39

textual problems   7, 12
Titus   28, 30, 31, 32, 34, 120
Torah   46, 77, 110
Twelve   4, 17, 23, 25

Zealots   20